Media Reforms and Democratization in Emerging Democracies of Sub-Saharan Africa

Ufuoma Akpojivi

Media Reforms and Democratization in Emerging Democracies of Sub-Saharan Africa

palgrave
macmillan

Ufuoma Akpojivi
Department of Media Studies
University of the Witwatersrand
Johannesburg, South Africa

ISBN 978-3-030-09196-5 ISBN 978-3-319-75301-0 (eBook)
https://doi.org/10.1007/978-3-319-75301-0

Cover illustration: mvp64/iStock/Getty Images
Cover design by Tom Howey

Printed on acid-free paper

This Palgrave Macmillan imprint is published by Springer Nature
The registered company is Springer International Publishing AG
The registered company address is: Gewerbestrasse 11, 6330 Cham, Switzerland

To Linda and Oghenemaro

Foreword

The topic and issue of democratization and media reforms is one that reached the top of the African agenda in the late 1980s and into the 1990s, after decades of one party state or one party dominant or military government since the 1960s when most African countries became independent of political colonial rule. It was also a period after decades of economic decline and stagnation caused by a plethora of factors, chief among them, a failure by these governments who were not a product of free choice by the people to choose the kind of policies that would lead to a thriving economy that addressed structural issues, while delivering sustainable livelihoods across the social spectrum.

The call for media reform and democratization was both an agenda of Africans themselves and external forces including but not limited to foreign governments, aid agencies, multilateral financial and other institutions and civil society actors focused on democratization and media freedom. The actions of some of the actors when scrutinized critically, often ironically seem to negate the very idea of freedom to choose that is central to the narrative of democratization.

On the face of it, given the context in Africa, this coincidence of agendas should have been seen in the most positive light. Such a positivist approach to political, economic and social dynamics and change in society would at best be naïve and reductionist. In fact, it would mimic the era of an exclusive focus on development that was used as a justification for the suppression of civil and political rights, including media freedom and democracy, by the post-independence governments in Africa and in Asia, Latin America and other regions of the world.

An appropriate approach is to critique not only notions of media reform and democratization and how real actors in various contexts mobilize them, but also the motivations of the multiple local and external actors and the unequal power relations that obtain in such situations. In this exercise, critical skepticism should be the attitude to the dominant paradigms of liberal, neo-liberal and Marxist thought that Africans or those writing on Africa can often consciously or unconsciously lock themselves into.

Ufuoma Akpojivi, in this book, *Media Reforms and Democratization in Emerging Democracies of Sub-Saharan Africa* performs this critical analytical task in ways that enrich our attempts to understand African societies trying to carve a trajectory of shaping a new society without any shackles. Very few texts in the under-researched area of media and communication in Africa, break with a positivist narrow focus on the absence of media freedoms as compared to what is posited as the ideal in Northern industrialized societies.

Akpojivi constructs an argument which seeks to bring in forms of African philosophy and thinking about building and organizing society and its institutions in ways that people understand and are able to participate as a more substantive democratization process, as opposed to a process of democratization that is a superficial modernization project that seeks to mirror other societies. This is an ambitious task fraught with all sorts of pitfalls including whether one can posit an African philosophy and thought after the violent, in multiple senses of the word, encounter with slavery, colonialism and apartheid.

Akpojivi's focus on communication and media policymaking and the interactions, encounters and intersections of the various local and external actors is narrative of the complexity of what goes for democratization. The comparative case studies of Ghana and Nigeria, some of the first countries to gain independence and to fall under military rule, is rich and fairly reflects similar processes across the continent despite some local specificities. It also reveals the limits of notions or processes of media reform and democratization outside a broader context of decolonization of the social structures, political systems and creativity in re-thinking the organization of institutions.

While Akpojivi is contributing to an existing debate, he has opened a line of thinking that invites other scholars to engage him and each other in robust critical thinking that can make a significant contribution not only to intellectual ideas but to processes unfolding to create of Africa, 'new' societies that can best fulfill the potential of its inhabitants' futures.

University of the Witwatersrand
Johannesburg, South Africa

Tawana Kupe

Preface

This book is a product of two life experiences: first from the everyday conversations with my father, who is a staunch news addict. He is always keen to know what is happening around the world and its implications on the socio-economic and political developments. He often criticised and questioned the hegemonic flow of ideas, policies from the Global North to the South, and why African countries would rely so much on the West. Such conversations always left me wondering why African countries would always depend on the West for policy frameworks despite objections from the populace. This ignited my passion and interest in policy and democratization in African countries. Second, this work is centered on my PhD thesis from the University of Leeds, United Kingdom. My interest in this topic was further shaped by the politics and economics of communication policy and regulation course taught by Prof. Dr. Katherine Sarikakis. In her classes, one engages with the policy complexities associated with the globalization of ideas. This made me reflect upon why African countries are not leap frogging through developments despite embracing liberalism and neoliberalism, following re-democratization in the early 1990s.

Therefore, this book examines the media reform processes that characterize the democratization processes of emerging democracies of Ghana and Nigeria. Policymakers and media analysts in both countries are quick to refer to Western countries' frameworks either when deciding on policy initiatives or when evaluating the progress made in the democratization processes. This is further compounded by reports from international organizations such as Freedom House, Article 19 and the Mo Ibrahim Index of African Governance (IIGA), which are often used as proof or validation of media reform processes. While these reports or the yardsticks used by these organizations or Western governments might present a simplistic picture of the state of the reform and democratization process, I argue that in order to understand the true state of the reform processes and democratization project of emerging democracies there is need for a holistic assessment of the process which involves asking a series of questions:

Where are the media reform ideas emanating from? Do these ideas recognize the complex political, economic and socio-cultural factors of these emerging democracies that are characterized by ethno-cultural, religious, political and economic tensions? To what extent does the local context of emerging democracies influence the media reform and re-democratization processes? And who is involved in the process?

Emerging democracies like Ghana and Nigeria have not been able to make significant progress because the reform process was not driven by local needs and context but by Western influence and the need to be perceived as democratic. I have shown the contestation between the different actors in the media reform and re-democratization process by portraying how these contestations, coupled with the historic antecedence of both countries in turn, shape policy formulation and implementation, and the actualization of policy goals. Consequently, policies formulated and implemented during the reform processes have been problematic owing to complexities of policies due to interpretation and the clash of ideas and insincerity of governments to protect their authoritarian enclave. For instance, in Ghana this Western influence has posed a challenge to what Article 162 of the constitution meant. That is, whether licencing is required to operate electronic media or press? Who among the regulatory bodies (i.e. National Media Commission (NMC) and National Communication Authority (NCA)) should regulate media? Similarly, in Nigeria, due to both Western influence and the antecedence of the media in the country, the policy processes are meant to protect national interests. Due to the complexity in establishing what is of national interest, this concept is being used by the state to protect the authoritarian enclave of the state.

In addition, my argument is that the media reform processes are instruments to advance the neocolonialism project of the West in emerging democratic counties. This neocolonialism is facilitated by the use of aid, and technical assistance in pushing ideas of freedom, accountability, public trust and universal accessibility in the policies. Consequently, this leads to dependency and the haphazard nature of policymaking. Therefore, I argue that there is a need to re-think media reform processes in emerging democracies and this should involve what Cabral (1966) called the 'ideological weapon' against dominant ideology that has failed to recognize other ideas in the reform process. I argue that this act of providing an alternative ideology in the reform process should involve critical African thoughts that would enable thinking of viable alternative ideas that will recognize the realities of emerging democracies in order to achieve the realization of policy goals.

As earlier mentioned, this is based on my PhD thesis. However, significant revision has been carried out, as new chapters have been added, and previous arguments substantively built upon. Also, some sections have previously been published as journal articles and book chapters. The arguments in these sections have been developed further. I want to acknowledge the editors of African Journalism Studies formerly known as Ecquid Novi: African Journalism Studies, Journal of Global Communication and New Media Influence on Social and Political Change in Africa for their permission to re-use these materials.

This book would not have been possible without the assistance of certain people. I am indebted to my supervisors Dr. Chris Paterson and Prof. Katrin Voltmer for their intellectual rigour. Others include Prof. Tawana Kupe for writing the foreword, and the support since I joined Wits University; Prof. Pumla Dineo Gqola for her encouragement and support and for the intellectual conversations during our usual lunch. Prof. Gary Rawnsley, for encouraging me to write this book. You made this process of writing interesting. Lastly, my thanks go to the amazing team at Palgrave Macmillan for making the process smooth and easy for me.

University of the Witwatersrand
Johannesburg, South Africa

Ufuoma Akpojivi

Contents

List of Figures

CHAPTER 1

Introduction

The early 1990s witnessed what Huntington (1991) called the 'third wave of democracy' in the African continent. This period witnessed the move of most African countries from a single-party structure to a multi-party democratic system. To facilitate and consolidate this democratic process, these new democratic African countries were expected to formulate and implement reforms that would strengthen human rights, freedom of speech and freedom of the mass media.

Part of this reform, according to Price (2002), entails devising communication policies that will advance the democratic process, as media freedom and freedom of expression are considered vital ingredients to the sustenance of any democracy. Bennett and Serrin (2007), while extending this thought further, noted that the mass media play an active role in developing, building and strengthening democratic principles and institutions. Consequently, Moyer (a US journalist) added that 'the 250-year-old experiment in self-government in America will not make it.... As journalism goes, so goes democracy' (2008: n/p). From the above assertions, it can be inferred that the mass media are the central nervous system of democracy, hence the notion that the quality of any democracy is dependent on the quality of mass media and reforms in operation (Blankson 2007).

Voltmer (2008) argues that emerging democracies are made to abandon anti-democratic tendencies (e.g. suppression of free speech and censorship of the media) and embrace reforms that significantly contribute to and

U. Akpojivi, *Media Reforms and Democratization in Emerging Democracies of Sub-Saharan Africa*,
https://doi.org/10.1007/978-3-319-75301-0_1

promote competitive and participatory political systems (Rozumilowicz 2002), and as such, these reform initiatives should reflect universal norms and ideologies of media freedom. Consequently, policymakers from these emerging democracies transplant established democracies' blueprints or frameworks (Price and Verhulst 2000). The ability of these emerging democracies to implement these neoliberal reforms form the basis for ascertaining and appraising the democratic processes in these countries. Most media watchdog organizations such as Article 19, Reporters without Borders (RSF) and Freedom House use these as the yardsticks for measuring or ascertaining the state of democratization in these countries.

This approach is problematic as the implementation of neoliberal policies and reforms without an understanding of the interplay of the socio-political, economic and cultural factors in the democratization processes is misleading. This is because, according to Voltmer (2008), transplanting Western neoliberal policies into emerging democracies will not necessarily produce the desired results due to the influence and role of past history and inherent political, economic and cultural factors in the reform process. In addition, Jakubowicz (2002) posited that policies alone cannot guarantee the needed change in strengthening these emerging democratic institutions.

Rationale for Case Studies of Ghana and Nigeria

Most studies on media reforms and democratization processes have focused on South Africa, Zimbabwe, Cameroon and Kenya among others. In addition, these studies also focus on either the role of political actors in the democratization process (Voltmer 2008), or adopt the normative approach of evaluating media reforms based on a set of conditions as earlier noted (Mabadeje 2004; Kwame 2004). It is therefore necessary to examine the democratization process in relation to the struggle between media actors (political and economic) and the media themselves with particular focus on Ghana and Nigeria which are often neglected. The focus on Ghana and Nigeria cannot be overemphasized as they both share similar historical and developmental backgrounds.

Apart from having a similar history of being colonized by the same country, Ghana and Nigeria started their re-democratization processes in 1992 and 1999 respectively after prolonged authoritarian military regimes lasting over two decades, which weakened their democratic constructs (Clapham 1993; Ojo 2003; Ogbondah 2004). During this authoritarian period, weak state institutions such as the media were built and structured to support the military enclaves, leading to the underdevelopment of both countries. In the early 1990s, in the wake of the economic recession, both countries implemented the neoliberal policy of structural adjustment program (SAP) (Boafo-Arthur 1998; Onwumechili 2007). Both countries have similar media structures and the mass media played a significant role in the struggle for independence and re-democratization processes.

Therefore, in the wake of re-democratization, policymakers and other political actors were made to formulate policies that will help build strong institutions, and promote democratic cultures of media freedom and freedom of expression which are considered a major bane in both countries. Hence, the holistic formulation and implementation of policies that will facilitate the re-democratization process, as this was made a condition for the continuous support of Western aid and assistance (LaMay 2007). However, most studies that have examined the reform processes have produced different positions and arguments. Radelet (2010), in his study, argues that with the current reform processes in Ghana there is a clear break from the past, which will facilitate a vibrant democracy, good governance and economic development. On the other hand, Campbell (2011) stated that the current reforms being implemented in Nigeria are not producing the desired results due to the government's failure to create an holistic policy framework that will strengthen the democratic process. Consequently, the assertion that Nigeria is dancing on the brink of becoming a failed state and that the nascent democracy is being undermined.

Both statements reflect the dominant perspective upon which scholars and policymakers often judge reform processes in emerging democracies based on the approach of ticking boxes to ascertain whether certain criteria are in place to aid the reform process, and if governments allow journalists to exercise their responsibilities without being arrested or brutalized. Therefore, we need to go beyond the periphery of ascertaining the success of media reforms based not on conditionality, but on the need to examine compatibility of these reform policies with the antecedents of these emerging democracies. Likewise, we need to examine the challenges encountered and the interest reflected in the media reform process to determine if the new media systems are under political and economic pressures associated with emerging democracies. Using a comparative approach to ascertain whether there are common patterns between these two emerging democracies that have similar histories, I seek to address the following pertinent questions: what is the state of the media reforms in Ghana and

Nigeria? What are the fundamental principles guiding these reforms? What criteria can be used in evaluating media reforms in emerging democracies? Are these criteria culturally bound or universally applicable? And whose interest is reflected in the whole reform exercise?

Democracy and Media Freedom: Revisiting the Debate

The debate on democracy and media freedom is as old as man. I have been exposed to arguments that democracy is a Western concept and that its features are not compatible with the African continent. Likewise, the counter argument that democracy actually started in Africa and attempts at promoting and enforcing another form (i.e. a 'Western form') has led to the failure of most African states. What is striking in this debate is the idea that democracy is never African and if Africa has its own form of democracy, as most Africanists claim, then how is it that there has never been a success story about an African democracy? According to Adebanwi and Obadare (2011: 314) there is always the debate whether 'Africa's total environment, its history, politics, economics and culture, are conducive to democracy and supportive of democratic life'. This question echoes the pessimistic views of democracy in Africa. Therefore, I argue that in the conceptualization of democracy there is the need to recognize that there are different forms of democracy practiced (see Chap. 2), and the imposition or attempt at universalizing democracy has led to the unsuccessful reforms and democratization in the African continent which Adebanwi and Obadare (2011) and others have discussed.

As earlier stated, democracy is a complex and ambiguous concept to define due to the many perspectives from which it can be conceptualized. Despite the certitude of any definition, such definition is subject to debate and contention (Rozumilowicz 2002). One such debate is the idea of what constitutes democracy. Most often in the debate about democracy, reference is made to Abraham Lincoln's definition of 'government of the government by the people and for the people'. From this definition comes the issue of which people: in other words all the people who constitute the society or a majority that agrees on the same thing. This, therefore, brings about the need to problematize the minority, and its function in society since it is excluded based on the definition. In addition, there is the complexity of which form of democracy, as in most discourses on democracy there is the assertion that there is a universal democracy that is applicable in all countries (Nyerere 2000).

According to Nyerere (2000), different countries have their own forms of democracy which are unique to them and differ from others. For instance, the British type of democracy is intricately different from the American style, and likewise from that of post-independent Tanzania. Thus, the current concept of a common and universal form of democracy that is applicable to all countries irrespective of cultural boundaries is problematic. Diamond (2008a) perceives democracy to be a Western concept rooted in Western beliefs and practices which are currently being universalized. This claim is questionable and stirs debate, as the word 'democracy' originates from the Greek which means rule of the people (Ake 1996, 2000). This invariably means democracy as postulated by most scholars is not Western but European, and within the current structure of the European Union the different member states were once practicing different forms or types of government such as monarchy, aristocracy and theocracy.

Similarly, African scholars such as Ake (1991) argue that democracy was actually rooted in African cultural practices before colonization, as colonization brought with it a normative perspective of democracy which is currently being forced onto the continent. Kwesi (1995) posited that before colonization African societies were governed by chiefs and kings, and within this system every adult (male and female) had the opportunity to contribute and participate towards community discourse. Although critics will see this to be authoritarian due to the powers ascribed to these kings and chiefs, Kwesi stated that unlike the Western form of democracy no organized opposition group is needed to act as regulator as the council of chiefs or elders performed checks and balances within the system.

Another salient debate within the conceptualization of democracy is the format of democracy. Should democracy be limited to 'procedures', in other words equal and universal adult suffrage as Keane (1991) argued (see also Dahl 1971), or 'substantive', in other words regular conduct of elections which involves the development of democratic principles that will allow for civic and political liberties such as media freedom and freedom of expression which are central to any democratic society (Diamond 2008b). This is salient because most often democracy has been reduced to regular conduct of elections as its level of maturity based on how frequently governments have changed and the frequency of elections conducted (Voltmer 2008; Diamond 2008a). This is further reflected in Adebanwi and Obadare (2011: 312) where they conceived of democracy from the perspective of multi-party elections, 'regular, free and fair elections'. Although all these perspectives are right approaches to seeing democracy, they are myopic and reflect the dominant approach to democracy which ignores other forms or cultures of democracy. However, in spite of the complexity in the conceptualization of democracy as highlighted above, I will approach democracy from two basic principles (i.e. competition and participation (Rozumilowicz 2002)) which every democracy must exhibit. These two principles are considered as the underlying objective of democracy. According to Nyerere (2000) democracy is about participation, the ability of people to engage and be involved in making decisions that impact on their wellbeing and development and in the overall development of society. Therefore, the restriction and limitation of people's involvement in whatever form is undemocratic as it will not only hinder the growth of society but the development of citizenry.

For this participation to take place a free and independent media that will provide citizens with relevant, adequate information 'to make decisions, as well as ensure a forum for the development of ideas and opinions' (Rozumilowicz 2002: 13) is needed. The provision of relevant information, according to Silverstone (1999), is crucial to the sustenance of democracy and ensuring good governance, hence making the debate on media freedom fundamental in the discourse of democracy. Just like democracy, the concept of media freedom has been interpreted from different perspectives (Wasserman and Boloka 2004) because media freedom constitutes both philosophical and political debates (see Chap. 2 for an in-depth discussion). This freedom is imperative to the attainment of democracy as it ascribes power and legitimizes the process, and allows for competition. Competition will enable the diversity of views and opinions which occur during partition (Chomsky 2011; McChesney 1999). Normatively, when the idea of competition is discussed it is always from the perspective of multi-party systems, and diversity of views and opinion (see McChesney 1999). However, the way this competition is approached within Africa is different from the West. According to Ake (1996), this competition has to reflect and be grounded in the collective interest of the public. In other words, everyone is entitled to compete and express their views and opinions, but this should be done in the overall interests of community which is often considered as 'Ubuntu' (Fourie 2008). This is evident in the political and democratic processes of democracies in Africa where most often elective positions are 'zoned' or 'zeroed' to an ethnic group or to people or organizations that have helped in advancing the interests of the society. For instance, in Nigeria, where elective positions are zoned to the different regions in the country, or in South Africa where the public is admonished to 'do it' for Nelson Mandela and the African National Congress, and likewise in Ghana where reference is always made to the 'big six', the founding leaders of Ghana who fought against colonialism. Although active competition is allowed, such competition is dependent on the collective interest of society which is most often not the case in universalized forms of democracy that are promoted on the African continent. Therefore, the problems that have characterized the practice of Western democracy in Africa led to the debates of democracy not being compatible in Africa and the need to embark on what Adebanwi and Obadare (2011) called 'crafting African democracy', which must recognize the economic, socio-political and cultural differences in these African countries which will, to a large extent, determine how they approach, conceptualize and practice democracy.

Structure of the Ghanaian and Nigerian Mass Media

The purpose of this section is to discuss and examine how the structure of the mass media in the colonial and post-colonial eras have continued to influence the operation of the mass media in the current era or re-democratized era.

Synopsis of the Ghanaian Mass Media

The mass media in Ghana can be classified into press and broadcasting. The press in Ghana is regarded as the second oldest press in English speaking West Africa, as it started in 1822 as a sequel to the press in Sierra Leone that started in 1801 (Jones-Quartey 1960). The development of the Ghanaian press has always been associated with the struggle for political renaissance, i.e. the period between '1874–1930, also between 1931 and the attainment of self-government in 1957' played a significant role in the growth and development of the Ghanaian press (ibid: 33). According to Bourgault, the *Royal Gold Coast Gazette* was the first newspaper to be published in Ghana, then known as Gold Coast, in 1822. This newspaper was published by an ex-American slave called Charles L. Force (Bourgaul 1995: 154). And years later, Bannerman Charles published the *Accra Herald* in 1858 by handwriting every copy, and was regarded as the first true African editor (Ainslie 1966: 22).

The early 1930s witnessed the flourishing of the press in Ghana, as this period saw the establishment of two additional dailies: the *Gold Coast Spectator*, later known as the *Spectator*, which started in 1927, and the *West African Times* which started in 1931. Both dailies had an impact on the international scene as they featured international news alongside local news. Most of the content of the early press, according to Ainslie, was meant to educate and entertain the public (1966: 22). However, the year 1947 witnessed the participation of foreign organizations and individuals in the production and distribution of prints. Cecil King of the 'Mirror Groups' started the *Gold Coast Daily Graphic* and the *Sunday Mirror of Accra* (Ainslie 1966: 56). The arrival of Cecil King Mirror Groups brought dynamism and innovation to the press in Ghana. According to Bourgault, the press adopted 'tabloid page makeup, liberal use of illustrations and photos, human interest stories', consequently affecting the indigenous press which could not cope with such innovations (1995: 156).

However, the success story of Cecil King was short lived as Kwame Nkrumah and his Convention People Party (CPP) started the *Accra Evening News*, which was mainly a political paper, to attack the ideologies of Cecil King and his Western views (Bourgault 1995: 157). In the wake of independence, Nkrumah and his party purchased the Guinea Press that later published the *Ghana Evening News* and the *Ghanaian Times*, so at the dawn of independence there were four dailies, three owned by Nkrumah and his party and the *Daily Graphic* owned by Cecil King (Bourgault 1995: 157). The attainment of independence shaped the media environment significantly as Nkrumah openly opposed the press and instituted a culture of censorship. This affected the operation of the press. Consequently, this necessitated the sale of Cecil King's *Daily Graphic* to the Nkrumah government, thereby consolidating the government's desire to control the press (Bourgault 1995: 157). Ainslie further added that this control of the press by government created a precedent for the future of the press in Ghana (1966: 63). Other problems that confronted the early press during this era included lack of capital to invest in modern printing equipment to cope with the challenges confronting them and a lack of trained journalists who could effectively report and examine every news item critically (Ainslie 1966: 64). Jones-Quartey (1960: 38) summed up the Ghanaian press by stating that 'it can be said without doubt or hesitation that before the year 1950 there was not and had never been in Ghana a press that is financially sound'.

Consequently, the present structure of the press in Ghana has been affected by the pre-colonial and post-independent legacies. The present structure shows a press that is widely diffused in order to overcome its outright control by government in the pre-colonial and post-independence era. The present attempts of press liberalization started in 1992, when the country embraced re-democratization following the long years of military rule that saw press suppression and promotion of a 'silent culture' in the media environment (De Gale 1999: 2). Therefore, at present, ownership of the press cuts across the government, private individuals and political parties as there is a proliferation of daily newspapers such as the *Daily Graphic*, *Ghanaian Times*, *Daily Dispatch*, *Ghanaian Chronicles* and *Daily Statesman*. In addition, there are weeklies such as the *National Democrat*, and *The Lens*, and bio-weeklies including *Ashanto Pioneer*, *The Insight*, *Ghanaian Voice* and *Public Agenda*. This diversification of media ownership, it can be argued, is an attempt to avoid a repeat of history when the press became state property.

The story of broadcasting is no different from the press. Broadcasting started in Ghana in 1935, and it was established by the then Governor Arnold Hudson to relay messages from London to Accra (Akpojivi and Fosu 2016; Bourgault 1995). In time, more relay stations were established across other cities such as Kumasi, Sekondi and Korofidua to reach the public with information regarding the colonial administration (Bourgault 1995: 69). However, it should be noted that the establishment of these relay stations was not to meet the information needs of the public but to serve the needs of the colonial leaders in order to aid effective administration and to entertain them (Ansu-Kyeremeh and Karikari 1998: 2). Ansah, while supporting this position, held that the introduction of broadcasting into Ghana was to serve as a propaganda tool for educating the public about policies and activities in the British Empire and the need for the public to embrace such policies and their ideologies (cited in Alhassan 2005: 212).

Radio Zoy, which later became the name of the relay station, was place under the direct control of the colonial administration through the Public Relations Department, which later metamorphosed into the Information Service Department. The department was charged with the responsibility of utilizing the media for the realization of the economic and developmental plan of the Gold Coast nation (Ansah 1985 cited in Alhassan 2005: 212). The content for Radio Zoy was mainly British Broadcasting Corporation (BBC) programs. The effects of the Second World War impacted on the development of broadcasting in Ghana as more efforts were geared towards propaganda (Mackay 1964).

At the end of the Second World War, the broadcast media witnessed unprecedented growth and development as more re-diffusion stations were opened and the colonial masters encouraged the indigenes into broadcasting, and so provided training through the BBC. For instance, by 1956 there were over '445 radio technicians and 163 radio mangers in Ghana' (Tudesq 1983: 23). In addition, Radio Zoy began broadcasting in five major languages (Ewe, Akan, Hausa, Ta and Dagbani (Bourgault 1995: 69)). The introduction and use of indigenous languages helped to reach out to the public, and so by 1945 there were more than 5850 subscribers (Ansah 1985 cited in Alhassan 2005: 212). The year 1953 witnessed a lot of fundamental and structural changes in broadcasting, and one such was the re-naming of Radio Zoy to Gold Coast Broadcasting Service (GCBS) (Alhassan 2005).

At independence in 1957, Kwame Nkrumah and his political party (the CPP) further restructured GCBS into what is presently known as the Ghana Broadcasting Corporation (GBC) under the National Liberation Council Decree (NLCD 226) of 1968. This decree tasked GBC to assist in the government's developmental plan, invariably empowering it to inform, educate and enlighten the public (Alhassan 2005). Also, in 1965, television services were added to the operation of GBC (Donkor 2007). However, since the inception of radio and television in Ghana the broadcasting industry has been subjected to undue government interference and control right from colonialism (refer to the earlier discussion) to the post-independence era. The post-independence era saw Nkrumah tightly controlling the media and using them to promote his socialist ideology (Tudesq 1992: 36), and this trend followed through to the military era until the current wave of democratization that aided freedom of the media.

The re-democratization era facilitated the liberalization of the airwaves in 1992 following the institution of a democratic government which brought some changes to the broadcast industry. This liberalization 'broke the monopoly enjoyed by GBC for over seventy years since its establishment' (Donkor 2007), as there is presently private ownership alongside government ownership structures in Ghana. Government owned media organizations are funded by the government, and this includes Ghana Radio and Ghana Television, all under the umbrella of the Ghana Broadcasting Corporation (GBC). It should be noted that Ghana Radio and Ghana Television work on the network system as signals are mainly created in the capital cities and transmitted to the regional zones for redistribution (Bourgault 1995). According to Anaglate (1985) all ten regions in Ghana are presently covered by GBC (cited in Donkor 2007).

On the other hand, private owned media are proliferating, as there are diverse radio and television stations scattered across Ghana's main cities, and their arrival has brought a new style of journalism that has been lacking since independence, consequently re-invigorating the media sphere (Hasty 2005).

In order to strengthen broadcasting in Ghana and avoid the culture of censorship that characterized the pre-colonial and post-independence era, two regulatory agencies—the National Media Commission (NMC) and the National Communication Authority (NCA)—regulate the Ghanaian media environment. Both agencies were established following the liberalization of the airwaves that was facilitated by the 1992 constitution. Article 167 of the constitution created the National Media Commission to protect and guarantee the mass media's freedom and prevent interference from government. The commission was charged by the constitution to regulate the media based on its guidelines, and to investigate, monitor and settle every complaint made against the mass media (NMC Act 1993). Based on this provision, the NMC is the only body responsible and mandated to check the media. In addition, the commission is to report to parliament directly, and the 15 board members that compose the commission are not directly appointed by the president or minister. Ten of them are nominated by civil societies, three by media practitioners and parliament, and two by the president. Also, the 15 board members elect their own chairman (Article 167, of Ghana 1992 Constitution). The purpose is to avoid the previous scenarios when government appointed all the board members, interfered in their activities and sacked them without due consultation (Donkor 2007).

On the other hand, the National Communication Authority (NCA) was established by Act 524 of 1996 to grant telecommunication licences (i.e. cable, radio, television, telephone and other telecommunication services) in line with public interest. In addition, the NCA advises the government on communication policies and the best measures and practices for regulating the telecommunication industry (NCA Act 524 of 1996). However, the president appoints all eight board members including its chairman and director general, and the commission reports to the minister of information. This has placed the commission under the direct management of the Ministry of Information and thus the autonomy of the organization is threatened. Based on the history of Ghana's media, as already discussed, this trend needs to be re-considered. Before the establishment of both regulatory organizations (i.e. the NMC and NCA), regulation of the media was tied to the Ministry of Information as it decided and dictated the way the media should operate, just as was the case in the colonial era and the post-independence era (Alhassan 2005). It is often the case that the president appoints all the board members, decides their functions and relieves them of their appointments when he deems fit without questioning (Donkor 2007).

Synopsis of the Nigerian Mass Media

The Nigerian press is often regarded as the most vibrant in Africa as a result of its massive and extensive media infrastructure (Bourgault 1995) that has made it possible for the media to withstand every challenge. The history of Nigeria's press started in 1859 when the first newspaper, *Iwe Irohin*, was produced in Abeokuta by a missionary called Reverend Townsend. This paper, first written in Yoruba and later in English (Bourgault 1995), was basically meant to educate and entertain the public.

Years later, in the wake of political consciousness, a series of other newspapers were produced such as the *Lagos Weekly Record* of 1891 by Jackson Payne John (Bourgault 1995). The active participation of Nigerians in the early press began in 1925 with the likes of Herbert Macaulay and Ernest Ikoli influencing the early press greatly (Coker 1960: 73). Herbert Macaulay established the *Daily News* in 1925 and used this paper to project his political ideologies and that of his political party, the National Democratic Party, thus making it the first political newspaper (Coker 1960: 74; Bourgault 1995: 145–155). However, the *Daily News* went out of print in 1936 because of political, economic and social factors. Politically, Macaulay's political party was waning; economically, the paper was faced with financial difficulties as the cost of production could no longer be subsidized by the party; and lastly the paper's style no longer appealed to the public due to the arrival of other competition (Coker 1960: 74).

The *Daily Service* and the *Comet* newspapers were established in 1933, the former, and others, being politically motivated in their establishment. The *Daily Service*, edited by Ernest Ikoli, started as an instrument for the Lagos wing of the Nigerian Youth Movement which principally opposed the ideologies of Herbert Macaulay, while the *Comet* was published by Duse Mohamed Ali (Bourgault 1995). Most of these newspapers were concentrated in Lagos, hence neglecting the other regions of the country (Bourgault 1995: 73). However, with the arrival of Nnamdi Azikiwe from Gold Coast (Ghana) in 1940, the Eastern region was covered by his chain of newspapers. The *Eastern Nigeria Guardian* covered Port Harcourt, the

Nigerian Spokesman covered the Onitsha area, the *Southern Nigerian Defender* covered the Warri zone, and the *West African Pilot* newspaper had national coverage (Bourgault 1995: 155; Nyamnjoh 2005). The arrival of the *West African Pilot* helped in the struggle of political renaissance and brought with it a new style of journalism that impacted greatly on the practice of journalism in Nigeria (Bourgault 1995: 155). According to Coker, the 'Pilot brought an entirely new emphasis on aspects which had almost completely been ignored by its predecessors, namely, the human interest angle of evaluating the news in anything, and the bold spirit of adventure in reporting and editorial comments' (1960: 76).

The Northern region was largely neglected by these entrepreneurs because of their high levels of illiteracy and the fact that Hausa and Arabic were the main languages, in contrast to the Western region where English and Yoruba are the dominant languages, and most of these early newspapers were produced in English (Coker 1960: 77). Nevertheless, with the establishment of *Gaskiya* by the Northern Nigeria government and the introduction of Azikiwe's *Comet* newspaper in Kano, the information needs of the Northerners were met (Bourgault 1995: 155). The establishment of Gaskiya Corporation by the Northern government aimed to encourage the development and growth of the region's vernacular languages. Hence the *Nigerian Citizen*, a periodical from Gaskiya, was produced in the Fulani, Tiv and Kanuri languages (Bourgault 1995: 155). The development of the press across all regions contribute to the development of the press in Nigeria. Ainslie buttressed this fact by saying that the need to meet the diverse requirements of a large multi-ethnic society coupled with the difficulty of distribution due to the size of the Nigerian state, led to the development of the Nigerian press (1966: 56, see also Bourgault 1995: 156).

However, the early press suffered from financial and technical difficulties (Coker 1960: 79). Newspapers were mainly established for political reasons, and to promote ethnic lines of ideologies (Bourgault 1995: 156). For instance, Azikiwe established his chain of newspapers to serve the interests of the Eastern region and his political party, the National Council of Nigeria and Cameroon party (NCNC). Likewise, Obafemi Awolowo established the *Nigerian Tribune* to project the Western region's ideologies and the ideology of the Action Group (AG) party, to counter the views of the national government and other regions. Similarly, the *Gaskiya* of the Northern region was established by the Northern government to promote its cause and that of its political party, the Northern People

Congress (NPC) (see Hachten 1993: 16). This accounted for insufficient funding as most of these entrepreneurs ran out of money, and this lack of funds prevented the various newspapers from buying printing machines to cope with the challenges confronting them.

The present structure of the (print) press in Nigeria still reflects the attributes of the early period. The press in Nigeria is still divided along ethnic ideologies and political affiliations, and is mostly concentrated in Lagos state, the commercial capital of Nigeria. For instance, a quick glance at the press reveals that the establishment of most of the present national dailies was meant to promote the political ideologies of their owners. The *Nigerian Guardian*, owned by the Ibru dynasty, was established to position the family politically. Likewise, the *Nigerian Compass* was established by Daniel Gbenga to serve and promote his political ideas. Also, the *Vanguard* newspaper promotes the cause of the Itskeri ethnic group in the Niger Delta region; the *Punch* newspaper was established mainly to counter the views of Awolowo's *Nigerian Tribune*, and the former *Nigeria Concord* newspaper was used to promote and project M.K.O. Abiola politically.

Although there are several other weekly, bi-weekly, ethnic and regional newspapers or magazines, these listed above are the nationally and internationally recognized newspapers or magazines which have helped to shape, or have influenced, the socio- political and cultural patterns of Nigerian society. It is pertinent to state that there are presently no nationally owned dailies due to a lack of funds and poor management, as the national *Daily Times* newspaper went out of business because of mismanagement and poor circulation since the public perceived it to be a mouthpiece of the federal government. However, some government controlled newspapers can be found at the state and regional levels, for example the *Pointer* newspaper owned and funded by the Delta State government, the *Chronicles*, owned and sponsored by the government of Cross River State, the *Observer* owned and funded by the government of Edo state, and the *New Age* newspaper owned and funded by the Northern governments of Nigeria to cover all the Northern region.

The history of broadcasting is similar to that of the press. Broadcasting started in Nigeria in 1932 and it was introduced by the colonial masters (the British) to serve their interests and to aid in the administration of the colony. Most of the programs were from BBC and were re-distributed and re-transmitted from London to Lagos (Mackay 1964: 1). ThePosts and Telegraphs Department began by distributing programs to Lagos, Ibadan and Kano, which were the main populated centers (Mackay 1964: 2). As the years went by, the Post and Telegraphs Department began to experiment with wired and wireless, thus leading to the development of Radio Distribution Services (RDSs), charged with transmitting 'programmes primarily to serve a particular area' (Mackay: 26).

As radio broadcasting began to grow, all the RDSs were incorporated into government control under the Nigerian Broadcasting System (NBS) in 1949 (Kolade 1974: 87; see also Bourgault 1995), and the Nigerian Broadcasting System was given a new mandate to promote Nigerian unity through its programs and likewise reflect 'linguistic and cultural differences in the regions'. Thus, NBS stations were established in Lagos, Abeokuta, Enugu and Kano, and re-diffusion stations were established in Kaduna, Warri, Sokoto, Calabar and Maiduguri (Bourgault 1995: 70). These NBS stations and re-diffusion stations were structured along the BBC model of Public Service Broadcasting (PSB), as they were charged to inform, educate and entertain the public in line with their mandatory objective of promoting national unity (see Tudesq 1983: 19; Mackay 1964: 1; Bourgault 1995: 70).

The political crisis between Obafemi Awolowo and the national government over the use of NBS resulted in the establishment of the first television service in Nigeria and Africa as a whole. The television station, known as the Western Nigeria Television (WNTV), was established in 1959 at Ibadan to serve as a political instrument in propagating the ideologies of the government of the Western region (Action Group). The coming of WNTV changed the media environment completely, as broadcasting later became a political tool to advance the cause of each region (see Bourgault 1995). The Eastern region's government established the Eastern Nigeria Television (ENTV) in 1960 to promote its cause; likewise in 1962 at Kaduna, the Northern region established its television service, known as the Northern Nigeria Television (NNTV) with the aid of two British companies, Granada and EMI. Consequently, upon independence in 1960, the three regions all had television stations helping to promote their different ideologies (Bourgault 1995: 132).

The political tension and crisis between the North and South immediately after independence led to the destruction of the PSB model as governments directly interfered with the operation of the broadcast media (Mackay 1964: 53; Bourgault 1995: 70, 72). In addition, the military takeover of the Nigerian state in 1966 led to the creation of states that witnessed a proliferation of television stations as each state clamoured for its own television and radio stations. However, Decree 24 of 1977 created the Nigeria Television Authority (NTA) as the sole body authorized to broadcast signals, so all regional and state-owned television stations were merged into NTA (Bourgault 1995: 132).

In 1979 Decree 24 was again abolished, causing the return of the media to states, and each state was allowed to create and own its media (ibid: 133). The establishment of the National Broadcasting Commission in 1992 by General Babangida witnessed the licencing of private individuals or corporations to participate in the broadcast media, and hence the growth and development that followed (Onwumechili 2007).

The present structure of broadcasting in Nigeria shows that broadcasting is divided into three formal levels—federal, state and private (Ekpu 1990: 116; Ojo 2003; Musa and Mohammed 2004: 244). Each level shows the ownership structure and its funding mechanism.

The **federal level** is comprized of media organizations that are owned and funded by the Federal Government of Nigeria. They include the Nigerian Television Authority (NTA) and the Federal Radio Corporation of Nigeria (FRCN). The federal government appoints and constitutes the board of each organization, and these organizations are directly under the Ministry of Information, and therefore report to the Minister of Information (Musa and Mohammed 2004). NTA and FRCN work on the network system as signals are mainly created in the capital cities and transmitted to the regional zones for re-distribution (Ekpu 1990: 116; Ojo 2003; Bourgault 1995). These organizations' programs fall into three categories, 'public enlightenment, news and current affairs and entertainment', and all are produced in English, although local NTA and FRCN stations produce programs in local Nigerian languages such as Hausa, Yoruba and Igbo (Bourgault 1995: 135–137). These organizations are also mandated to promote Nigerian culture and unity, hence the huge amount of developmental programs produced by both organizations (Bourgault 1995: 137). This, according to Tudesq, has made Nigeria the principal producer of local media content in the African continent (1992: 147). However, both organizations are viewed as the mouthpiece of the Nigerian government and, as such, propaganda tools; hence they lack credibility among the Nigerian people.

State level of ownership is comprized of media organizations owned and funded by the various state governments of the federation. Just like the federal media, these media organizations are directly under the state governments and are meant to serve the information needs of the states (see Musa and Mohammed 2004). State television makes use of ultra high frequency (UHF), and the radio stations use frequency modulation (FM), thus restricting coverage to the boundaries of the states. The board of directors and members of each state media are constituted by the governor of the state and are accountable to the commissioner for information in that state. Such a structure has placed the various state media under the direct control of the state governments, thus the low patronage. It is pertinent to point out that almost all 36 states in Nigeria own one medium of communication (i.e. radio or television).

On the other hand, **private level** of ownership started in 1992 following the establishment of the National Broadcasting Commission (NBC) by General Babangida. The coming of NBC witnessed a proliferation of the media due to private participation in the media sphere (see Jibo and Okoosi 2003: 182). According to Opoku-Mensah, the opening up of the media sphere in any country will lead to the growth and development of the mass media (1998: 9). Presently, the Nigerian media sphere has a huge array of private cable networks and private television stations. The arrival of both private television and cable has helped to meet the information needs of the public since it distrusts both the federal and state-owned media. Nonetheless, these private media are being criticized for focusing more on entertainment programs to achieve good ratings and standing before the public and advertisers. To Paterson, the programming of these private television broadcasters revolves around 'sport, American movies, European and American newscasts' and has little to offer with regard to the local culture of the public (1998: 575). In such scenarios, democracy will be endangered as the public will not be adequately informed.

However, the regulatory structure in Nigeria has not helped in strengthening the media sphere as the regulatory structure of the Nigerian mass media revolves around the National Broadcasting Commission (NBC) and the Nigerian Press Council (NPC). The NBC was established by Decree no 38 of 1992, now amended and known as Act 38 of 1992 (NBC 2009a, b). The commission was charged with the responsibility of regulating the activities of the mass media (i.e. radio, television and satellite) as stated in Section 2 of the NBC Act. Other functions include 'licensing of broadcasting stations, monitoring of broadcasting stations, regulating the broadcasting industry, arbitrating on broadcasting disputes and issuing and enforcing the broadcasting code' (NBC 2009a, b). Consequently, the commission drafted the Nigerian Broadcasting Code which acts as the framework and guideline for regulating media contents, and dealing with complaints arising from the activities of the broadcast media.

The structure of NBC reveals that the board and its members are appointed by the president, and the commission reports directly to the minister of information, thus lacking autonomy. The present organizational structure has been criticized, as it is perceived by critical thinkers that the government exercises undue interference and control over the commission and indirectly influences the operation of the broadcast media (Ojo 2003). On the other hand, the Nigerian Press Council (NPC) is the regulatory body in charge of regulating the activities of the (print) press. The NPC was established by Decree 85 of 1992, now Decree 60 of 1999 (NPC Act 1999). The objective of this decree serves as the framework by which the press is regulated. According to Section 17 of the NPC Act, all practicing journalists should be registered and they must have the necessary qualifications and required experience in order to be recognized by the Nigerian Union of Journalists (NUJ). In addition, to improve accountability and professionalism, the NUJ adopted a code of conduct, the NUJ Code of Ethics of 1998, to regulate the activities of journalists in accordance with the principles of the NPC Act.

However, the lack of autonomy regarding funding and member composition has made scholars argue that the government indirectly interferes with the operation of the NPC and in the affairs of the press (Nyamnjoh 2003, 2004), as the regulatory body sometimes lacks the courage to exercise its authority based on its constituted authority. The manner in which the government appoints members of regulatory agencies has made the public and scholars see such action as an attempt by the government to interfere with regulators' independence (Andrea and Shaw 2009). Before the establishment of both regulatory agencies, regulation of the media in Nigeria was tied to the Ministry of Information, as it decided and dictated the way the media should operate, just as occurred in the colonial era and in the post-independence era (Alhassan 2005). With a tendency to government interference, as earlier highlighted, it can be argued that the colonial legacy of control is still playing out in a refined democratic way.

Complexities in Conceptualization Democracy

Many readers will be wondering why a study of this nature that seeks to critique and examine the nature of policy flow and liberal democracy in Africa would adopt such a title or use the terminology of an 'emerging democracy'. One might ask whether this is wrong or misleading, hence the need to clarify this misconception. My usage of the words 'emerging democracy' in this context is metaphoric as the purpose of the book is to critique the importation of Western liberal ideas such as democracy into the post-colonial African states of Ghana and Nigeria, and to show the irony of the democratic projects through media reforms. This is evident in the complexity of conceptualization of democracy as shown by different scholars such as Diamond, Voltmer, Lindberg and Orock. Diamond and Voltmer, in their standardization of democracy, classified democracy as consolidated democracy, new/emerging democracy and transitioning democracy. According to Voltmer (2008), emerging democracies are democracies that recently embraced democratic practices and are yet to establish these democratic practices into becoming a consolidated democracy. Therefore, there is the need to problematize this conceptualization by asking the following questions: when is democracy consolidated and when is it emerging? What yardsticks have to be met or what is the basis for classifying a nation as a new or emerging democracy? Are these yardsticks culturally, politically and economically inherent to post-colonial states or universally applicable? Using the works of Lindberg, Ake, Orock, Obadare and Nyamnjoh who have argued that there is no single variable of democracy, and critique democratic evaluation based on indicators, we need to understand that within the African context, the democratic model practiced is significantly different, as the space or arena of democracy has its cultural logics of ethno-regionalism in the production of values associated with the ethics of democracy. Hence the metaphoric usage of 'emerging democracies' in the book's title as a way of showing the complexities associated with the universal acceptance of ideas across the world.

Bibliography

Adebanwi, W., & Obadare, E. (2011). The Abrogation of the Electorate: An Emergent African Phenomenon. *Democratization, 18*(2), 311–335.

Ainslie, R. (1966). *The Press in Africa: Communications Past and Present*. London: Gollancz.

Ake, C. (1991). Rethinking African Democracy. *Journal of Democracy, 2*(1), 32–44.

Ake, C. (1996). *Democracy and Development in Africa*. Washington DC: The Brookings Institution.

Ake, C. (2000). *The Feasibility of Democracy in Africa*. Dakar: CODESRIA.

Akpojivi, U., & Fosu, M. (2016). Indigenous Language Broadcasting in Ghana: Retrospect and Prospect. In A. Salawu & M. Chibita (Eds.), *Indigenous Language Media, Language Politics and Democracy in Africa*. New York: Palgrave Macmillan.

Alhassan, A. (2005). Market Valorisation in Broadcasting Policy in Ghana: Abandoning the Quest for Media Democratization. *Media Culture and Society, 27*(2), 211–228.
Andrea, M., & Shaw, C. (2009). *Accountability and the Public Interest in Broadcasting*. London: Palgrave Macmillan.
Ansu-Kyeremeh, K., & Karikari, K. (1998). *Media Ghana: Ghanaian Media Overview, Practitioners and Institutions.* Accra: University of Ghana Printing Press.
Bennett, W., & Serrin, W. (2007). The Watchdog Role of the Press. In D. A. Graber (Ed.), *Media Power in Politics.* Washington DC: CQ Press.
Blankson, I. (2007). Media Independence and Pluralism in Africa Opportunities and Challenges of Democratization and Liberalization. In I. Blankson & P. Murphy (Eds.), *Negotiating Democracy Media Transformations in Emerging Democracies.* Albany: State University of New York.
Boafo-Arthur, K. (1998). The International Community and Ghana's Transition to Democracy. In K. Ninsin (Ed.), *Ghana: Transition to Democracy.* Dakar: CODESRIA.
Bourgault, L. (1995). *Mass Media in Sub-Saharan Africa.* Bloomington: Indiana University Press.
Campbell, J. (2011). *Nigeria Dancing on the Brink.* New York: Rowman & Littlefield Publishers Inc.
Chomsky, N. (2011). *How the World Works.* New York: Penguin Group.
Clapham, C. (1993). Democratization in Africa: Obstacles and Prospects. *Third World Quarterly, 14*(3), 423–438.
Coker, I. (1960). "The Nigerian Press: 1929–1959", in Committee on Inter-African Relations "Report on the Press in West Africa", prepared for the International Seminar on Press and Progress in West Africa. University of Dakar.
Dahl, R. (1971). *Polyarchy Participation and Opposition.* London: Yale University Press.
De Gale, C. (1999). *Ghana Media Report.* Available online at: http://journ.ru.ac.ac/amd/Ghana.htm. Accessed 20 Feb 2007.
Diamond, L. (2008a). Consolidating Democracy. In L. LeDUC, R. Niemi, & P. Norris (Eds.), *Comparing Democracies 2 New Challenges in the Study of Elections and Voting.* London: Sage Publications.
Diamond, L. (2008b). Progress and Retreat in Africa the Rule of Law Verse the Big Man. *Journal of Democracy, 19*, 138–149.
Donkor, P. (2007). *Self Censorship in Ghana Broadcasting Corporation (GBC)* (M. A. Dissertation). University of Leeds.
Ekpu, R. (1990). Nigeria's Embattled Fourth Estate. *Journal of Democracy, 1*(2), 106–116.
Federal Republic of Nigeria. (1999). *The Nigeria Press Council (NPC) Act.* Lagos: Federal Government Press.

Fourie, P. (2008). Ubuntuism As a Framework for South African Media Practice and Performance: Can it Work? *South African Journal for Communication Theory and Research, 34*(1), 53–79.

Hachten, W. (1993). *The Growth of Media in the Third World: African Failures, Asian Successes*. Ames: Iowa State University Press.

Hasty, J. (2005). *The Press and Political Culture in Ghana*. Indiana: Indiana University Press.

Huntington, S. (1991). *The Third Wave: Democratization in the Late Twentieth Century*. Norman: University of Oklahoma Press.

Jakubowicz, K. (2002). Media in Transition the Case of Poland. In M. Price, B. Rozumilowicz, & S. Verhulst (Eds.), *Media Reform Democratizing the Media, Democratizing the State*. London: Routledge.

Jibo, M., & Okoosi, A. (2003). The Nigerian Media: An Assessment of Its Role in Achieving Transparent and Accountable Government in the Fourth Republic. *Nordic Journal of African Studies, 12*(2), 180–195.

Jones-Quartey, K. (1960). "The Ghana Press", in Committee on Inter-African Relations "*Report on the Press in West Africa*", Prepared for the International Seminar on Press and Progress in West Africa. University of Dakar.

Keane, J. (1991). *The Media and Democracy*. Cambridge: Polity Press.

Kolade, C. (1974). Nigeria. In S. Head (Ed.), *Broadcasting in Africa: A continental Survey of Radio and Television*. Philadelphia: Temple University Press.

Kwame, K. (2004). Press Freedom in Africa Challenges and Opportunities. *New Economy*.

Kwesi, Y. (1995). *Speaking for the Chief: Okyeame and the Politics of Akan Royal Oratory*. Bloomington: Indiana University Press.

LaMay, C. (2007). *Exporting Press Freedom Economic and Editorial Dilemmas in International Media Assistance*. London: Transaction Publishers.

Mabadeje, I. (2004). *The Nigerian Press Under the Military: A Compendium of Cases of Press Freedom Violations in Nigeria (1966–1999)*. Uyo: Robertminder International Ltd.

Mackay, I. (1964). *Broadcasting in Nigeria*. Ibadan: Ibadan University Press.

McChesney, R. (1999). *Rich Media, Poor Democracy: Communication Politics in Dubious Times*. New York: The New Press.

Moyer, B. (2008, July 11). Is the Fourth Estate a Fifth Column?: Corporate Media Colludes with Democracy's Demise. *In These Times*.

Musa, M., & Mohammed, J. (2004). The Political Economy of Media Ownership in Nigeria. In T. Pradip & Z. Nain (Eds.), *Who Owns the Media Global Trends and Local Resistances*. London: Zed Books.

NBC. (2009a). Management Structure of the National Broadcasting Commission. Online: www.nbc.gov.ng. Accessed 28 Nov 2009.

NBC. (2009b). Online: www.nbc.gov.ng. Accessed 23 Dec 2008.

NMC Act. (1993). *National Media Commission Act 1993, Act 449*. Accra: Government Printer.

Nyamnjoh, F. (2003). *Media Pluralism and Diversity: A Critical Review of Competing Models*. In Broadcasting Policy and Practice in Africa by Article 19.
Nyamnjoh, F. (2004). Media Ownership and Control in Africa in the Age of Globalization. In T. Pradip & Z. Nain (Eds.), *Who Owns the Media Global Trends and Local Resistances*. London: Zed Books.
Nyamnjoh, F. (2005). *Africa's Media Democracy and the Politics of Belonging*. London: Zed Books.
Nyerere, J. (2000). *Africa Today and Tomorrow*. Dar Es Salaam: The Mwalimu Nyerere Foundation.
Ogbondah, C. (2004). Democratization and the Media in West Africa: An Analysis of Recent Constitutional and Legislative Reforms for Press Freedom in Ghana and Nigeria. *West Africa Review, 6*, 1–36.
Ojo, E. (2003). The Mass Media and the Challenges of Sustainable Democratic Values in Nigeria: Possibilities and Limitations. *Media Culture & Society, 25*(6), 821–840.
Onwumechili, C. (2007). Nigeria: Equivocating While Opening the Broadcast Liberalization Gates. In I. Blankson & P. Murphy (Eds.), *Negotiating Democracy Media Transformations in Emerging Democracies*. Albany: State University of New York.
Opoku-Mensah, A. (1998). *Up in the Air? The State of Broadcasting in Southern Africa. Analysis and Trend in Six Countries*. South Africa: PANOS.
Paterson, C. (1998). Reform or Re-Colonisation? The Overhaul of African Television. *Review of African Political Economy, 25*(78), 571–583.
Price, M. (2002). *Media and Sovereignty the Global Information Revolution and Its Challenge to State Power*. Cambridge: MIT Press.
Price, M., & Verhulst, S. (2000). Introduction. In M. Price & S. Verhulst (Eds.), *Broadcasting Reform in India Media Law from a Global Perspective*. Oxford: Oxford University Press.
Radelet, S. (2010). Success Stories from Emerging Africa. *Journal of Democracy, 21*(4), 87–101.
Rozumilowicz, B. (2002). Democratic Change: A Theoretical Perspective. In M. Price, B. Rozumilowicz, & S. Verhulst (Eds.), *Media Reform Democratizing the Media, Democratizing the State*. London: Routledge.
Silverstone, R. (1999). *Why Study the Media?* London: Sage Publications.
Tudesq, A. (1983). *La Radio en Afriqua Noire*. Paris: Editions A. Pedone.
Tudesq, A. (1992). *L'Afrique Noire et ses Television*. Paris: Anthropos.
Voltmer, K. (2008). Comparing Media Systems in New Democracies: East Meets South Meets West. *Central European Journal of Communication, 1*, 23–40.
Wasserman, H., & Boloka, M. (2004). Privacy, the Press and the Public Interest in Post-Apartheid South Africa. *Parliamentary Affairs, 57*(1), 185–195.

CHAPTER 2

Hegemony and Neo-Liberalism: Democracy and Media Freedom

The purpose of this chapter is to provide the theoretical foundation of the study, by discussing the different theoretical frameworks surrounding democracy and freedom, and how these theories have helped in propagating and promoting the normative idea of democracy and freedom. Likewise, this chapter will further establish how these ideas of democracy and media freedom flow from the Global North to the Global South as instruments of aid and technical assistance (Packenham 1973), hence furthering the principles of neoliberalism that have characterized emerging democracies and their democratization processes.

However, before discussing these theories, we need to start by conceptualizing the democratic media structure in Africa as this will provide the background information for contextualization and contesting the ideas of the different theories.

African Democracy: A Basis for Democratic Media System Development

A very brief recounting of the genesis surrounding this work and this particular section is very relevant for two salient reasons. Firstly, according to Packenham (1973) personal experiences are the best ways in which one is able to describe, discover and critique liberal ideas. Secondly, personal

U. Akpojivi, *Media Reforms and Democratization in Emerging Democracies of Sub-Saharan Africa*,
https://doi.org/10.1007/978-3-319-75301-0_2

experiences will help establish the systematic flow of imperialists' ideas which are normalized in society (see Ake 1982).

My interest in this topic, treated in this section of the book, began in 2015 at a postgraduate student presentation at the Media Studies Department, University of the Witwatersrand, South Africa. A colleague of mine, during a question and answer session, criticized the presenter's idea of an African democracy by asking whether we have an African democracy, or a media system that is functional. 'Can you tell me one African country that has been successful with normative democracy or with African democracy?' he asked. Despite the student's explanation tapping into the Botswana, Rwanda, Tanzanian and Ghanaian experiences, his views were dismissed. In addition, during my doctorate studies at the University of Leeds, United Kingdom, I had on numerous occasions discussed the problems of democracy in Africa and attributed these to the attempt at transplanting Western concepts into Africa, which has not been feasible. On these occasions my ideas were dismissed and I was seen as someone who is overtly African and who loves to critique Western societies and ideologies, and so labelled 'Marxist'. This made me reflect on what democracy means and its culture in African realities, and wonder how an African democratic culture is inherently unique and often dismissed, despite this playing out daily and influencing the media system and media culture. Chomsky (2011) posited that the democratic culture and realities of most African states are different from the 'special' form of democracy advanced by the West, which people are familiar with due to the imperialistic nature of the concept (Ake 1982).

I have often asked: what is so special about the Western notion of democracy that America and other European countries are interested in transplanting these ideas into other countries without recognizing the unique characteristics of these countries (Voltmer 2008; LaMay 2007), and being blind to other forms of democracy? Numerous funds and extensive research has been channeled into exploring the concept of democracy which, in most cases, is presented as the yardstick or framework of development (Ake 1996). Consequently, this leads to the assertion that most African countries are underdeveloped as the result of not being democratic according to Western norms (Ake 1982). Staffan Lindberg and Michael Coppedge, and others in their study of democracy entitled 'Varieties of Democracy', acknowledged that there are different forms of democracy as democracy manifests itself differently. However, I will deviate from their standpoint on the varieties of democracy but focus on the cultures of

African democracy and how these determine how people communicate, and what the role of the media in the democratic process should be.

As stated in Chap. 1, I have approached democracy from the perspective of participation (Nyerere 2000). Participation is central to any democratic institution as it is a procedure that guarantees equality within an unequal society. To Rozumilowicz (2002) such participation allows democratic principles, such as civil and political liberties like freedom of expression and media freedom, to thrive. Nevertheless, the participation which I want to emphasize is communal participation, which is different from Western democratic participation, which is individualistic. According to Ake (1993), African communities focus on communal participation (i.e. participation that will enhance and promote the good of society). This participation cuts across the different age grades, gender and class of the people. Within African communities, men and women meet to deliberate on issues affecting the community through the different age grades composition for men/boys and women/girls in society. For instance, in the Urhobo culture, age grades are called 'otu', which are different based on the practicing community. Likewise, in Igbo tradition age grades are named differently such as OtuOgbo, NdeUke or NdeEbiri according to the specific community (see Amdiume 1987). Otite (1972: 306) argues that such communal participation through the age grades affords community members the opportunity to meet and deliberate collectively on issues affecting the political, economic and cultural developments of the community. In such deliberations, the 'community interests are placed above those' of individuals or lineage group.

Similarly, Obadare (2006) argues that ethno-religious formations and ethno-culture groups are other forms in which citizens' participation seeks to promote communal interests over individual interests. For instance, in Nigeria ethno-cultural groups such as the Arewa Consultative Forum (ACF), Arewu Youth Forums (AYF), Ijaw Youth Congress (IYC) and Oodua Peoples Congress (OPC) are groups in which democratic participation occurs. These shape the wider political and economic development of the country. Almost every ethnic group in Nigeria has a forum where issues affecting the collective interests of the community are discussed before being projected into national polity. Consequently, Obadare (2006) argues that these ethno-cultural groups and ethno-religious groups, such as the Pentecostal Fellowship of Nigeria (PFN) and the Christian Association of Nigeria (CAN), influence the democratic structure of the Nigerian state. This is similar to other post-colonial African states where participation is rooted at the grassroots level and subsequently at national level.

Therefore, the premise that Africa's democracy is rooted in participation at the communal level, which enriches democratic discourse, must be recognized because such participation promotes not only freedom but accountability, due to the cycle of participation. That is, communal participation influences national discourse and participation, and national discourse and participation feed back to the communal level (see Fig. 1). Otite (1972: 307–308), while supporting the above fact, stated that within an African community all:

> participate in one form or the other in settling their own affairs through free discussion and act as final arbiters for the governmental processes as directed by the elders. It must be noted that the age grades have their different leaders whose opinion is always sought by the town council or court on matters peculiar to the age grades or concerning certain aspects of town government such as the execution of administrative decisions. It is therefore obvious that the town rulers and politicians are in close social contact with the various members of their community

Therefore, ignoring these fundamental features of democracy or level at which democracy is practiced and displayed within African societies and focusing only on the regular conduct of elections, free speech as the basis of ascertaining the functionality of democracy in Africa is misleading

Fig. 1 An illustration of the cycle of participation

(see Akpojivi 2013). And this has been the focus of most studies on democracy and media development in the African continent over the past two decades (see Adebanwi and Obadare 2011; Tettey 2001). An understanding of the dynamic nature of the democratic cultures and principles in Africa is fundamental not only to the sustenance of democracy, but to media development in the continent. The mass media is alleged to be at the center of socio-cultural, economic and political development of humans and of the African states due to the role it plays (see Hyden and Okigbo 2002). However, Mano (2011) argues that the media in Africa are not meeting the realities of the people and community that they reach. Most often people are not involved in the everyday activities of the media, consequently Chinweizu (1999) posited that Africa is in dire need of a media system that is socially constructive and will reflect the ideological needs of its people.

Therefore, one way of achieving such a media system is through a democratized media system, i.e. one which reflects the realities of the people and community. This democratized media is inherently linked to principles of communal participation, although the concept of a democratized media is highly contested because people view it differently. Principally, when people talk about democratized media, reference is always made to institutional organization of the communication process and this institution is difficult to democratize due to political and economic reasons (Akpojivi 2014). However, I have approached democratized media as being the ability of citizens to participate actively in the communication process. This means guaranteeing everyone the right to participate in the construction of truth in society and this is only viable when everyone is given the opportunity to participate by expressing themselves through sharing ideas and information that will facilitate the development of society (Hackett 2000). To this end, a democratize media should provide the space for citizens to engage with each other, address issues of public interest devoid of personal interest and nurture debate whether or not such debates will generate controversy. By acting as a site for contestations about the common good for community, truth will be derived (Mill 1859) and this will lead to the overall development of the society.

This means democracy and democratized media is structured on 'voice', that is everyone being invited to participate on issues affecting the development of society and not placing a premium on the voice of a select few in the development of society. This, however, raises questions of who gets to participate or speak within the democratized media. How does this participation or voice manifest itself within national and community discourse?

And in what shape does it manifest itself within the African context? With Nyerere (2000) and Ake (1993) expounding ideas of communal participation, one would assume that everyone is given a voice and everyone is heard. However, this is not the case as even within the different ethno-cultural groups such as age grade and ethno-religious groups which Obadare (2006) elucidated, certain voices are suppressed or marginalized due to seniority, social status or other factors (see Otite 1972). Nevertheless, within the African context, 'all voices are welcomed but some voices are given priority over others' and this informs and shapes the communication process. Although this can be considered as bad, as all voices are not placed on equal footing (Ngugi 2017), the mere fact that there is egalitarianism within the process strengthens democratic culture and media democratization.

The dynamics in which this participation or voice is manifested in Africa has changed dramatically. This voice is not only limited to elites who by status of their social, economic and political conditions are invited to participate but it is also individualized, in other words the interests of the community are not the overall motive of such participation. This has led to the dependency approach of post-colonial states (Mbembe 2017) because society now depends on these elites for guidelines, and these elites depend on normative Western framework for addressing societal problems: hence the mishaps confronting African societies. Hackett (2000), while promoting the need for African growth and development, posited that having a democratized media which encourages active participation will enable society to improve on practices, institutions and context (especially policies) that will drive democratic principles and values of participation, and accountability, which is a bane in Africa. In addition, this will be more relevant for a continent where the majority of its citizens reside in rural areas and are invariably excluded from all spheres of society. Therefore, this democratized media will enable and facilitate the inclusion of these excluded people in both local and national discourses. Chibita and Salawu (2016) argue that such participation will lead to media and democracy development in Africa.

However, this form of democratized media is currently not obtainable within the mainstream media as participation is limited to elites or people who the media thought were relevant to society (see McChesney 2002, 2008). Although with the emergence of new media technologies most ordinary people can contribute and participate in the media sphere (Fosu and Akpojivi 2015), nevertheless such participation is still limited. And this has contributed significantly to the weakening of the democratization processes on the continent and reliance on the Western model for development. Consequently, the praxis of most African states in achieving the intended policy goals or objectives of these Western liberal notions of democracy and media reforms in their states.

Nyamnjoh (2005: 25), while summing up the impact of this dependency and transplanting liberal democracy without understanding Africa's democratic culture discussed above, held that:

> implementing liberal democracy in Africa has been like trying to force unto a body of a fully figured person, rich in cultural indicators of health with which Africans are familiar to a dress made to fit a slim, de-fleshed Hollywood consumer model of a Barbie-doll entertainment icon...then when the dress fails to fit the African body, instead of blaming the tiny dress or its designer, the tradition has been to fault the popular body for emphasising too much bulk, for parading the wrong size, for just not being the right thing. Not often is the experience of the designer or dress maker questioned. Such high levels of insensitivity is akin to the behavior of a Lilliputian undertaker who would rather trim a corpse than expand a coffin to accommodate a man-mountain or a carpenter whose only tool is a hammer and to whom every problem is a nail.

The above from Nyamnjoh (2005) calls for the need to allow and recognize that different societies have different traditions and cultures and this should be allowed to shape and negotiate the forms of democracy and communication that suit a society's context. This means that democracy and media democratization in Africa is not absolute and individualistic but is rooted in citizens' participation, which is not abstract or based on elitist participation but conceived on the assumption that everyone must participate in policy decisions and implementation. The inability to exercise this active participation is what has led to policy complications where emerging democracies such as Ghana and Nigeria are unable to achieve the desired policy objectives due to the flawed policy formulation and implementation of policies that have not recognized the unique inherent African democratic practice. This book is on a trajectory to juxtapose the experiences of Ghana and Nigeria and identify lessons that could be learnt from both countries. These lessons could be applied in understanding the democratic patterns of new democracies in the region.

Revising Media Freedom: The Philosophical Debate

The concept of media freedom and its meaning is highly contested as it means different things to different people. Most often when media freedom is debated and discussed it is seen from the negative freedom perspective that is (ideas of absolute freedom) without recognizing that freedom needs to be regulated and that there is no absolute freedom in any country, even in the most liberal nations of the world such as the United States, Britain and Canada. Despite this, the legitimacy of any government is centered on the government's ability to protect free speech and media freedom because free speech is considered the foundation of any democratic state because of its ability to facilitate accountability within the state and consolidate democratic principles (Richards 1999). Consequently, there are annual reports from media watchdog organizations such as Mo Ibrahim, Article 19 and Reporter without Borders which highlight the state of the media and democracy in developed, developing and underdeveloping countries. Such reports are often criticized by nation states, policymakers and scholars (see Levitsky and Way 2010: 60–61). Therefore, within this section I seek to examine and discuss the different philosophical and political debates of media freedom and how this has influenced how emerging democracies such as Ghana and Nigeria conceptualize and understand media freedom.

Barendt (1985) argues that media freedom constitutes both a philosophical and political debate. Philosophically, there are two approaches to the concept of media freedom (i.e. a negative freedom perspective and a positive freedom perspective). However, most often in the debate of media freedom scholars are aligned to the negative freedom approach which is premised on freedom from state control. This approach is rooted in the principles of truth, democracy and self-fulfillment advanced by John Stuart Mill and Alexander Meiklejohn. The principles of truth and self-fulfillment are associated with John Stuart Mill who posited that the pursuit of truth through free and unregulated discussions will lead to individual self-fulfillment and development (Mill 1869 [1974: 33]). Likewise, the principle of democracy postulated by Alexander Meiklejohn held that democracy will be enriched when people are free to express themselves as the unrestricted flow of information will provide citizens with valuable information to hold governments accountable (Lewis 2004).

Nevertheless, the philosophical foundation for the debate of media freedom is rooted in John Stuart Mill's classical work entitled *On Liberty*, as Mill addressed salient issues confronting media freedom debates such as :is freedom absolute? When can nation states interfere or intervene, and what kind of intervention can be of public and national interest? These issues are still relevant in contemporary societies as states are confronted with these issues, in other words the need for a balance between freedom and regulation (Lichtenberg 1990a, b; McQuail 2003; see Akpojivi 2012). Mill in *On Liberty* examined the extent to which states can exercise legitimacy over individuals and limit or protect individuals from the tyranny of the state (1869 [1974]). According to Mill, everyone has the right to form an opinion and be free to express such opinion(s). As such, free expression will lead to the discovery of truth as 'truth is more likely to emerge from uninhibited discussion than from the exercise of freedom subject to occasional government restraint or regulation' (cited in Barendt 1985: 8). The above statements indicate that society will benefit more from a marketplace of ideas as this will facilitate human and societal developments. Mill attests to this by arguing that the suppression of an opinion will rob society of human development as the suppressed idea or opinion could have been the truth that would have assisted the state and government in developing society (1869 [1974: 34]). Consequently, Kant stated that denying citizens the freedom to express themselves is like 'withholding from the ruler all the knowledge of those matters which if he knew about them he would himself rectify' (cited in Holmes 1990: 29).

Nevertheless, Mill further stated that this right to freedom of expression of citizens can be withdrawn when such rights pose a threat to the public as human activities could occasionally affect society (1869 [1974: 23, 100]). The democratic nature of society confers rights and freedom to citizens thereby exposing society to danger as these citizens could exceed their freedom and cause harm to others in society, hence the need for regulation (Mill 1869 [1974: 101]; Kendall 1966: 34; Lichtenberg 1990a, b: 12; Holmes 1990: 37). According to Mill, the only freedom devoid of restraint is that which does not affect other members of society: therefore the conduct of every individual must be in line with the interests of others (1869 [1974: 27]). Hegel buttressed this argument further by stating that man is by nature an evil being and cannot make right decisions or judgments, thus the need for the state to regulate man's activities (1869: 35). Therefore, society is believed to have jurisdiction over the conduct of man which may affect the rights or activities of others. And when the jurisdiction of the state is questioned by the public, such jurisdiction should be subjected to public debate (Mill 1869 [1974: 135]).

On the other hand, Lichtenberg (1990a, b) posited that this has informed the contemporary demands for regulations as the rationale behind national states' government regulation of free speech and the media is centered on the need to protect the national interest, which has to a large extent informed the need for content and structural regulation of the media. For the sake of national interest certain information and activities have to be excluded from media debates and the rights of individuals to participate in the media discourse restrained (Holmes 1990). Although this call for regulation has been criticized, the need for regulation in society cannot be overemphasized because, according to Holmes, if there are no regulations, society will be subjected to the dictates of the few, and monopolies and autocracy of the private interests of the selected few will be promoted (1990a, b; see Fiss 1990; McQuail 1992). Nevertheless, the premise of regulation is centered on three fundamental arguments. The positive right argument holds that state intervention and regulation are necessary to protect both the speaker and the public rights of access to media. The teleological argument posits that freedom of speech is a means to achieving certain societal values such as fairness and truth which are pivotal to the development of society. According to this view, interventions from the state could sometimes help states in achieving these values more effectively than when there is no state intervention. The democracy argument states that state regulation of the media will enable the media to provide the necessary information required by informed citizens and electorate (Kelley and Donway 1990).

Despite these positions, the idea of regulation has been widely criticized by liberal theorists such as Milton, Locke, Tocqueville and Spinoza. According to these political theorists, who have contributed to the development of liberal theories, freedom is a catalyst for democracy consolidation and development (Curran 1979: 68; Holmes 1995: 13; Ocitti 1999: 9). According to these theorists, democracy bestows on everyone the right to express views and opinions whether dissenting or not, and such views or opinions should not be silenced by the state in its attempt to regulate (Ambrose 1995). Sketch, while extending this thought further, posited that democracy thrives within the premise of plurality of political views and active public participation and discussion (cited in Holmes 1995: 15). This can only be achieved within an unregulated media as they will be free to actively carry out their functions as watchdogs or holding governments accountable, and provide a platform for people to engage with each other (Tettey 2001; Feintuck 1999; McQuail 2003).

This idea of regulation is always disputed in society because regulation is often seen as pursuing the selfish interest of state and states cannot be trusted to act as a mechanism for enforcing regulation because, according to critics, governments hide behind the complex nature of society to overestimate the threat free speech and media freedom has on national security in order to justify regulation (Scanlon 1990; Ungar 1990).

Most often in African states, governments have used simple but contested words of public interest and national interest to regulate free speech and media freedom, and both concepts have influenced policy formulation and implementation in contemporary societies. According to Netshitenzhe (2002), national interest connotes the totality of things that ensure the survival of a nation and it is the responsibility of the democratic government to make such decisions which should reflect the wishes of the public (McQuail 2003). To Freedman, public interest is the 'realisation of the desires of the public as a collection of individuals' (2008: 64). However, this idea has been jettisoned by the media which argue that most often national interest and public interest reflect the interest of a selected few and a means by the state to limit critical media and views (Wasserman and de Beer 2006: 67). Likewise, the state has rejected the media claims of public interest to mean the media's own selfish ambition. On the other hand, the citizens demand accountability from the media as they are perceived to hold the public trust by engaging in their watchdog functions and responsibility using the freedom granted to them. Hence the need to ascertain the extent to which the mass media are living up to their responsibility as most often the ills in society are attributed to the media for failing to effectively fulfill their responsibility.

However, Madison added a new dimension of free speech to the philosophical argument of media freedom. According to him, free speech is an 'inalienable human right' bestowed to man and this right should be protected from being hijacked by 'abusive censorship of political debate' by the majority who might want to suppress the rights of others (Richards 1999: 1, 24). To him the concept of free speech is an abstracted concept that is rooted in the normative philosophy of natural rights and denying people this right to freely express themselves is a structural injustice (Richards 1999). Therefore, Madison advocates for tolerance of speech whether dissenting or not. This call for tolerance, according to Richards, 'extends the protection of free speech as broadly as the underlying right to conscience and threats thereto' (1999: 26). However, Bollinger (1986) posited that this concept of tolerance under free speech might facilitate the possibility of civil disobedience due to entertaining all views and opinions. Consequently, critics have criticized this idea of tolerance arguing that it is a utopian concept as there are no governments in the world, even the liberal states of the United States, Canada, etc. that will translate the theory of tolerance into practice or reality (Marcuse 1969). For instance, the United States, known as a firm believer and promoter of freedom, has been very critical of WikiLeaks' and Julian Assange's activities in revealing classified information. Likewise, the espionage and security laws such as the Patriot Act and Incitement Law have been used to arrest and detain people such as Chelsea Manning for disclosing information which was regarded as sensitive.

On this basis Marcuse (1969) argues that the concept of tolerance is used to strengthen the tyranny of some over others since the concept has changed its political meaning from being 'an active into passive, from practice to non-practice', consequently the belief that the public tolerate every activity of the government and the government does not tolerate public activity. Meiklejohn substantiated the above argument further by stating that the mere fact that most liberal states have constitutional provision for freedom does not guarantee that such speeches from everyone will be entertained but speeches should be in line with the requirements of the law (1966: 23). This further establishes the arguments for regulation that are earlier discussed. Emerson (1982: 62), while summing the different contestations between free speech and tolerance, concludes that 'powerful forces will surely seek to contain the outer boundaries of expression by prohibiting speech that challenges the underlying political, economic and social structures'.

These different contestations surrounding free speech, tolerance and regulation supports Hegel's criticism of the notion of negative freedom. According to him, the argument for a negative freedom is 'one sided', hence the need to recognize the ideas of positive freedom. According to him, there is no single country in the world whose citizens and media enjoy absolute freedom as there will always be some form of restriction or regulation to check excesses in society. These restrictions are essential to safeguard the security of the nation state (Richard 1999) even though such concepts are contested and controversial (see Freedman 2008). However, the ability to contextualize positive rights within the domain of negative rights will lead to progress and development of society (Hegel 1896: 37). In other words, states should guarantee the freedom of media and speech as this will lead to a marketplace of ideas and enable the media to fulfill their watchdog roles, but should likewise allow for regulation that will limit the excesses of the media. This is in accordance with Benjamin Franklin's assertion that 'the liberty of the press should be left untouched but balanced with the liberty of the cadgel' (cited in Clark 2005: 33).

Despite these, Barendt and Hitchens (2000: 15) argued that the concept of media freedom is different from free speech because media freedom is conditional and institutional, which is different from unconditional free speech. In other words, freedom of the media is centered on them being committed to performing certain responsibilities and when such responsibilities cannot be met the need for media freedom protection cannot be justified (Lichenberg 1990a, b: 104). Therefore, rethinking or revising the concept of media freedom is required. What does it really mean? How can media freedom be approached in an emerging democracy with inherent political, economic and cultural conditions?

Keane (1991) conceives media freedom as absolute freedom from government control and the rights of citizens to freely express themselves. This position was equally supported by Ojo (2003: 825) who sees media freedom as 'the right or ability of practitioners to express their views, opinions or report events as they are without seeking approval from any person(s) and without being subjected to any form of intimidation, molestation, persecution or harassment'. The ideas surrounding these definitions are most often used in the debate and discourse of media freedom across the world. However, such understanding of media freedom is myopic as there is always the tendency of nation states to interfere (control, or censor) information which they regard as unfavorable although the level of such control differs from country to country (Pillai 1999–2000: 198). Also, if media freedom is seen from the perspective of freedom from government control or interference, scholars need to address the growing trend of government sponsored or owned international media and the global flow of information from organizations such as Voice of America, Al Jazeera, BBC World Service and Deutsche Welle, and whether such acts are repressive to media freedom (Gunaratne 2002: 344), which have also been instruments for public diplomacy.[1]

However, McQuail sees media freedom differently. He viewed media freedom as the ability of the media to meet the needs and demands of the public as their sole responsibility (cited in Tettey 2006: 229). This is in line with the Royal Commission on the Press (1997) ideology which advocates freedom for the media (journalists, editors and proprietors) to meet the demands of the public, as such informed publics are needed in order to sustain and grow the democratic processes (cited in Curran 1979: 76). Curran added that the central role that the mass media plays in society as the watchdog and fourth estate of the realm, has influenced the normative idea of freedom of the media from political and economic influences (1979). Because it is only when the media is granted this freedom (from political and economic pressures) that they can effectively act out and fulfill their responsibilities to society by reflecting diversity of views and opinions that will ensure a well-educated public which will be able to sustain democracy (Curran 1979: 68). Nevertheless, this perspective has been criticized by Graber et al. (1998: 3) who argued that such a perspective ignores the problems associated with concentrated media ownership and commercialization of the media. These associated problems, coupled with inherent political and economic factors, will hinder the media from acting as a marketplace due to the interplay of these factors in the activities of the media (Wahl-Jorgensen 2007).

This idea of media freedom is grounded in the liberal theory (i.e. the absolute freedom perspective of media freedom earlier discussed). Gunaratne (2002) alluded that media freedom is usually associated with the feature of Siebert's theory of liberalism or what Merrill (2000a) referred to as CHAOS—'Competition, Heterogeneity, Autonomy, Openness and Selfish paradigm'. This perspective sees the openness of society (i.e. the implementation of a liberalization policy) and media (i.e. freedom from government control and monopoly) as a means of judging media freedom (Ocitti 1999: 9). The basis for such argument is based on the ideas that developed and modernized societies have opened up (liberalized), hence their development, unlike underdeveloping and authoritarian states which lack development. Consequently, Tettey (2001) stated that this idea has informed the current wave of democratization taking place in the developing world due to the benefits presented to them. Tettey (2006) further added that such openness is central to the political and economic developments of emerging democracies because it will help institute and promote good governance and societal values such as truth and fairness (see also Cammack 1994; Leftwich 1993; Tettey 2001).

Thussu (2000) believed that the mass media are the driving force of such development and modernization; hence the importance of media freedom to drive such a process cannot be overemphasized. To him, the media help to pass such ideologies (democracy, development and modernization) onto the African continent, and only a free and independent media can facilitate this (see also Kareithi and Kariithi 2005). From the above, it can be posited that this idea of media freedom revolves around the features of government not having a monopoly of information, relative absences of government restraints on the media, the existence of conditions to ensure the dissemination of diverse ideas and no concentrated ownership (McQuail 1992 and Price 2002a, b). These features or characteristics of media freedom as encapsulated in the Western frameworks are not reflective of the unique African experiences. A lucid review of the media freedoms in African countries shows that they do not follow or subscribe to those features. According to Haynes (2001a, b) and Huntington (1991) the mass media in Africa reveal some culturally unique features such as dominance of state-owned and controlled media, private ownership alongside government ownership, lack of public service as understood in the West, regulatory bodies under government supervision, a large-scale culture of corruption, incomprehensive legal frameworks and government interference with the judiciary.

Consequently, Nyamnjoh (2005) argues that the generalized features of the West are too 'simplistic' and 'unrealistic' as they do not take into consideration the socio-cultural, political and economic situations of each country. In addition, these unique features in Africa are intangible features which have influenced emerging democracies' understanding of media freedom and concepts such as public and national interest. In a bid to be perceived as democratic, emerging democracies such as Ghana and Nigeria, which are the focus of this study, have embraced and embarked on the rhetoric assertion of media freedom. Therefore, the question arises of what counts as the present state of media freedom after embarking on such policies following the re-democratization processes that started in 1992 and 1999 respectively. This is relevant because there have been increased cases of intimidation and assault on media practitioners and attempts by the state to censor or regulate mainstream media including new media (see Nyarko and Akpojivi 2017).

From the above, it can be inferred that the Western model of media freedom has not been effective in emerging democracies. This does not mean that media freedom ideas as contained in the Western framework should be dismissed but that in emerging democracies such as Ghana and Nigeria there is the need to recognize and consider the unique features of these African states, as already discussed above. Therefore, we need to explore the degree of universality of the Western concepts of media freedom in these countries, and to examine the extent of the conditions under which the universal standards can be applied, since the *values* of media freedom cannot be transplanted from one country to another, although attempts have been made to transplant the *ideas* of media freedom (see Ake 1979).

In line with the above assertion, I will approach media freedom in Ghana and Nigeria in this book as the ability of the media to act as a space or arena for participation (see Van Belle 2000: 138). That is, the ability of the media to encourage and act as a public sphere for discussion without interference of editorial positions, and the free exchange of information among the public and within the media sphere without restrictions. This criterion best suits the African context for two fundamental reasons. Firstly, most scholars have ignored the issue of accessibility and participation in the debate of media freedom on the African continent, but focus more on the ideas of interference and restriction from government. In the discourse of media freedom it is useful to examine who are participating and who have access to participation. This is in relation to earlier discussion that African societies are communal and participation of all is central in decision making. However, in most societies participation in the media sphere is restricted to the elite, thus the interest of the minority supersedes the interest of the majority who are excluded from such participation.

McQuail (1992: 8) argues that there has been a continual conflict between the media, elites and non-elites, as 'all these voices want control or access to the media channel for their purpose'. In this competition for access and participation, the non-elite are at a disadvantage since they cannot afford access due to their low social status (McQuail 1992). According to statistics, the majority of the populace in Africa resides in rural areas (World Bank 2015), consequently making participation and accessibility a mirage for them. Secondly, in Africa the 'parameters of freedom of expression and press continue to be determined by how well the content of that particular print, or electronic medium portrays powerbrokers in a positive or at least neutral light' (Tettey 2001: 12), and not on the basis of the constitutional provision facilitated by liberalism.

These elements as contained in my conceptualization and definition of media freedom will aid in the contextualization of media freedom in Ghana and Nigeria as it will enable a critical reflection of how emerging democracies understand media freedom and how such an understanding influences their policy formulation and implementation processes.

Media Policy Making and the Dependency Approach

Marshal McLuhan (1964), in his book *Understanding Media: The Extensions of Man*, posited that we live in a global village where information is expected to flow freely irrespective of boundaries. The mass media is regarded as a strategic tool in the attainment of this global village because people can only access information about their immediate environment and the world at large via the media (Taylor 1997: 3). To this end, media and communication policies are formulated to enhance this free flow and exchange of information across countries, even though it is naïve to say such guiding principles are well implemented without any form of restriction by nation states (Price 2002a, b). Ideally communication and media policies are influenced by institutional dynamics, technological innovation and democratization, which constantly mold and shape the dynamics of policy debates (Mansell and Raboy 2011: 2). These factors to a large extent determine the pattern of information flow within a country and between countries, and whether a society will be an information society or knowledge-based society where information is readily available to the general public irrespective of geographical location, or an exclusive society. Therefore, the rise in nation states' demand for communication policies in the twenty-first century to address the challenge of the globalized media sphere with regard to the unprecedented scale of impact that the political, economic and cultural structures of societies have on the context and content of media policies.

Voltmer (2008: 26), while extending this point further, stated that policymakers are expected to formulate policies that will address the various dimensions by which the principles of free speech or media freedom might be endangered. These include ownership laws to limit media concentration and laws to protect cultural identities, among others. Although the struggle for media policies to share the global ideology of media freedom and free speech has never been a neutral one but a 'tactical argument in socioeconomic and ideological struggles, these policies are drafted to reflect and promote the universal ideology of free flow of information' (Nordenstreng 2011: 84, 86; Freedman 2008).

Historically, the idea of media freedom is an age-old concept in which policymakers have engaged since the start of the Cold War (Schiller 1976). This is explicitly stated in John Foster Dulles' (the American architect of the Cold War) statement 'if I were to be granted one point in foreign policy and no other, I would make it the free flow of information' (cited in Schiller 1976: 30). Packenham (1973), while substantiating this view, posited that ideas such as democracy and media freedom are used by America as instruments of foreign policies in pushing and spreading American ideology. This makes the idea of media freedom as a tool of achieving a marketplace of ideas an old idea, not one that had started with the World Summit on the Information Society (WSIS 2003, 2005) as most scholars tend to argue. John Foster Dulles' statement reveals the strategic importance of media freedom in the global media environment and in the policy arena (Nordenstreng 2011: 79). Therefore, the doctrine of free flow of information or media freedom has been an ideological concept and struggle in the global scene as suggested by Dulles and Packenhams' statements, and has influenced media policy formulation and implementation in developed and developing countries alike.

Consequently, this makes media freedom a concept whose construct 'is made up of political and ideological elements derived mainly from the United States geopolitical interest' (Nordenstreng 2011: 79). To Chuma and Moyo (2010: 1–2), the reforms embarked upon by developing countries since the 1990s reflect the new focuse of a unipolar world dominated by the United States after the Cold War. Price argued that the supremacy of the United States in this ideological struggle has influenced the conceptualization of media freedom in line with the beliefs of the United States, and is presently being universalized (2002a, b: 47). In other words, the guiding principles of the United States built around its historic context of promoting 'freedom' (as contained in its constitution) has shaped how communication policies are approached in the global arena. The influence of the United States through media and communication policies is constantly felt through the 'process of interaction, through treaty or agreement on the flow of ideas, information', which is intensified on a daily basis (Price 2002a, b: 3).

This is done via the hard and soft approaches which have made nation states dependent on the United States (see Ake 1996; Mbembe 2017). Melody reasoned that 'it is increasingly difficult for countries to make national policies without coordinating with international organisations' (2011: 69) such as UNESCO, ITU, the IMF and the World Bank. Since the Cold War, UNESCO is a major organization that has helped in the spread of universal ideas like 'freedom' across nations. Chakravartty and Sarikakis (2006: 7) argue that UNESCO and other multi-lateral bodies were pivotal tools for promoting neoliberal policies and the ideology of modernization and Westernization during the Cold War. Although UNESCO portrays 'itself as a defender of freedom' and not 'press freedom' as contained in Article 1 and 2 of its constitution, pressure from the West has made media freedom its focus or agenda since 1990 (Nordenstreng 2011: 82–83). Consequently, UNESCO and other international agencies have become tools for pushing and promoting the ideological interests of the United States and allies of developing countries primarily because they receive overwhelming support from these countries (the United Kingdom,

France and Germany among others) (Chakravartty and Sarikakis 2006). The formulation of policies that are contrary to the beliefs of these supporting countries and funders of UNESCO would amount to withdrawal of support for UNESCO as witnessed in 1980 Macbride reports in 'Many Voices One World' which saw the United States pull out of UNESCO and other aggressive campaigns against UNESCO (see Winseck 2002; Chakravartty and Sarikakis 2006). Also, recently the United States under President Donald Trump pulled out of UNESCO because of UNESCO's recognition of Palestine; recognition considered to have an anti-Israel bias (Shugerman 2017).

To this end, most UNESCO policy documents have emphasized the development and modernization of the media environment in developing countries using neoliberal policies (Manyozo 2011). However, in the wake of the emergence of telecommunications towards the end of the twentieth century, the emphasis moved from UNESCO to the International Telecommunication Union (ITU) (Chakravartty and Sarikakis 2006). Consequently, the ITU hosted a series of meetings such as the World Summit of the Information Society (WSIS) in 2003 and 2005 with the central goal of achieving an 'Information Society' where information is readily available across borders. Hence, deregulation and liberalization of the telecommunication and media sectors became a necessary policy agenda for countries, as evident in the WSIS summits in Tunis (2005) and Geneva (2003) where individual rights to communication was recognized as a fundamental tool in the attainment of an information society (see Chakravartty and Sarikakis 2006). Therefore, Nordenstreng (2011: 86) asserted that 'WSIS stands as a culmination of post-Cold War globalisation' which Western countries have used to export and transplant their ideological interests of freedom to other countries. Developing countries and emerging democracies today look at these international organizations for frameworks or blueprints of their policy formulation and implementation. Hence, Price and Verhulst (2000) posited that the inevitable practice of developing countries looking to international organizations and developed countries for reform practices has further enhanced international dominance in policymaking processes (2000: 89).

This hegemony is further strengthened by soft approaches from international organizations in the form of media assistance programmes and granting of loans to influence policymaking processes of transitioning, and emerging democracies in luring them to embrace neoliberal policies of the West (Packenham 1973). LaMay (2007) alleged that the United States and allies export Western ideas of media freedom to countries through media assistance packages and loans from the World Bank and the IMF. Such media assistance packages and loans not only help to further the ideological interests of the United States, but those of other associated countries with shared ideologies (LaMay 2007). Countries that adopt democracy and are willing to promote freedom are rewarded with 'heavy political and economic incentives' while those opposed to such dominating ideas are deprived of incentives (Mertus 1999 cited in Price 2002a, b: 60; Onwumechili 2007). America or the Western ideology of free flow and doctrine of non-intervention is centered on 'free market capitalist politico-economic system' (Taylor 1997: 38).

Therefore, LaMay (2007) argues that political and economic incentives for media assistance have become a hugely attractive mechanism for encouraging emerging and transitioning democracies to formulate and implement communication and media policies that will facilitate media freedom and democracy. This is evident in the vast budget spent by these Western countries on media assistance. LaMay (2007: viii) stated that, for example, 'USAID spent over $264 million on media assistance between 1985 and 2001, the great majority of that after 1989 when the agency spent an average of $33 million annually on such assistance, with amounts ranging from a low of $13 million in 1992 to a high of $61 million in 1999; the total of all US media assistance, governmental and non-governmental is estimated to be at least $600 million over the same period, with the bulk of it going to former soviet and communist countries in Europe'. This increase in media assistance to emerging democracies is because these democracies need these funds to tackle economic depression in their countries. As Taylor puts it, emerging democracies 'obviously find it difficult to survive independently in an increasingly interdependent world economically delineated by the Bretton Woods system, unless they become part of the system' (1997: 38). Packenham asserted that this aid and media assistance was perceived as an instrument that will contribute to the growth and development of these countries. This process became a dominant approach for the hegemonic transfer of Western ideas such as freedom and democracy to emerging democracies. Hence the fundamental questions in the policymaking processes of these countries are: who is involved? Is there active participation of the public in the policymaking that affects their lives? Whose interests are reflected in the policymaking processes? These questions are salient because, according to Melody, we live in an internationalized policy environment and 'national sovereignty with respect to communication policies is being steadily eroded' (2011: 69).

Therefore, the need to critically examine the dependency approach that has characterized media policy processes in emerging democracies and assess whether these policies are able to address the salient developmental issues in the media environment of emerging democracies as the political, economic and cultural antecedents of these democracies are not recognized in this globalized media freedom ideology. According to Gilson and Raphaely (2008), an evaluation of policymaking in emerging democracies shows that the ruling elite readily accepts these Western ideas of liberalization, privatization and commercialization in the wake of re-democratization without consultation with the vast majority of the public to ascertain how these values are compatible with the inherent values of the nation state; or what the impact of such policies on the socio-political, economic and cultural patterns of the state is (Tunstall 1977; Chakravartty and Sarikakis 2006).

Ideological homogenization has been widely criticized because it has become the yardstick for measuring the state of media freedom and democracy in nation states by these Western states and media assistance donors (Dahl 1971; 1956) without understanding how uniquely different nation states are. This difference and hegemonic flow of ideology makes policy-making processes in Africa complex. Emerging democracies seek to reform their media industries in line with these Western ideologies because it is believed that these policies will certainly work in their countries since they worked in developed societies, but without understanding the interplay of the political, economic and socio-cultural factors of each nation state (Melkote and Steeves 2001: 78). Also, there is a desire to maintain media aid and other economic and technical assistance that accompanies such policy reforms, even when they are unsustainable in the society due to cultural clashes (LaMay 2007). Claude Ake (1996, 1979) captured this validly by stating that African leaders want to assert their independence by formulating their own policies and ideas and likewise embrace these Western ideas due to the economic and other assistance which they consider vital to developing their countries. Milton (2000: 38) ascribes this dilemma to the fact that some people are benefitting from the status quo, hence the unwillingness to allow for reforms to recognize the unique political, economic and socio-cultural dynamics of these countries. Therefore, Nyamnjoh argues, this has not led to the development of the media sphere in these emerging democracies due to the cultural and societal clashes about policy values. According to him, the ideas reflected in the policies of these emerging democracies are myopic and a false representation of the realities in the African media environment, and thus unrealistic (2005: 257).

Tomaselli (2009) argues that it will be difficult for these emerging democracies to achieve the desired goals contained in the policy documents with hegemonic ideologies because templates in which these policies are crafted differ from the practices in these new emerging democracies in Africa. Therefore, it is very important for policymakers in these emerging democracies to go outside borrowing and accepting of ideas from Western or international organizations and formulate policies that engage with everyone (elite and non-elite); by so doing recognizing the prevailing socio-economic and cultural realities of their societies (Melkote and Steeves 2001: 199). This calls for a paradigm shift from the dependency approach to a participation approach, as this will help identify potential policy implementation issues and other challenges to the policy process before and during policy formulation. This is not usually identified with the dependency approach because of the linear flow of ideologies built into such imported policies. Therefore, the participatory approach involves an in-depth understanding of the problem through the active participation of all stakeholders, which will help prevent pre-determined ideologies in policy process, seeing that the effectiveness or realization of policy goals is largely affected by the complex interplay of societal values identified in the policy process (Hill 2005: 184).

Framework for Understanding Policymaking

Following the previous sections, which looked at the hegemonic flow of policy into emerging democracies and its impact, it is now relevant to examine the policymaking processes useful for the development of emerging democracies. This section throws more light onto this process and provides an ideal framework for understanding this process.

Policy research stems from the desire to ascertain the effectiveness of policies in societal reforms (Walt et al. 2008: 308). It has become common in academic research activities because of its multi-disciplinary nature that cuts across many fields such as political sciences, media and communications, economics and health (Buse 2008). Consequently, the stereotypical approach of most policy research has failed to look at the holistic policymaking process. For instance, some focus on the role of actors, in other words the actor-centric approach which focuses only on the role of actors and their ideologies in the policy process thereby ignoring other aspects of the policy process such as policy content and the policy implementation process (see Reich 1995; Buse 2008). Likewise, others focus on policy content and its likely impact on the media environment, while neglecting other aspects (i.e. actors and process) (Gilson and Raphaely 2008: 295). Therefore, Mansell and Raboy posited that focusing on these aspects alone neglects fundamental issues surrounding the policy process (2011: 5).

Consequently, in order to understand the holistic policymaking process, I will adopt the Walt and Gilson (1994) framework which recognizes the totality of the policy process (i.e. policy context, policy content and policy process). The framework understands that policy is a product of political and social processes which are most often ignored in the dominant policy framework used in the field of media studies. For instance, Brewer and deLeon (1983) present a linear, six-stage, policy process that is difficult to conceptualized as policy formulation does not necessarily follow linear stages in society. Likewise, Lasswell's (1956) heuristic stages of policymaking that view the process as neutral is not suitable. Policymaking is a highly contested process in which contrasting political and economic actors fight for material advantage (Freedman 2008). According to Walt and Gilson's framework of policy processes, there is interaction between all the elements and actors in policymaking. To them, the effectiveness of any policy with regard to evaluation (i.e. if policy goals and objectives have been achieved) is dependent on all three elements of context, content and process. Policy context refers to the historical and immediate environment and the problems that the policy seeks to address (Walt 1999). The context is also the genesis of the policy process as problems are identified based on the historical background or present environment (Brewer and deLeon 1983: 31). These problems, coupled with the vested interests of the different stakeholders/actors, will determine the policy objective (Gilson and Erasmus 2008: 362). Policy content means the wording of the policy or provisions of the policy as a means of addressing the problems identified in the policy context. This is usually influenced by the policy context (i.e. the historical and societal values) (Walt 1999). The policy process involves the implementation of the policy in order for the policy goals to be realized (Walt and Gilson 1994). This policy process could be affected by political, cultural and economic factors which will, to a large extent, determine the effectiveness of the policy and the implementation mechanism (see Hutchison 1999).

Although this framework (see Fig. 2) looks simple, it reveals the interaction and interplay between each element in the policy process, and a problem with just one element in the framework will impact on the overall effectiveness of the policy process.

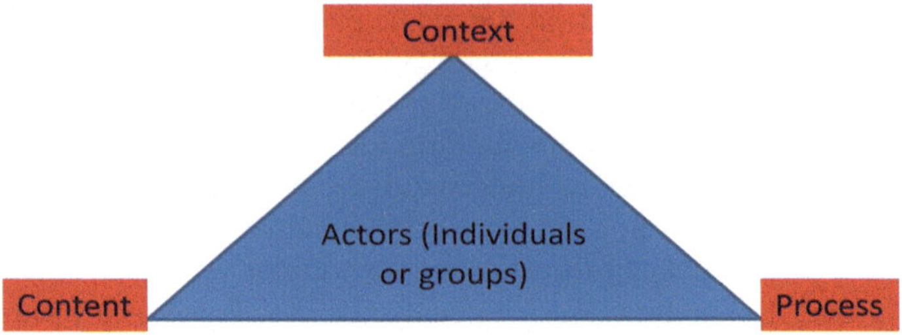

Fig. 2 Walt and Gilson's (1994) Framework of policymaking (see also Akpojivi 2014)

Using this framework will help explain and establish the policymaking processes in the emerging democracies of Ghana and Nigeria. Insights into how both countries approach media freedom will be provided through lucid review of the rationale for the present policy content, how policy content is being implemented and the challenges confronting implementation will be highlighted (Akpojivi 2014). In addition, this will reveal if the process of policy formulation is flawed due to the dependency approach and hegemonic flow of ideas in the policymaking process, or the failure of political actors to allow for full media reform (see Milton 2000; Haggard and Kaufman 1997). The focus of this book is to examine the media reform processes in emerging democracies, therefore it is important to look at the policymaking processes (i.e. policies formulated) to establish the extent to which universal ideas of media reforms and democracy are applicable and the degree to which internal factors such as political, economic and cultural factors influence the policy process.

In conclusion, this chapter begins to look at the different theories around media freedom. It establishes that the concept of media freedom is an idea that flows from developed Western societies and their various agencies to emerging democracies. These emerging democracies are expected to embrace not only the ideas but the framework, as it forms the basis on which a nation's growth and development is judged. The chapter further argues that this dependency approach which has characterized emerging democracies is not facilitating the growth and development of these emerging democracies because of the exclusive nature of the process which does not recognize the unique inherent political, economic and socio-cultural values of these emerging democracies.

Note

1. In the Qatar-Gulf crisis of 2017, Gulf states such as UAE, Bahrain, Saudi Arabia and Egypt demanded that Qatar news channel Al Jazeera be shut down as part of the conditions to restore relationships with Qatar.

Bibliography

Adebanwi, W., & Obadare, E. (2011). The Abrogation of the Electorate: An Emergent African Phenomenon. *Democratization, 18*(2), 311–335.

Ake, C. (1979/1981). *Social Science as Imperialism: The Theory of Political Development.* Ibadan: Ibadan University Press.

Ake, C. (1982). *A Political Economy of Africa.* London: Longman.

Ake, C. (1993). The Unique Case of African Democracy. *International Affairs, 69*(2), 239–244.

Ake, C. (1996). *Democracy and Development in Africa.* Washington DC: The Brookings Institution.

Akpojivi, U. (2012). Community Radio Regulation and Its Challenges in Ghana. *Journal of African Media Studies, 4*(2), 193–207.

Akpojivi, U. (2013). Looking Beyond Elections: An Examination of Media Freedom in the Re-Democratization of Nigeria. In A. Olorunnisola & A. Douai (Eds.), *New Media Influence on Social and Political Change in Africa.* Hershey: IGI.

Akpojivi, U. (2014). Democratizing the Media in the New Democracies of Ghana and Nigeria: Challenges and Prospects. Ecquid Novi: African Journalism Studies, *35*(3), 87–105.

Ambrose, B. (1995). *Democratization and the Protection of Human Rights in Africa: Problems and Prospects.* London: Praeger.

Amdiume, I. (1987). *Male Daughters, Female Husbands.* London: Zed Books.

Barendt, E. (1985). *Freedom of Speech.* Oxford: Clarendon Press.

Barendt, E., & Hitchens, L. (2000). *Media Law Cases and Materials.* Harlow: Pearson Longman.

Bollinger, L. (1986). *The Tolerant Society: Freedom of Speech and Extremist Speech in America.* New York: Oxford University Press.

Brewer, G., & deLeon, P. (1983). *The Foundations of Policy Analysis.* Illinois: Dorsey Press.

Buse, K. (2008). Addressing the Theoretical, Practical and Ethical Challenges Inherent in Prospective Health Policy Analysis. *Health Policy and Planning, 23,* 351–360.

Cammack, P. (1994). Political Development Theory and the Dissemination of Democracy. *Democratization, 1*(3), 353–374.

Chakravartty, P., & Sarikakis, K. (2006). *Media Policy and Globalization.* Edinburgh: Edinburgh University Press.

Chibita, M., & Salawu, A. (2016). Introduction: Language, Structure and Agency: Optimising Media Diversity in Africa Using the Indigenous Languages. In A. Salawu & M. Chibita (Eds.), *Indigenous Language Media, Language Politics and Democracy in Africa*. New York: Palgrave Macmillan.

Chinweizu. (1999). Towards the African Renaissance Media. In M. W. Makgoba (Ed.), *African Renaissance*. Cape Town: Tafelberg Publishers Limited.

Chomsky, N. (2011). *How the World Works*. New York: Penguin Group.

Chuma, W., & Moyo, D. (2010). Policying the Media in Southern Africa in the Global Era: An Introduction. In D. Moyo & W. Chuma (Eds.), *Media Policy in a Changing Southern Africa Critical Reflections on Media Reforms in the Global Age*. Pretoria: University of South Africa Press.

Clark, C. (2005). The Press the Founders Knew. In T. Cook (Ed.), *Freeing the Presses the First Amendment in Action*. Louisiana: Louisiana State University Press.

Curran, J. (1979). Press Freedom as a Property Right: The Crisis of Press Legitimacy. *Media Culture & Society, 1*, 59–82.

Dahl, R. (1956). *A Preface to Democratic Theory*. London: The University of Chicago Press.

Dahl, R. (1971). *Polyarchy Participation and Opposition*. London: Yale University Press.

Emerson, T. (1982). The First Amendment in the Year 2000. In S. Halpern (Ed.), *The Future of Our Liberties: Perspectives on the Bill of Rights*. Westport CT: Greenwood.

Feintuck, M. (1999). *Media Regulation, Public Interest and the Law*. Edinburgh: Edinburgh University Press.

Fiss, O. (1990). Why the State. In J. Lichtenberg (Ed.), *Democracy and the Mass Media*. Cambridge: Cambridge University Press.

Fosu, M., & Akpojivi, U. (2015). Media Convergence Practices and Production in Ghana and Nigeria: Implications for Democracy and Research in Africa. *Journal of Applied Journalism and Media Studies, 4*(2), 277–292.

Freedman, D. (2008). *The Politics of Media Policy*. Cambridge: Polity Press.

Gilson, L., & Erasmus, E. (2008). How to Start Thinking About Investigating Power in the Organizational Settings of Policy Implementation. *Health Policy and Planning, 23*(5), 361–368.

Gilson, L., & Raphaely, N. (2008). The Terrain of Health Policy Analysis in Low and Middle Income Counties: A Review of Published Literature 1994–2007. *Health Policy and Planning, 23*, 294–307.

Graber, D., McQuail, D., & Norris, P. (1998). Political Communication in Democracy. In D. Graber, D. McQuail, & P. Norris (Eds.), *The Politics of News, the News of Politics*. Washington DC: CQ Press.

Gunaratne, S. (2002). Freedom of the Press: A World System Perspective. *International Communication Gazette, 64*(4), 343–369.

Hackett, R. (2000). Taking Back the Media: Notes on the Potential for a Communication Democracy Movement. *Studies in Political Economy, 63*, 61–86.

Haggard, S., & Kaufman, R. (1997). The Political Economy of Democratic Transitions. *Comparative Politics, 29*(3), 263–283.

Haynes, J. (2001a). Sustainable Democracy in the Third World. In J. Haynes (Ed.), *Towards Sustainable Democracy in the Third world*. London: Palgrave Publishers.

Haynes, J. (2001b). Conclusion. In J. Haynes (Ed.), *Towards Sustainable Democracy in the Third World*. London: Palgrave Publishers.

Hegel. (1896). *Hegel's Philosophy of Right*. (S. W. Dyde, Trans.). London: George Bell and Sons.

Hill, M. (2005). *The Public Policy Process* (4th ed.). London: Pearson Longman.

Holmes, S. (1990). Liberal Constraints on Private Power?: Reflections on the Origins and Rationale of Access Regulation. In J. Lichtenberg (Ed.), *Democracy and the Mass Media*. Cambridge: Cambridge University Press.

Holmes, S. (1995). *Passion and Constraint on the Theory of Liberal Democracy*. London: University of Chicago Press Ltd.

Huntington, S. (1991). *The Third Wave: Democratization in the Late Twentieth Century*. Norman: University of Oklahoma Press.

Hutchison, D. (1999). *Media Policy: An Introduction*. Oxford: Blackwell Publishers.

Hyden, G., & Okigbo, C. (2002). The Media and the Two Waves of Democracy. In G. Hyden, M. Leslie, & F. Ogundimu (Eds.), *Media and Democracy in Africa*. New Brunswick: Transaction Publishers.

Kareithi, P., & Kariithi, N. (2005). Introduction. In P. Kareithi & N. Kariithi (Eds.), *Untold Stories Economics and Business Journalism in African Media*. Johannesburg: Wits University Press.

Keane, J. (1991). *The Media and Democracy*. Cambridge: Polity Press.

Kelley, D., & Donway, R. (1990). Liberalism and Free Speech. In J. Lichtenberg (Ed.), *Democracy and the Mass Media*. Cambridge: Cambridge University Press.

Kendall, W. (1966). The Open Society and Its Fallacies. In P. Radcliff (Ed.), *Limits of Liberty: Studies of Mill's On Liberty*. California: Wadsworth Publishing Company Inc.

LaMay, C. (2007). *Exporting Press Freedom Economic and Editorial Dilemmas in International Media Assistance*. London: Transaction Publishers.

Lasswell, H. (1956). *The Decision Process: Seven Categories of Functional Analysis*. College Park: Bureau of Governmental Research: University of Maryland.

Leftwich, A. (1993). Governance, Democracy and Development in the Third World. *Third World Quarterly, 14*(3), 605–624.

Levitsky, S., & Way, L. (2010). Why Democracy Needs a Level Playing Field. *Journal of Democracy, 21*(1), 57–68.

Lewis, T. (2004). Democracy, Free Speech and TV: The Cases of BBC and Profile Alliance. *Web Journal of Current Legal Issues*, 1–21.

Lichtenberg, J. (1990a). Introduction. In J. Lichtenberg (Ed.), *Democracy and the Mass Media*. Cambridge: Cambridge University Press.

Lichtenberg, J. (1990b). Foundations and Limits of Freedom of the Press. In J. Lichtenberg (Ed.), *Democracy and the Mass Media*. Cambridge: Cambridge University Press.

Mano, W. (2011). Why Radio Is Africa's Medium of Choice in the Global Age. In L. Gunner, D. Ligaga, & D. Moyo (Eds.), *Radio in Africa: Publics, Cultures, Communities*. Johannesburg: Wits University Press.

Mansell, R., & Raboy, M. (2011). Introduction: Foundations of the Theory and Practice of Global Media and Communication Policy. In R. Mansell & M. Raboy (Eds.), *The Handbook of Global Media and Communication Policy*. London: Wiley-Blackwell.

Manyozo, L. (2011). Rethinking Communication for Development Policy: Some Considerations. In R. Mansell & M. Raboy (Eds.), *The Handbook of Global Media and Communication Policy*. London: Wiley-Blackwell.

Marcuse, H. (1969). Repressive Tolerance. In R. Wolff & H. Marcuse (Eds.), *A Critique of Pure Tolerance*. London: Beacon Press.

Mbembe, A. (2017). *Critique of Black Reason*. Johannesburg: Wits University Press.

McChesney, R. (2002). *Our Media Not Theirs: The Democratic Struggle Against Corporate Media*. New York: Seven Stories Press.

McChesney, R. (2008). *The Political Economy of the Media, Enduring Issues, Emerging Dilemmas*. New York: Monthly Review Press.

McLuhan, M. (1964). *McLuhan Understanding Media*. London: Routledge.

McQuail, D. (1992). *Media Performance Mass Communication and the Public Interest*. London: Sage Publication.

McQuail, D. (2003). *Media Accountability and Freedom of Publication*. Oxford: Oxford University Press.

Meiklejohn, A. (1966). Freedom of Speech. In P. Radcliff (Ed.), *Limits of Liberty: Studies of Mill's On Liberty*. Belmont: Wadsworth Publishing Company.

Melkote, S., & Steeves, L. (2001). *Communication for Development in the Third World Theory and Practice for Empowerment* (2nd ed.). London: Sage Publication.

Melody, W. (2011). Whose Global Village? In R. Mansell & M. Raboy (Eds.), *The Handbook of Global Media and Communication Policy*. London: Wiley-Blackwell.

Mill, J. (1859). *On Liberty*. London: Penguin Group.

Mill, S. J. (1869). *On Liberty* (4th ed.). London: Longman.

Milton, A. (2000). *The Rational Politician Exploiting the Media in New Democracies*. Aldershot: Ashgate.

Netshitenzhe, J. (2002). *Should the Media Serve the Public or National Interest?*", presentation to the Goedgedacht Forum for Social Reflection, Cape Town. www.gcis.gov.za.

Ngugi, W. (2017, March 2). *Secure the Base: Decolonising the Mind*. Lecture at the University of the Witwatersrand.

Nordenstreng, K. (2011). Free Flow Doctrine in Global Media Policy. In R. Mansell & M. Raboy (Eds.), *The Handbook of Global Media and Communication Policy*. London: Wiley Blackwell.

Nyamnjoh, F. (2005). *Africa's Media Democracy and the Politics of Belonging*. London: Zed Books.

Nyarko, J., & Akpojivi, U. (2017). Intimidation, Assault, and Violence Against Media Practioners in Ghana: Considering Provocation. *Sage Open, 7*(1), 1–12.
Nyerere, J. (2000). *Africa Today and Tomorrow*. Dar Es Salaam: Mwalimu Nyerere Foundation.
Obadare, E. (2006). Playing Politics with the Mobile Phone in Nigeria: Civil Society, Big Business and the State. *Review of African Political Economy, 33*(107), 93–111.
Ocitti, J. (1999). *Media and Democracy in Africa Mutual Political Bedfellows or Implacable Arch-Foes*. Cambridge: Weatherhead Center for International Affairs.
Ojo, E. (2003). The Mass Media and the Challenges of Sustainable Democratic Values in Nigeria: Possibilities and Limitations. *Media Culture & Society, 25*(6), 821–840.
Onwumechili, C. (2007). Nigeria: Equivocating While Opening the Broadcast Liberalization Gates. In I. Blankson & P. Murphy (Eds.), *Negotiating Democracy Media Transformations in Emerging Democracies*. Albany: State University of New York.
Otite, O. (1972). Continuance and Change in an Urhobo Age-Grade Organization in Nigeria. *Cahiers d'etudes africaines, 12*(46), 302–315.
Packenham, R. (1973). *Liberal America and the Third World: Political Development Ideas in Foreign Aid and Social Science*. New Jersey: Princeton University Press.
Pillai, M. (1999–2000). Freedom of the Press: Is the Western Press Listening to its colleagues in the Third World Countries? *Nieman Report*, 53/54.
Price, M. (2002a). *Media and Sovereignty the Global Information Revolution and Its Challenge to State Power*. Cambridge: MIT Press.
Price, M. (2002b). Bosnia-Hercegovina and Post-conflict Media Restructuring. In M. Price, B. Rozumilowicz, & S. Verhulst (Eds.), *Media Reform Democratizing the Media, Democratizing the State*. London: Routledge.
Price, M., & Verhulst, S. (2000). Introduction. In M. Price & S. Verhulst (Eds.), *Broadcasting Reform in India Media Law from a Global Perspective*. Oxford: Oxford University Press.
Richards, D. (1999). *Free Speech and the Politics of Identity*. Oxford: Oxford University Press.
Rozumilowicz, B. (2002). Democratic Change: A Theoretical Perspective. In M. Price, B. Rozumilowicz, & S. Verhulst (Eds.), *Media Reform Democratizing the Media, Democratizing the State*. London: Routledge.
Scanlon, T. (1990). Content Regulation Reconsidered. In J. Lichtenberg (Ed.), *Democracy and the Mass Media*. Cambridge: Cambridge University Press.
Schiller, H. (1976). *Communication and Cultural Domination*. New York: White Plains.
Shugerman, E. (2017, October 12). US Withdraws from UNESCO Over 'Anti-Israel Bias'. *Independent Newspaper*.
Taylor, P. (1997). *Global Communications, International Affairs and the Media Since 1945*. London: Routledge.

Tettey, W. (2001). The Media and Democratization in Africa: Contributions, Constraints and Concerns of the Private Press. *Media Culture & Society, 23*(1), 5–32.
Tettey, W. (2006). The Politics of Media Accountability in Africa: An Examination of Mechanisms and Institutions. *International Communication Gazette, 68*(3), 229–248.
Thussu, D. (2000). *International Communication Continuity and Change*. London: Arnold.
Tomaselli, K. (2009). Repositioning African Media Studies: Thoughts and Provocation. *Journal of African Media Studies, 1*(1), 9–21.
Tunstall, J. (1977). *The Media Are American*. New York: Columbia University Press.
Ungar, S. (1990). The Role of a Free Press in Strengthening Democracy. In J. Lichtenberg (Ed.), *Democracy and the Mass Media*. Cambridge: Cambridge University Press.
Van Belle, D. (2000). *Press Freedom and Global Politics*. WestPoint: C.T. Praeger.
Voltmer, K. (2008). Comparing Media Systems in New Democracies: East Meets South Meets West. *Central European Journal of Communication, 1*, 23–40.
Wahl-Jorgensen, K. (2007). *Journalists and the Public Newsroom Culture, Letters to the Editor and Democracy*. New Jersey: Hampton Press Inc.
Walt, G. (1999). Implementing Health Care Reform: A Framework for Discussion. In R. Saltman, J. Figueras, & C. Sakellarides (Eds.), *Critical Challenges for Health Care Reform in Europe*. Philadelphia: Open University Press.
Walt, G., & Gilson, L. (1994). Reforming the Health Sector in Developing Countries: The Central Role of Policy Analysis. *Health Policy and Planning, 9*(4), 353–370.
Walt, G., Shiffman, J., Schneider, H., Murray, S., Brugha, R., & Gilson, L. (2008). Doing Health Policy Analysis: Methodological and Conceptual Reflections and Challenges. *Health Policy and Planning, 23*, 308–317.
Wasserman, H., & de Beer, A. (2006). Conflicts of Interest? Debating the Media's Role in Post Apartheid South Africa. In K. Voltmer (Ed.), *Mass Media and Political Communication in New Democracies*. London: Routledge.
Winseck, D. (2002). The WTO, Emerging Policy Regimes and the Political Economy of Transnational Communications. In M. Raboy (Ed.), *Global Media Policy in the New Millennium*. Luton: University of Luton Press.
World Bank. (2015). http://data.worldbank.org.
World Summit on the Information Society "Geneva Report 2003". Online: http://www.itu.int/wsis/documents/index.html. Accessed 12 Oct 2007.
World Summit on the Information Society "Tunis Report 2005". Online, http://www.itu.int/wsis/documents/index.html. Accessed 12 Oct 2007.

CHAPTER 3

Media Reforms, Democratization in Ghana: From Policy Ambition to Implementation

Following the re-democratization process that started in 1992 in Ghana, the country embarked on numerous reforms, such as formulating and implementing policy, that will help achieve the overall objectives of opening the media sphere and facilitating democratic consolidation. Therefore, this chapter seeks to examine these policy processes by ascertaining the extent to which Western ideas were encapsulated based on the different policies formulated and implemented following the re-democratization process. Also, it will analyze the impact of these policies on the media sphere by examining the rationale behind the key media policies, identify and analyze the policy concerns and the impact of these on the Ghanaian media environment.

Foreign Influence on Ghana Media Reform

Media reforms in Ghana have largely been influenced by international charters and provisions of media freedom and free speech. This also influenced their approach and understanding of media reform, which has mainly been taken for granted, and trivialized without questioning. Therefore, in order to comprehend the underlying principles behind Ghana's media policies, it is imperative to begin this chapter by examining the impact of foreign influences on policy formulation and the impact of these ideas on the Ghanaian media sphere. Ghana is a signatory to the

U. Akpojivi, *Media Reforms and Democratization in Emerging Democracies of Sub-Saharan Africa*,
https://doi.org/10.1007/978-3-319-75301-0_3

Universal Declaration of Human Rights (1948), and the African Charter on Human and Peoples' Rights (1986), and the central theme among these policy documents is the need to protect the inalienable human right of free speech, which is considered a universal entitlement that should be protected, and the democratic progress of a nation is measured by its ability to protect this inalienable right of free speech (Diamond 2008a, b) and embrace principles of liberal democracies (Ake 2000).

The Universal Declaration of Human Rights which was adopted in 1948 was set as a common standard by which countries are to protect the inalienable human right of freedom of speech and expression. Article 19 of the declaration holds that:

> Everyone has the right to freedom to opinion and expression, this right includes freedom to hold opinions without interference and to seek, receive and impact information and ideas through any media regardless of frontiers (Universal Declaration of Human Rights 1948).

The idea encapsulated in this provision is a vital requirement that liberal democracies are expected to live up to, as the ideas in the above provisions are adhered to in most democratic nations although the rationale behind each law and provision might differ: however, they all share similar ideas and principles about the need to protect dissenting views and allow plurality and diversity of opinions. This idea likewise influenced the conceptualization of the African Charter on Human and Peoples' Rights of 1986 also known as the Banjul Charter, which can be regarded as an offshoot of the Western ideas encapsulated in the Universal Declaration of Human Rights. Article 9 of the charter identified the need to protect the rights of everyone to receive information and the right to freely express his/her opinion(s) within the law (African Charter on Human and Peoples' Rights 1986).

Nevertheless, it is important to note that although Ghana is a signatory to the above charter, these international provisions are subject to the laws and provisions of the Republic of Ghana, so they are neither compulsory nor enforceable due to the African Union policy of non-interference. However, it is pertinent to state that the ideologies behind these provisions, to a certain extent, have influenced policy formulation and implementation in Ghana. This is because according to Kafewo (2006) the Ghanaian state is largely dependent on aid and technical assistance from Western countries for its economic survival so it was compulsory for

Ghanaian political actors and policymakers to recognize and incorporate these ideas into policy formulation following the re-democratization process. Failure to incorporate these ideas will have a huge impact on the economic development of the country (Boafo-Arthur 1998: 167–177), as these donor countries and countries offering technical assistance would cease such assistance (LaMay 2007).

Consequently, during the re-democratization process that started in 1992, policy formulation was geared towards embracing the Western ideology of promoting free speech, diversity and plurality in order to continue enjoying aid from donor countries. One policymaker asserted that 'the major donors to Ghana's economy made the concept of media freedom and independence and freedom of speech or expression for the citizens a condition for the government to access loans and have economic ties with Western countries' (Monney Affail, Interview 2010). The above assertion shows the process of policy formulation was largely influenced by economic pressures. According to Packenham (1973: 5) the 'assumption here was that aid should be used not so much to achieve economic development and with a host of congenial political results'. Therefore, the conditionality of aid was used as a tool for promoting liberal democracy and its principles of free speech and plurality and diversity within the media sphere. This means that the re-democratization process of policy formulation to reform the media industry was not a neutral process but induced by the West using economic tools such as aid and technical assistance as a way of pushing the Western ideologies of freedom and democracy into emerging democracies.

Consequently, it can be argued that this economic assistance influenced the policy formulation and implementation processes in Ghana. For instance, an examination of policy documents giving birth to the re-democratized era and institutionalizing the media reform (i.e. the 1992 constitution of the Republic of Ghana), one sees that the ideas of freedom of speech and expression, and freedom of the mass media, were recognized as fundamental tools for the socio-political, economic and cultural development of the country in order to achieve the Millennium Development Goals (MDGs). These MDGs have been a challenge for most African countries. The extent to which these MDGs have been achieved in Ghana is debatable as the country still experiences some developmental challenges such as gender equality, child mortality and universal education, which the MDGs seek to achieve. According to the United Nations Development Programme (UNDP) (2015), attempts are being made to find ways to initiate a development framework that will be used in the period after the MDG deadline of 2015 to meet and address these challenges.

The 1992 constitution is widely considered a model for Africa due to its explicit provisions for both human rights and media freedom and independence. The constitution separated the normative human rights (life, speech, religion and property) from that of the media, which is the norm in most post-colonial African states where the provision of media freedom is usually merged with and derived from fundamental human rights. According to Article 162 of the 1992 Ghanaian constitution, freedom and independence devoid of censorship and interference in the mass media is guaranteed. The constitution states that:

> (3) There shall be no impediment to the establishment of private press or media; and in particular, there shall be no law requiring any person to obtain a licence as a prerequisite to the establishment or operation of a newspaper, journal or other media for mass communication or information. (4) Editors and publishers of newspapers and other institutions of the mass media; shall not be subject to control or interference by government, nor shall they be penalised or harassed for their editorial opinions and views, or the content of their publications. (5) All agencies of the mass media shall, at all times, be free to uphold the principles, provisions and objectives of this constitution and shall uphold the responsibility and accountability of the government to the people of Ghana (Article 162 Subsection [3–5], of the 1992 Ghana Constitution).

From the above provision, it can be argued that the constitution was framed to promote freedom and independence of the media structured along the negative freedom perspective which, in most cases, is misconstrued to mean absolute freedom by media practitioners due to the context of freedom from 'government interference'. This idea of freedom and independence was further promoted within Article 167 of the constitution which calls for the establishment of an independent regulatory agency, the National Media Commission (NMC), which is charged with the responsibility of regulating the mass media without interference from government and ensuring that the mass media are well able to discharge their constitutional duties.

Outside the constitution, other policy documents that were formulated after the 1992 constitution such as the National Telecommunication Policy (2005), National Media Policy (2000) and Ghana ICT for Accelerated Development Policy (2003) were also framed along these ideas. The impact of this Western influence on policy formulation could either be positive, leading to a more liberalized and developed media environment in which the principles of freedom and independence will facilitate media growth and societal development, or have a negative effect in that these policies are incompatible with the realities of the Ghanaian society, hence, the difficulty in actualizing the policy goals and objectives.

To establish this argument further, which is the premise of this book, I need to examine and discuss the various policy documents in Ghana in relation to the goals and how this to a large extent has impacted on the Ghanaian media sphere.

Media Reforms and Policy Framework

Following the re-democratization process that started in 1992, the government embarked on media reforms by formulating different media policies such as the National Media Policy (2000), the Information and Communication Technology for Accelerated Development Policy (2003) and the National Telecommunication Policy (2005) as a way to open up the media sphere. According to Heath (1999: 512), outside the constitution, which is considered the fundamental and 'definitive voice of broadcasting policy' in Ghana because of its influence in the framing of the other policy documents, these other policy documents provided a detailed framework for the media reform processes. Therefore, we need to examine these policies in relation to the reform processes. The rationale is not to determine who was involved in the process (i.e. given a voice or not) or why and what impact these voices could have had on the policy formulation process. However, the focus is to ascertain the issues and underlying reason(s) behind each policy document formulation and implications on the media sphere. As Bacchi (1999) posits, effective policy formulation and implementation process involves the identification of policy concerns and the interest reflected in policy formulation. This approach is salient as it will facilitate an understanding of the problems and help in addressing them by identifying measures and committing to addressing the policy concerns (Bacchi 1999: 1–2).

Below is a brief discussion of the different policy documents in Ghana.

National Media Policy (2000) This policy document can be regarded as the first detailed one outside the constitution that provided directives and guidelines for the media environment following the confusion that confronted the reform process due to explicit directives. This policy document explicitly stated the expectations and roles of the mass media in society because it outlined the framework for the operation of the mass media in Ghana. The regulatory body, the NMC, drafted the policy so that it could serve as a framework not only for the operationalization of the media but provide guidelines for regulating the media and yardsticks for measuring media performance. The findings of the policy document resulted from previous policy documents or discussion such as the 1995 preparatory committee for independent broadcasting, the 1996 film policy seminar, submission from individuals and corporate organizations, and consultation with media operators and experts (National Media Policy 2000). According to the policy, its fundamental objective is to 'promote and ensure a free, independent, dynamic and public spirited media that will provide access for all, and not only some of our people to participate freely, fully, and creatively at the community, national and global level' (National Media Policy 2000). In addition, the policy calls for the all-round development of citizens in relation to the media providing and meeting the information needs of the citizens and advancing the democratic process. This is in line with the overall policy objective in which the mass media are considered a public trust whose overall goal should be to reflect public interest irrespective of the media ownership structure (i.e. public, commercial or community owned). Therefore, it can be argued that this policy document objective was influenced by the universal guidelines or principles of independence, public trust and accessibility of the media (National Media Policy 2000).

Consequently, the policy calls for a free and independent media as a means of meeting and sustaining the public trust as freedom from political and economic actors will enable the media to focus on satisfying the needs of the public. A specific and general guideline for each medium of communication was set out by the policy; among the general guidelines are the promotion and development of local culture, and balance between the diverse interests of cultural, political and economic factors. On the specific guideline for the media, the policy sets out comprehensive criteria that programming content should meet (National Media Policy 2000).

National Telecommunication Policy (2005) This policy document was drafted by the Ministry of Information in Ghana in 2004 and was adopted by the cabinet of the Republic of Ghana and published in 2005. The policy document was developed and influenced by the findings from consultations with stakeholders (i.e. civil societies and policymakers in the telecommunication industry) and broadcasters (National Telecommunication Policy 2005). According to the policy, its primary objective is to promote the issue of communication rights, in other words the ability of the public to have access to information irrespective of geographical location and to bridge the information gap that exists between those with access to information and those denied access due to infrastructural and institutional deficits that have characterized the country since independence. According to the policy, its fundamental objective is 'that every citizen and resident of the Republic of Ghana shall have available, high quality and affordable access to information and communication services, to help transform Ghana into a knowledge based society and technology driven economy' (National Telecommunication Policy 2005).

From the above policy objective, one can infer that opening the media sphere to accessibility and participation by the public was considered as the yardstick of citizens and communal development. This embodies the notion of information as a fundamental human right as encapsulated in the Universal Declaration of Human Rights and the African Charter on Human and Peoples' Rights as previous discussed. This idea was further explained by a regulator and policymaker George Sarpong who held that the policy was formulated to address the problem of access to information and communication across Ghana, thus serving as the telecommunication industry's perspective on broadening universal access (Interview 2010). To this end, the policy calls for the liberalization of the telecommunication industry to open the sector to investment, transparent principles and licensing procedure (National Telecommunication Policy 2005). However, it should be noted that this policy focus was centerd around the telecommunication industry and not broadcasting. Nevertheless, in relation to broadcasting the policy calls for the establishment of a three-tier broadcasting system—public, commercial and community media—which previously had excluded the Ghanaian media environment due to institutional and infrastructural deficits. According to the policy, public media are media organizations that are wholly and partially funded by the state. They must reflect the public interest in their reportage and must be accountable to the people via the independent regulatory body (NMC). Commercial media, according to the policy, are media organizations that are privately and independently owned for profit purposes, while community media are meant to represent a specific community or group of persons who are excluded from the public and commercial media domain. Therefore, the primary objective of community media is to promote the cause of the community by pursuing a 'participatory social development agenda, which is non-profit, non-sectarian and non-partisan' (National Telecommunication Policy 2005).

To this end, the policy proposed a comprehensive review of the current broadcasting policy in Ghana as a way of expanding and increasing accessibility of the media to all citizens despite barriers of cultural diversity and language. This is because the policy recognized community media as a vital tool in bridging the information gap that exists in Ghanaian society and in accelerating universal access. Therefore, the National Communication Authority (NCA) had to adopt this policy within six months and speedily review all applications for community media in the public interest.

Consequently, it can be argued that this policy document was largely influenced by the desire to meet the interests of the public and their right to communicate, which is considered a fundamental human right as the policy further added that universal access to the media should be attained by all citizens by 2010. One mechanism to achieve this universal access is by opening the media industry to active participation by interested stakeholders, and this is only possible when freedom and independence can be guaranteed.

Ghana ICT for Accelerated Development Policy (2003) The desire to develop the socio-political and economic landscape of the country led to the setting up in 2002 of the information and communication technology (ICT) policy and plan development committee chaired by Professor Clement Dzidonu (a computer science professor and member of many global information technology forums such as ICANN and IDRC commission experts for West Africa). At this time, the Ghanaian economic landscape was considered to be largely underdeveloped due to the prolonged military rule which restrained political and economic growth (Jebuni and Oduro 1998: 21, 29). Therefore, policymakers' realized that the usage of ICT due to its vast potential would help in leapfrogging through development and assist with the attainment of the Millennium Development Goals (Zongo 2001; Thapisa and Birabwa 1998). According to the policy, the need to facilitate development in Ghana has necessitated the desire to harness ICT for the 'development, deployment and exploitation of ICTs within the economy and society' (ICT4AD 2003).

The above position ascribes the success and growth of Ghana's economic and political development to the usage of ICT. The dominant belief is that for underdeveloped countries to leapfrog through development they have to embrace democracy and implement liberalization policies that will lead to embracing ICT for developmental initiatives. For this to occur, the policy calls for the creation of an enabling environment that will allow for a massive roll out of ICT in all sectors of the economy. This enabling environment includes the development and implementation of the entire necessary legal, institutional and regulatory framework and structure. According to the policy, the establishment of a good regulatory framework will help 'restrict regulation to the necessary minimum and reinforce competition within the industry and sector, while ensuring that the basic rights, choices and preferences of consumers continue to be protected, and the principle of universal access and service reinforced' (ICT4AD 2003). The enabling environment can only be created when the concept of media freedom is appreciated by all stakeholders (i.e. government, policymakers, civil societies and the public), who should be ready and willing to allow freedom and keep to the underlying principles of freedom and liberalization, since this is the key factor that can bring about the change required by the policy.

A Discussion: From Policy Ambition(s) to Implementation

From the above discussion on the rationale behind the media policies in Ghana, there are common themes that cut across the different media policies that have been reviewed. These themes include freedom and independence, universal access, media accountability and media as a public trust—and these will form the basis of the discussion. This is because, to a large extent, these themes shape the context and structure of the media policies already discussed.

Independence and Freedom of the Media

From all the policy documents discussed, it can be inferred that independence and freedom is a core theme that cuts across these policy documents as these documents stated that only when there is independence and freedom in the media environment can the different policy goals be achieved. For instance, the ICT4AD policy stated that an enabling environment in the media sphere and an independent media free from restraint are both needed. However, as earlier stated, the concept of media freedom is difficult to conceptualize due to its philosophical and political nature, and this to a large extent has influenced people's understanding of the word. Nevertheless, for the purpose of this discussion and to effectively nuance the policy goals in relation to implementation, I shall discuss media freedom as the ability of the media to carry out their constituted functions of information, education and entertainment without interference in the editorial positions of the media from government or media owners (William 1979: 267). The rationale behind this definition is premised on the ideas in Article 162 of the 1992 constitution and other policy documents that provided for absolute freedom from government interference or other restrictive measures. Therefore, it is appropriate to examine how the media reforms embarked upon have facilitated this freedom and independence of the media from government interference or other restrictive measures.

In order to effectively evaluate the media reform process in relation to media freedom and independence, it is salient to examine how media practitioners in Ghana conceptualize media freedom and independence in the re-democratized era. Most media practitioners' understanding of media freedom and independence is centered on their understanding of the 1992 constitution. The constitution provided for no censorship or impediment to the operation of the media. This means the media have been charged to carry out their constitutional functions of responsibility and accountability without interference from government or other private interests. Most often this could be seen as absolute freedom for media practitioners. According to the manager of Ghana Broadcasting Corporation (GBC), 'I think the framers of the 1992 constitution realized that the media has to be free for the dissemination of information for the wider public hence the constitutional provisions and framing of the constitution from that perspective' (Peggy Ama Donkor, Interview 2010). Similarly, one policymaker puts it 'Article 162 or the entire Chapter 12 of the 1992 constitution is the essence of the journalistic profession in Ghana today and gives the journalists the latitude to operate and carry out their mandate to society' (Affail Monney, Interview 2010).

The above means that media practitioners construed this freedom from the right perspective of absolute freedom to engage in all kinds of activities without recognizing that freedom comes with the responsibility to be truthful, and to promote societal development as argued for by social responsibility theorists. This construction of freedom from the right perspective could be problematic in an emerging democracy as this right could be abused and hinder the development of the media environment and democratic process. For instance, some media practitioners have been critical of government and security agents for attempts at gagging the media and their actions without ascertaining if their actions or those of the government are allowed within law. For example, in 2010, the police invited the editor of Joy FM, located in Accra, in for questioning about news reports that were alleged to have caused fear and panic in the public. The news organization reported that government threats to business investors led to the loss of investment opportunities. Consequently, the invitation by the police generated wide controversy about the state of media freedom in the country. Whereas some media practitioners saw the invitation as a threat to media freedom, others did not. According to an editor in GBC 'I think that the recent trend of some media practitioners being arrested in the name of telling stories that seem to be creating so called fear and panic in the system is a stab in the back of press freedom' (Edward Nyarko, Interview 2010). Such an opinion highlights media freedom from the right perspective as it places the media as an institution whose actions cannot be questioned or concerns raised. This limits the meaning or understanding of media freedom as freedom comes with responsibility. Media practices and journalism are not only about the freedom of expression entitled to every citizen but are also about respect for ethics and responsibility within the media sphere and towards society, as anything outside of this will endanger democracy (Akpojivi 2014). This idea of 'responsibility' challenges the normative ideas of media freedom and free speech which is always from the right perspective. Therefore, the onus lies on the mass media and media practitioners to recognize this and not to assume that the media reforms embarked upon mean an absolute right but for them to work within the constitutional provisions. As the minister of communication elucidated, 'in Ghana we have liberalized the media to allow for absolute freedom by putting the necessary structures in place to facilitate this freedom. Nevertheless, journalists must be responsible in order not to jeopardize this freedom' (Harune Iddrisu, Interview 2010).

To this end, to effectively examine the media freedom and independence theme in relation to policy implementation, I will examine it through two subthemes of government-media relationship and media ownership, because the relationship that exists between the government and media speaks a lot about the success of the reform activities.

Government-Media Relationship

According to Teeter and Loving (2004: 1) 'a major test of a nation's freedom is the degree of liberty its people have in speaking, writing and publishing'. This alludes to the nature and level of relationship that exists between the government and the press, as this relationship (rosy or dissenting) between the government and the media will influence the working environment of the media, in other words if the government sees the media as partners the environment will be liberal and instruments needed to foster the growth of the media will be promulgated. However, if the media are perceived as enemies, restrictive laws that will hinder the operation of the media will be formulated and implemented. Voltmer (2006: 7) argues that the relationship between the media and government during the transition process can be problematic and complex due to new orientations and new rules of engagement with political actors. The media are confused as to whether or not to challenge state authorities and liberate society from repressive tendencies and, at the same time, challenge the fragility of the new regime's call for caution (Voltmer 2006). Therefore, there is a need to examine if the present democratic space promotes freedom and independence of the mass media and allows them to engage in their responsibilities, whether the current legislations and policies enhance freedom, and what the implications are in the media sphere.

Since the attainment of independence in 1957 to date, various regimes have responded to the media differently. Most often the media were considered an enemy of the state, one whose powers of promoting accountability and transparency should be curtailed. In the early 1990s, Ghana's minister of information alleged that society does not need a 'critical media but a media that will partner with government' (The Democratic Journalist 1990 cited in Eribo and Jong-Ebot 1997: x). Similarly, Nyarko and Akpojivi (2017) asserted that in some instances media practitioners have been arrested and intimidated for carrying out their constituted functions. Consequently, a strained relationship often occurs between the media and government. According to Adebayo (2001), this strained relationship has contributed significantly to the underdevelopment of the media industry. As the editor of *Concord* newspaper states 'since independence most of the regimes from the early years of Nkrumah's government to the various military regimes and the post democratic era that started in 1992, have promoted a media environment known as the culture of silence that restricted media activities and made the media terrain difficult for media organisations to operate in' (Alfred Ogbamey, Interview 2010). The culture of silence was legitimized using legal instruments such as criminal libel and civil libel laws, therefore making the media operate in a stringent environment which suppressed their ability to engage in their watchdog functions and monitoring of government activities.

Alhassan (2005) opined that the media environment between 1957 and 1991 was characterized by excessive monopoly, centralization of the media, statist ideology and economic depression; hence most media practitioners were forced to leave the profession or go underground. According to an editor:

> Prior to 1992 few newspapers were allowed to operate and exist because we had the newspaper licensing law which the authorities used to decide which newspapers they wanted to operate and not to operate. We eventually had a situation where no political or private newspaper existed. All the existing newspapers were forced to do sport which was seen as a safer area if they wanted your licence renewed because if you do politics they [the government] will follow you up and your licence will not be renewed, and in regard to broadcasting GBC was the sole station providing government information (Alfred Ogbamey, Interview 2010).

The above experiences from both the independence and post-independence eras therefore influenced the context of media freedom and independence in present day Ghana. Section 4.1. of the National Media Policy 2000, while attesting to the above, held that the pre- and post-independence media environment had a negative impact on the media due to undemocratic tendencies, thus the need to address this issue coupled with the need to be in tune with global practices. Alhassan (2005) postulated that most media reforms embarked upon by emerging democracies were intended to prevent previous practices where dissenting views were suppressed by governments in order to hold onto power. This explains why all the media policies formulated upon re-democratization call for the opening of the media industry to allow for the attainment of John Stuart Mill's and John Milton's concept of a 'marketplace of ideas' where information from both public and private media will compete for attention. Consequently, Article 162 of the Ghanaian constitution brought about the framework that re-defines the relationship between the government and the mass media. This was also facilitated by former President John Kufuor who repealed the criminal libel laws in 2000 which were used by previous administrations to restrict the activities of the mass media.

Consequently, the media environment has drastically facilitated growth and development due to the nature of relationships that exist between the government and the media. According to an editor with GBC 'the media environment now is incomparable to earlier years. Prior to 1992, the environment was a bit hostile to press freedom but after 1992, especially in 2001 when the criminal law was repealed, the media landscape dramatically changed because we now have the freedom to express ourselves not only as media men but as the public also' (Edward Nyarko, Interview 2010). This sentiment was likewise shared by a policymaker, Bright Blewu, who added that the media environment following the liberal policies had made the environment tolerant and accommodating of diverse views and opinions, therefore aiding democratic advancement as the sole purpose of democracy is to accommodate and promote all views whether dissenting or not. This richness in the media environment can be attributed to the constitutional provision that guarantees freedom of all views, thereby giving the once excluded and marginalized political groups the opportunity to voice their opinions through the wide range of media available to them.

Hence, this has influenced how people and international organizations perceive media freedom and independence in Ghana without a detailed nuance. For example, Ghana has been recognized as having the most free media environment in Africa and is a role model to other African countries because of the explicit provisions of freedom within the constitution and media policies. The former executive director of the NMC, George Sarpong, while explaining the rationale behind such recognition stated that 'devotion of Chapter 12 of the 1992 constitution to media freedom as against what is witnessed in other African countries has contributed largely to the present liberal environment reflected in the recent assessments by most international organizations even outside Ghana. We came up first in Africa on the RSF [Reporters Sans Frontières] scale, and we have also done very well on other assessments that have been done. So we consider ourselves one of the freest media environments in Africa today' (Interview 2010).

Such an assertion is problematic as media freedom is reduced to ticking boxes or meeting certain criteria as discussed in the previous chapter. Merely ticking boxes will not present a true reflection of the state of the media environment. For instance in Botswana, although there is no explicit provision for media freedom in the 1966 constitution, the media have witnessed growth and development and have contributed to democratic consolidation in the country. Consequently, Botswana is judged to have the most stable democracy in Africa (Mosaka and Kamaimba 1998). Likewise, the explicit provision of rights and freedom only provide the framework in which the mass media are to operate as this does not indicate the level of freedom in a society, as the level of freedom is based on implementation. Therefore, the only way to ascertain media freedom and independence in Ghana should be centered on the media's ability to perform their constitutional functions of holding government accountable and promoting democracy in Ghana in line with the provision. Implementation of the policy is based on the fact that the whole essence of media freedom is centered on media performance, in other words the ability of the media to carry out their rudimentary functions of informing, educating and representing the citizens as postulated by Barnett (1999).

In relation to media performance, there are numerous contestations as to whether the media in Ghana is living up to its responsibilities as stated in the various media policies. According to the Ghana Journalists Association (GJA) code of ethics (1994), every journalist must exercise his/her watchdog function with the utmost sense of responsibility to preserve democracy. However, the public perception of the media's ability to live up to their responsibility as contained in the GJA code of ethics is ambivalent due to the quality of their reportage. Often the mass media have been praised for significantly embracing active watchdog responsibilities despite the precedence of pre-independence and post-independence, as earlier stated. According to Karikari (1998) the media in Ghana have contributed significantly to expounding the political debates and transition in Ghana. There have been numerous instances in which the media have questioned government actions and policies, for example, the 'dumsor' crisis (an electricity crisis due to irregular power outages) and the waste management scandal of 2016 (Daily Guide Newspaper 2016).

This and many other examples show the dynamic shift in the media environment from an era when the media went underground and were less critical to a media that are proactive and critical of government. According to the editor-in-chief of GBC, Francis Sasu, the media's ability to exercise their watchdog role in Ghana's polity has showed that the environment is not only liberal but that the media are properly utilizing the favorable media environment and have moved away from antecedent influence (Interview 2010). This goes against the assertion of scholars such as Voltmer (2006) and Milton (2000) who argued that most media organizations in democracies emerging from one-party states such as Ghana face inherited problems that will shape the relationship between the media and government.

Therefore, it can be argued that one significant contribution that the media have made in relation to the media reforms embarked upon is the creation of a platform for debate on government politics and actions. Akpojivi (2012) and Fosu and Akpojivi (2015) argue that it is now a common phenomenon that most radio and television stations serve as platforms to engage with both ordinary citizens and government. This has brought government closer to the people as people can easily engage with it and hold it accountable. This platform is made possible by the emergence and convergence of information communication telecommunications (i.e. mobile phones and new media). This new media and technological convergence in the media sphere was facilitated by liberalization, which was the cornerstone of all the media policies previously discussed.

New media technologies have broadened citizens 'participation and allowed for debates to be raised...on almost every issue' on mainstream media such as radio, television, etc. (Kafewo 2006: 7), and likewise outside the mainstream media. According to Radsch (2013) this new media technology has given birth to what is called citizen journalism in which ordinary citizens without any formal education in journalism can report on national issues. And this has increased audience and citizens' participation in the media sphere. Likewise it has changed the face of journalism practices in Ghana from the linear flow of information to a multi-directional one, which has invariably affected democratic consolidation as participation is central to democracy (Ake 2000) and brings the public closer to government, and government closer to the public (Coleman et al. 2011). This new media technology has afforded people who were once excluded from the media and national discourse an opportunity to actively contribute to debates. According to an anonymous source, 'new media has made it easy for people to voice out their opinion about any political or socio-economic issues within the comfort of his/her home' (Interview 2017). Ransford Tetteh, editor of the *Daily Graphic*, while emphasizing the impact of new media on the democratic and media sphere, held that 'new media technologies had enhanced the democratic process as people are free to express their views, contribute to political debate and hold public officers to account, and by so doing participate in democracy and seeing that participation is a key element in democracy and the reverse of it would be catastrophic for Ghana's democracy' (Interview 2010). Similarly, Ajoa Yeboah Afari, the coordinator of the Ghana Media Standards Improvement Project states that 'this phone in phenomenon [on radio and television programmes] has afforded the average person who can afford the price of a phone card the opportunity to air his/her grievances without worrying about seeing or going through a middle man. This person can call into any radio station and air his or her views or talk about something going on in the community he wants Ghanaians to know about' (Interview 2010). As well as the freedom for ordinary people to participate in media debates, media practitioners themselves have integrated new media technologies into their everyday practice as they 'can integrate new media platforms into programming, for example with broadcast they can use tools such as Facebook, Twitter in their morning shows to enable listeners to air their views' (Anonymous, Interview 2017).

Daniels (2014), while developing this thought further, argues that journalists in the newsroom are now actively using social media platforms such as Twitter to engage with the public by examining and discussing issues affecting the political, economic and cultural developments of societies. Consequently, there is the assertion that almost every journalist has a social media account which is actively used for journalistic purposes. This has expanded the frontiers of media practices and freedom. According to an anonymous source 'before the emergence of the internet, and new media technology, the freedom of the media was limited but lately it is unlimited due to its potential to the media sphere' (Interview 2017). Henckes (2016), while summing up the opportunities of new media technologies in the media sphere and society in general, argues that new media platforms bridge the gap that exists between the governed and government as they provide the space for 'complaining, reassurance and interaction'. This platform of debate is one of the fundamentals of democracy and freedom in the media environment and is a crucial element in the democratization process which has contributed significantly to the sustenance of democracy in Ghana, owing to it being a transparent avenue for debate. This germane role of the media in building platforms for debate and promoting transparency was evident in the 2008, 2012 and 2016 elections as people would monitor and report on electioneering activities. Therefore, Boadi (2009) argues that this is the reason why Ghana's democracy has been growing and the media receive international and national accolades.

Despite these achievements, some media practitioners, policymakers and non-government organizations (NGOs) have contradicted the above achievements, arguing that the mass media in Ghana are irresponsible and not living up to their constitutional responsibilities. Such assertions are centered on the huge number of libel suits and complaints against the media (Arthur 1997: 12). This has led to the belief that the media are not adhering to the fundamental principles of the constitution and the GJA code of ethics on truthful reporting without bias, either in a bid to be the first to report news (i.e. for economic reasons or political motives). Aidan (2010) explains that freedom comes with responsibility and accountability, and if the media are not responsible and accountable to the public then they have no moral justification to act as watchdogs of society.

One major issue that has led to this feeling is the dominance and focus of politics in the Ghanaian media sphere. As an emerging democracy there are many issues confronting the socio-economic, political and economic development of the country, and the media have a responsibility to facilitate and ensure the all-round development of the country. However, Hasty (2005), Fosu and Akpojivi (2015) in their studies argue that the media focus is on political issues as almost every program on radio and television is politically inclined as discussions are centered around what government officials are engaged in and the perception of the opposition parties about the issue. This, to a large extent, has formed a kind of culture within the media sphere and society. Hasty (2005), while buttressing this fact, argues that it has become a common phenomenon to see Ghanaians listening or watching television every morning and late afternoon just to be aware of and participate in what is happening in the country.

Such a practice can be commended due to its contribution to the political development of the country, as leaders are easily held accountable, and the structure of governance is demystified or deconstructed. Ordinary citizens can now participate in the everyday governance of their society by participating in national discourse. However, this politicization of the media has a grave impact on the socio-economic and cultural development of the country as other sectors of the economy are neglected. Gifty Afenyur Dadzie, a senior policymaker, while highlighting this impact, posited that 'when people want water to drink, when people want affordable houses, the mass media are talking about who is opposing who in politics; will that put food on the table of the public?' (Interview 2010). The above assertion highlights the gap between the expectation of the public and what the mass media are actually doing. Fosu and Akpojivi (2015) argue that this gap is centered on the premise of the media thinking that society is interested in politics. Due to the antecedents of Ghanaian society when critical views were once suppressed by the state, in the re-democratized era every radio and television station and newspaper organization wants to cover or discuss politics.

Although such politicization might be considered an essential component of the democratization process, nevertheless the benefits of politics can only be achieved when it is policy oriented and centered around the development of society and not on personality. According to Karikari (1998: 205) the politicization of the media around personality and not on policy issues has a serious impact on the ability of the media to exercise their constitutional mandate as the vested interests of the different political divide—i.e. National Democratic Congress (NDC) and the New Patriotic Party (NPP)—influence the actions of the media as the media are more partisan oriented. Media scholars and commenters are worried about this trend in the media environment as it brings to mind the issue of balance between the constitutional provision and realities of society. For instance, Article 163 of the 1992 constitution states that 'all state-owned media shall afford fair opportunities and facilities for the presentation of divergent views and dissenting opinions'. These media organizations might claim that the act of politicization is centered around this provision: however, there is the need to balance this act in line with the realities of society, in other words the everyday needs of society, as Gifty Afenyur Dadzie elucidates earlier. If this constitutional provision is not effectively balanced the re-democratization process might be endangered. As one policymaker stated 'it is not by shouting or giving unfounded allegations on radio or television that the media will be known to be critical or vocal... if the media creates conditions for a coup d'état in Ghana as they are now doing, the media will get it...the media should not think that a coup d'état has vanished from Ghana, it depends on the media. What happened in Rwanda should serve as an example, the genocide can happen anywhere' (Gifty Afenyur Dadzie, Interview 2010).

This view might be considered a stern warning and sometimes an over exaggeration but it presents the reality. The overheated political debates could endanger democracy as most coup d'états and conflicts in Africa were facilitated by the media (Chari 2016) which provided the platform. Feintuck (1999) argues that principles such as a fairness doctrine could allow media organizations to broadcast present issues in a balanced, equitable and honest way, and is believed by scholars to help address this problem as was the case in the United States. Nevertheless, the complexity associated with a fairness doctrine in relation to deciding what is fair and balanced, especially in a country such as Ghana characterized by liberalism of speech and thought in the constitution, will pose a great challenge. Another challenge to the government-media relationship are the increasing cases of intimidation and harassment of media practitioners by the state following the re-democratization process. Nyarko and Akpojivi (2017) allege that there has been an increase in government harassment (by state security and politicians) of media practitioners where journalists are arrested or equipment destroyed in the course of them carrying out their responsibilities. This has caused Ghana to slip backwards in the ranking index of freedom of expression as by the close of 2016, Ghana's ranking on the index worsened to 26th place (see Nyarko and Akpojivi 2017). The government attributed this to the media not being responsible, hence its attempt to regulate even the new media.

Media Ownership Structure

The ownership structure of the media will directly or indirectly shape the political and economic structures of the media. Media ownership is regarded as a serious policy issue as it affects the ability of the media to fulfill their constitutional responsibility of holding the state accountable. Hence the constant challenge faced by policymakers is to address how they can insulate the media from both political and economic pressures. There is a belief that a broadcasting law will help address this ownership problem as it will state the extent to which media owners can influence their respective media organizations, and likewise outline the functions of the media. Although there have been recent attempts to pass a broadcasting law, this has generated contestations in the media sphere as the current broadcasting law is perceived to be contrary to the constitutional provisions that allow for freedom and independence of the media. For instance, the Ghana Independent Broadcasters Association (GIBA) challenged the broadcasting law in the Supreme Court over fears that the law will regulate content (Joy FM 2017). Thus there are worries about how the media ownership structure in Ghana can be made conducive to facilitate both the growth and development of the industry.

Numerous studies carried out by McChesney, Eribo, Ogbondah and McQuail, among others, have highlighted ownership influence over the operations of the mass media. However, these studies have failed to examine the degree and extent of media freedom available to the media in a liberal environment, which will be addressed in this analysis. Prior to the embrace of media reforms in 1992, the media environment was monopolized by the Ghana Broadcasting Corporation (GBC) serving as the main source of information (Alhassan 2005; Hasty 2005), and with the British Broadcasting Corporation (BBC) providing an alternative service. According to Boafo (1987), the monopolization of the media environment allowed government to interfere with the day-to-day operations of the media. The editor-in-chief of GBC describes this period by stating that 'GBC was being controlled by the government and it served as a government propaganda tool since it was being financed by the government, hence GBC was conscious of what they say in order not to step on the toes of the powers that be, i.e. they needed to be careful when releasing information, especially information against government' (Francis Sasu, Interview 2010). Such practice hindered media development and democratic advancement as the latter's dependence on the free flow of information enables the public to make informed political decisions.

However, with the embrace of re-democratization in 1992, the constitutional provisions on media freedom and independence resulted in a proliferation of media ownership, thus breaking the government's monopoly and opening the media sphere to private participation. However, Buckley et al. (2005: 6) argue that at the time of writing the 'liberal 1992 constitution, the issue of independent media ownership and the protection of the sparse radio spectrum was not fully considered, and hence the first problem was encountered with Radio Eye in 1994 when it broadcast without authorization based on the provision of Chapter 12 of the constitution that allows for ownership devoid of licensing'. This to a large extent has informed the constitutional interpretation in relation to media ownership, therefore changing the dynamics of the media environment in relation to the ownership structure. According to the former minister of communication Harune Iddrisu, 'tremendous progress has been witnessed in the Ghana media environment following the liberalisation of the media space, we have over 147 operational licensed FM stations and 48 licensed television stations in Ghana. This is unprecedented and it means that we have enhanced the frontiers of freedom of expression...and that we have true meaning to the particular requirement of the laws, i.e. constitution' (Interview 2010).

In line with the provisions of the reform processes, one could argue that with the proliferation of the mass media (i.e. print and broadcast industries), the diverse interests of the public in relation to an open, private and competitive industry as outlined in the National Telecommunication Policy 2004 are being met. To further protect the interests of the public in the reform process, the NMC was established on July 7,

1993 to help 'insulate state-owned media from government control, to investigate, mediate and settle complaints made against or by the media, promote and ensure the freedom and independence of the media and to make regulations for the registration of newspapers and other publications' (National Media Commission Act 1993). Although there are no specific guidelines as to how the NMC should carry out its mandate—as the Broadcasting Act, which should provide such information, has been contested in the Supreme Court—it can be inferred that the above functions are an acceptable framework by which the media are to be regulated to ensure their independence and freedom from ownership interference.

Despite these provisions that should guarantee independence and freedom of the media from ownership interferences, the media structures in Ghana are still struggling to insulate themselves from interference whether from the state or private individuals. One major obstacle to this is NMC's challenge in deciding who should be able to interdict the managers of the state-owned media outlets. NMC is allowed to appoint board members of state-owned media outlets to work alongside managers already in the system. This is a major problem in relation to implementation as there is confusion as to who has the powers to interdict. For instance, in 2010, the board members of GBC accused the director general and four other directors of financial mismanagement and wanted to sanction them. However, the director general and the directors alleged that the board has no power to sanction them. This power tussle between the GBC board members and directors reveals that the issue was not carefully considered during policy formulation. As one policymaker said, 'this problem was not envisaged during policy formulation because the focus at that time was the liberalisation of the airwaves and freeing it from government interference as there was the strong belief in the political and media sphere that a liberalized ownership structure will address the issue of ownership influence which is now not the case' (Affail Monney, Interview 2010).

The implication of Monney's assertion is that policy formulation during the transition process was quickly done just to free the media from government without a detailed examination or study of the long-term implication of such policies in the media sphere. Jacobson (2004: 65) reveals that the problem with policy formulation in developing societies, where policies are irreconcilable with the prevailing socio-economic and cultural considerations and are based on Western influence, is policy goal realization (see also Obadare 2006). Moreover, is media freedom and independence not endangered by ownership structure despite the policies' guarantee? This remains one very important unanswered question. Article 167c charged the NMC to insulate state media from government interference. Hasty (2005) and Alhassan (2005), in their study of the Ghanaian media, argue that the state-owned media continues to be subjected to government control due to the continual funding of state-owned media by government. The funding from government gives it room to interfere in the media by pressurizing the media to adopt its ideological position despite the constitutional provisions such as Article 162(4) which calls for each medium to set its own editorial opinion and be free from interference, thereby limiting media freedom to certain areas.

The manager of GBC, Peggy Ama Donkor, while attesting to this fact stated that:

> I work for a public service broadcaster, what we do is to service the government of the day, so we have no powers to do certain stories that other private media houses are doing...a reporter can go out and come and report exactly what happened but because of the interest of the government, we sometimes don't have the right to put the facts in the public domain (Interview 2010).

This claim is similar to Karikari's findings in his study of state-owned media's contribution to political discourse. According to Karikari (1998), media organizations owned by the state hardly allow for rational, rigorous debate on issues of national interest because of their desire to maintain the 'old regime' or culture of supporting their owner's ideology. Therefore, the need to question the effectiveness of Article 162 of the constitution that insulated state-owned media from interference and likewise ascertain why the status quo remains the same despite the reforms. Milton (2000: 38) argues that the reason the status quo remains in most emerging democracies is the selfishness and unwillingness of politicians to allow full institutional changes because of their desire to dominate the struggle for power. And this can be seen in the Ghanaian political sphere. For instance, the management of GBC was invited by the Ministry of Information following GBC's decision not to air the late President John Atta Mill's speech at the United Nations General Assembly. The actions of the Ministry of Information were widely criticized as many considered it to be a plot to interfere with GBC's operations because the government could have followed the due process of approaching the NMC, which is empowered to check and regulate the activities of the media in accordance with the NMC Act 1993. According to a policymaker, the government's attempt to test the constitutional provisions was based on the ideology that since it funds the media, it should have the right to question the failure of the media. The reaction of the media, civil society and the NMC is, however, an indication that democracy is still alive and growing in Ghana and issues like this should be expected in any transitioning democracy (Affail Monney, Interview 2010).

The above assertion that this is a common feature in emerging democracies supports the claim that allowing full reforms in an emerging democracy is often difficult due to the influence of antecedents (Milton 2000). This antecedent influence is often why the state-owned media are less critical and vocal. The previous atmosphere of fear and censorship, where media practitioners were arrested and sacked for their views, has continued to influence practitioners in state-owned media despite the reforms. According to the editor-in-chief of GBC, 'what I realize now is that government hardly dictates the kind of news that we put on air, government hardly interferes with that, it is up to the individual editor to determine which news they want to put on air. However, in doing so, they have to be mindful that stories which are not in the government interests are either removed or remodified to suit the government since they fund us and we cannot bite the fingers that feed us' (Francis Sasu, Interview 2010). In other words, a media manager's decision to exclude certain information from the public domain and be less critical of government is due to the years of censorship which has created a culture where state-owned media continue to follow the ideological standing of the government (Karikari 1998), since these media were all established by the government for a reason, and the government's continuous funding means the editorial position of the media is dependent on government ideology. Hence, Karikari posited that the issue of media ownership and its influence can only be addressed when media practitioners assert themselves and adhere to the constitutional provisions and not the ideological positioning of the media organizations for which they work. To him 'if a journalist cannot work within the editorial policy or belief in a state-owned media, then they should resign. It is like a journalist working for a Catholic media, and yet you want to promote abortion and contraceptives; your freedom in respect of the 1992 constitution is limited to the ideological principle guiding that media' (Interview 2010). This means media practitioners should not allow the culture of silence inherited from colonial and pre-independent eras to impact on their activities in this re-democratized era that has witnessed a reform of the media industry.

However, it is most often construed that the private media organizations are free to exercise their responsibilities. Contrary to this view, Karikari (1998: 204) argued that while the private media is seen to provide alternative views not covered in the public media (state-owned), the private media are more or less established for political or economic reasons which will, to a large extent, impact on their freedom and independence to fulfill their responsibilities. This is a view similarly shared by Chomsky and Herman (2002) who stated that beyond the private press image of freedom from interference, their practice shows that they seek to protect and defend the economic and political interests of society. According to Ben Ephsen, editor of the private press *Daily Dispatch* newspaper, the formulation of the 1992 constitution witnessed the proliferation of a private press with a different agenda and ideologies and these agendas dominate the public domain (2010). This is worrisome for the emerging democracy of Ghana as these private presses could be used to channel different ideologies in the country which could hinder the democratic consolidation process. Although scholars such as Hasty (2005) might consider these different opinions and views from each media owner to mean the media are vocal and critical, this poses a grave danger to democratic consolidation and the development of the media. According to Kuma Drah, managing editor for GBC News, we are currently witnessing the polarization of the media between the two major political parties (i.e. the NDC and NPP) because ownership of the media is divided along the lines of the political parties and this has given room to the media to voice different philosophical, ideological and partisan views in the private media sphere. A study carried out by RSF in 2016 established that the majority of the privately owned media are owned by people with political interests. For example, the owner of Excellence in Broadcasting Group Ltd, Dr. Kwabena Duffour was the former minister of finance and economic planning in the National Democratic Congress (NDC). Likewise, Frederick Blay who is the acting chairman of the ruling New Patriotic Party (NPP) is the majority shareholder of Western Publications Ltd which publishes some of Ghana's most popular newspapers such as *Daily Guide* and *News One* (RSF 2016).

This presents the issue of how to secure the independence and freedom of the private media from associated political and economic interest groups. George Sarpong, the former executive director of NMC, argues that this issue is a global phenomenon which is not limited to Ghana but the difference is centered on the extent and degree to which it occurs in Ghana compared to other countries (Interview 2010), which cannot be measured in this study. However, it is believed that the broadcasting law once passed will help address this problem. Likewise, effective regulation will help guarantee the freedom and independence of the media.

According to the various media policies, regulation is fundamental in a liberalized and reformed media sphere, hence regulation should be transparent. However, the issue of transparent regulation has been a dominant debate in Ghana and in most emerging democracies because of the constant balancing act between 'effective media regulation and the democratic right to freedom of expression' (Sarpong 2010: 7). There is a belief that the issue of regulation and the need to balance freedom with regulation was not effectively considered during the policy formulation process (see Buckley et al. 2005). This is evident with the broadcast from Radio Eye, and hence the need for government to quickly consider mechanisms for regulation. According to a policymaker Affail Monney, 'at the time of formulation, the desire of the framers was to free the media from any influence and this problem was not envisaged' (Interview 2010). Consequently, the NCA Act No. 524 of 1996 was enacted. The act empowers the NCA to regulate the telecommunication industry (i.e. wire, cable, radio and television). To this end, the President of the Republic of Ghana is to appoint the eight board members, and the body is to be under the direct management of the Ministry of Information.

However, there have been numerous issues around the independence of the NCA and how this might impact on the media. The structure above indicates a direct relationship between the agency and the government, which is unhealthy and not transparent. Tomaselli and Tomaselli (1989: 13) and Bourgault (1995) call this 'political patronage' where appointees are political sycophants who endeavor to serve the interests of their appointer, to the detriment of the wider public. And the composition of the board members can also be considered political patronage as these appointees could be viewed as acting in the vested interests of government. As one senior journalist with GBC puts it, the members of the NCA board are members of the political party in power; therefore they are there to do the government's bidding (Anonymous, Interview 2010). The implication of this kind of relationship between the government and regulatory bodies has been examined by Ekpu (1990) and Nyamnjoh (2005) in their studies. Nevertheless, this kind of structure creating two regulatory bodies has resulted in a conflict of interest and controversy over who has the mandate to regulate the media. For instance, Article 162(3) of the 1992 constitution requires no form of licensing to be met in order to own media; however, the NCA Act No. 524 of 1996 makes it compulsory to obtain a license before electronic media can be operated. While others see this licensing requirement as a fundamental necessity for media regulation in a democracy, placing this law within the constitution shows the problematic nature of the act. This has resulted in a series of legal actions challenging the NCA Act No. 524 of 1996. In one such case, the Supreme Court held that 'it was a restriction reasonably required for the protection of national security, public order, public morality and the reputation, rights and freedom of others within the meaning of Article 164' (cited in Buckley et al. 2005).

The above judgment limited licensing requirements to broadcasting and not print media due to the sensitive nature of the outlet. The former executive director of NMC, while endorsing the above judgment, held that 'the judgment reflects the fact that the radio spectrum is a limited resource and that the society cannot construe 162(3) to mean that everybody can set up any radio or television station. In any case, there is some approach to legal interpretation that tends to interpret general words from the context of the specific words used there' (George Sarpong, Interview 2010). This complexity or confusion in relation to what Article 162(3) means or permits can be attributed to the failure of reform processes to be holistic due to the haste to liberalize the media sphere: hence the issue of which medium requires or does not require a license. According to an editor at GBC, Edward Nyarko 'newspapers, radio, television, magazines are all part of the mass media, so you cannot say mass media, and then restrict some; that is the problem, therefore, giving politicians especially the appointing authority the NCA, the latitude to do whatever they want' (Interview 2010). The above assertion indicates the complexity of policy formulation, interpretation and implementation in Ghana which Buckley et al. (2005: 1) allude to as a gap between 'constitutional provisions and guarantees and actual regulatory practices in Ghana'.

Media as a Public Trust

All the policy documents facilitating the reform process call for the mass media to act as an agent of public trust in order for them to be valuable to citizens. This call, according to Higgins (2008), is necessary because of the struggle between maintaining a balance between the political and economic forces and the requirement to meet the needs of a diverse public. By the media acting as an agent of public trust this means they are rising above the challenge by balancing these different interests and putting citizens first in their activities. The citizens or public are considered a major constituent of the media industry since the media do not operate in a vacuum (Ekpu 1990). Over the years, the media have struggled to fulfill or meet the needs of citizens. Right from pre-colonial times, the media was used to serve the vested interests of the few colonizers and, in the post-independence era, the media are accused of serving the few interests of government, acting as the mouthpiece of the state (Nyamnjoh 2005).

Consequently, in the re-democratization era, the focus has been on how the media can be reformed to serve the interests of the public and not the selected few. This era facilitated the proliferation of the mass media. According to Charles Acheampong, spectrum manager at the NCA, there are over 300 newspapers, 37 public service media, 143 commercial media and 18 community media in operation in Ghana (Interview 2010). These various media outlets compete with each other, hence the question of how the policy goal of the media acting in the public trust can be achieved. George Sarpong posited that in this era of active competition between the various media outlets, the media can only achieve the goal of becoming a public trust by not focusing much on the interests of their owners but on the public (Interview 2010). In other words, the media should be interested in serving and meeting the diverse needs of the public such as information, education and entertainment 'in pursuit of a dynamic, equitable and culturally endowed national development' as stated in the National Media Policy 2000. This means that the programming of the mass media should satisfy the political, social and economic information quest of the public which will, in turn, facilitate or lead to self-development, as argued by John Stuart Mill.

To this end, the former minister of communication, Harune Iddrisu, stated that the 'Ghanaian media should perform their constitutional role of mirroring the society effectively, and give out comprehensive information in an objective and honest reportage in order to meet the information quest of the public, and by so doing gain the public's trust and confidence' (Interview 2010). The above means that public trust can only be achieved when the media fulfill their responsibility to the public in a professional and ethical manner and this idea was not reflected in all three major policy documents in Ghana. Although the Ghana Journalists Code of Ethics touches on the media being responsible (i.e. adhering to ethics), this is more from the perspective of being accountable to society. Therefore, the onus lies on the media to be credible, and adhere to the ethics of the profession as this is the only way they can win the public's trust. Persistent complaints based on an irresponsible media will have a grave impact on the ability of the public to trust the media as people will begin to question the credibility of the media and their activities.

According to Edward Nyarko, an editor with GBC, while substantiating the above, held that the public's trust in an organization can be lost over time when the public perceive that that particular media organization is always not reliable. The public will seek an alternative which can be trusted. According to him 'about 10 years ago, Being Blank Newspaper and the Chronicle private newspaper were held in high esteem, but as time passed, they lost the public confidence when people realized that they were not doing very well in terms of meeting expectations; today the public has voted and accepted the Daily Guide Newspaper as the most credible privately owned newspaper in the country' (Interview 2010). Similarly, there was judgement of the GBC state-owned media because of the perception that they are under the influence of the government and their interests are in serving the state rather than the public. According to the manager of GBC, Peggy Ama Donkor 'we are working so hard to win back the trust of the public. We lost this trust due to our perceived action of acting as a government mouthpiece or propaganda tool' (Interview 2010).

One factor that has continued to hinder the mass media acting as the public trust is resources (funding) to produce programming that will meet the diverse needs of the public and protect them from the interference and influence of owners. Following the proliferation of the media industry due to the breaking of GBC's monopoly coupled with poor economic conditions (Kafewo 2006), active competition between the various media organizations for limited resources resulted. Aside from the National Media Policy classification of the media into three tiers to reduce competition and meet the needs of the public at different levels, there is still active competition and the policy did not state how this competition can be effectively managed. As the managing editor of *Concord* newspaper, Alfred Ogbamey puts it 'the National Media Policy 2000 is one of those policies that speak in general terms, apart from the classification of the media, as a means to attain public trust, no machineries were put in place to facilitate it and ensure a balanced and healthy competition' (Interview 2010). According to the policy, the public media should operate as a non-profit organization which should be independent and professional in its activities. It is this level of professionalism that will win the trust of the public.

However, due to financial constraints the mass media are unable to act independently and in a professional manner as the funding from both government and private interests interfere with their activities; as the saying goes 'he who pays the piper calls the tune'. A lucid review of programming of the state-owned media GBC shows that the station is on a drive to boost its internally generated revenue through adverts, sponsorship and space rental. For instance, a 30-minute news segment is characterized by a series of advertisements every five minutes, thus making it difficult to differentiate between GBC and commercially owned media such as TV5 and Metro. Community radio stations are also caught in this dilemma and this reflects the complexities and difficulty in achieving policy goals in the re-democratized era of Ghana. According to the National Media Policy 2000, community radio stations are germane to the realization of public trust due to a mandate of local reach. Lewis (2006: 15) posited that the participatory and development oriented nature of community media allows for community media to serve the interests of the public by giving 'voice to the voiceless'. To this end, the National Media Policy 2000 calls for the creation of the Ghana Investment Fund for Telecommunication (GIFTEL) to fund and facilitate the growth and development of community media in Ghana. The extent to which this has been successful is subject to debate as at present, community radio stations in Ghana are still faced with numerous challenges in relation to establishment and sustenance. Therefore, this makes it difficult to distinguish between community media and commercial media as their programming and operations are similar (see Akpojivi 2012).

Conclusively, in the debate about the media acting as a public trust, the media and their practitioners always assume that they know what the public want. This is evident in the lack of active research and development carried out by the media to ascertain the needs and interests of the public and how these can be met. This creates a gap between the media and the public and, as such, assumptions from the media are centered around their editorial decisions (Coleman and Ross 2010). This is reflected in Ghana's media environment, as Edward Nyarko reinforced by asking 'what are we expected to do to continue to win the confidence of the people and maintain it? Are we going to continue to sit down in our offices assuming that we know what the public wants? The solution lies in continuous research, going out to find what the public wants, not what the politicians want or what I want to broadcast, because at the end of the day, what the public wants determine what will drive the market' (Interview 2010). Nyarko's assertion captures the realities of the Ghanaian media environment as Fosu and Akpojivi (2015) argue that this assumption of what the public wants has led to the politicization of the Ghanaian media sphere. The media assume, without carrying out research and development, that politics sells and Ghanaians are interested in politics, hence blatant overpoliticization of the airwaves.

There is also no evidence from the regulatory authorities (i.e. the NMC or the NCA) that they have carried out research and development to ascertain the needs and interests of the public and how these can be met. The only research carried out by NMC is a media monitoring project to determine the extent to which media houses are fulfilling their quotas in relation to news, music and accountability (Ghana Media Review 2006). Therefore, it can be argued that the incomprehensive nature of the reform process (i.e. policy formulation) has ignored this vital component. If the process had been holistic and participatory in nature (i.e. grassroots-driven and not imposed) this complexity and haphazardness would have been addressed. This is in line with Ake's (2000) position that democratization and reform has offered little fundamental change as the full potential of the process has not been utilized.

Universal Access to the Media

Nyamnjoh (2005) stated that access to information in most African countries is still a privilege, as the majority of Africans due to poverty are excluded from the information highway, and the further commodification and privatization of information and knowledge has made the reality of access to information a mirage. Nyamnjoh's assertion attests to the challenge of attaining universal access to the media which was encapsulated as a fundamental human right in the Universal Declaration of Human Rights of 1948. Although, universal access to the media is a major problem affecting both the developed and developing countries, it is more worrisome in developing African states such as Ghana because a modern and basic communication infrastructure is lacking.

Most often in the discussion of universal access to the media the focus is on the rights of the public to access information. However, it should be noted that there are two approaches to understanding universal access to the media: the right to access information and the right to participate in media discourse. The right to access the media will be incomplete without an understanding of the media content and citizens participation in the media discourse. Golding and Murdock (1986: 185) argue that 'no one should be barred from the means to communicate publicly or acquire communication because of circumstances beyond their control'. This means that accessibly to information can only be judged to be complete when such access encourages participation to broaden societal discourse. The call for universal access to the media cannot be overemphasized as, according to a UNESCO 2007 report, the majority of Ghanaians reside in the rural areas with a literacy rate of just 49% (Akpojivi and Fosu 2016). This means that due to the infrastructural deficit these people might be excluded from accessing and participating in a media discourse. Consequently, the media policies in Ghana advocate for the liberalization of the airwaves to encourage multiplicity of channels in the rural areas (see Buckley et al. 2005; Alhassan 2005).

In addition, the National Media Policy (2000) went further by insisting that these channels or media of communication should use local languages in broadcasting so that the excluded public (those who do not understand or speak English) can be accommodated. This is in line with the ICT4AD policy that sees the establishment of community media as a mechanism for empowering marginalized rural communities because of its reach and participation. In summary, the National Telecommunication Policy (2005) insists that by 2010 'every citizen and resident of the Republic of Ghana shall have available, high quality and affordable access to information and communication services, to help transform Ghana into a knowledge-based society and technology driven economy'. Seven years beyond the deadline, this is still a dream yet to be realized as universal access to the media is still an abstract concept due to numerous challenges and conceptual issues. George Sarpong, former executive director of NMC, held that this idea of universal access within the reform processes is limited to telecommunication services and not the mass media (Interview 2010). Such an interpretation of the National Telecommunication Policy is problematic as Section 5.1 of the National Telecommunication Policy entitled 'principles and objectives of universal access' reveals that this is inclusive of 'signal coverage of mobile and broadcast network'. Sarpong's assertion only highlights the difficulty in realizing policy goals, which most often can be attributed to the unwillingness of stakeholders such as the government, media and investors to fulfill. According to Bright Blewu, executive secretary of the GJA and media practitioner, the inability of most stakeholders to put machinery in place for the actualization of the policy goal of universal access has caused Ghana to continually lag behind despite policies being in place to address the issue (Interview 2010).

Outside the conceptual issue based on the interpretation of the policy, two fundamental issues were identified by the media policies in Ghana as a way of achieving universal access to the media. These are the use of local languages specifically to address the issue of literacy, which impacts on the ability of Ghanaians to understand and participate in media discourse, and building the communication infrastructure. To encourage citizens' participation and facilitate universal access to the media, the National Media Policy and ICT4AD policy charged the mass media to use indigenous language in media production and broadcasting of content. In a similar light, the NMC in partnership with the UNDP formulated a policy document entitled 'Guidelines for Local Language Broadcasting 2009'. This document provides the framework for procedure and processes underpinning local language broadcasting for media organizations for the procedure and processes underpinning local language broadcasting (see Akpojivi 2012; Akpojivi and Fosu 2016).

This approach is central to the realization of universal access to the media as Kwame Karikari opines that universal access will only be feasible when the mass media uses mother tongues in broadcasting. According to him 'the more we use our mother tongue the more we empower people to be able to communicate properly and effectively...if we don't encourage the use of our mother tongues in communication, the issue of free speech and right to communication will always be seriously limited' (Interview 2010). Karikari's idea is similar to Frank Ugboajah's (1985, 1986), who argued for an integrated media system that will be favorable to the locals and recognize their realities. Some media organizations such as Ghana Television, Metro television, Joy FM and Peace FM have taken advantage of this policy and provided comprehensive programming in which the uneducated could participate in societal discourse. This, according to Kafewo (2006), has changed the face of broadcasting in Ghana, because it has led to a more participatory and inclusive broadcasting culture. In as much as this trend is commendable, Akpojivi and Fosu (2016) have noted that the languages used by these media organizations are usually Akan and Ewe instead of all the official languages of English, Hause, Ewe, Akan, Nzem and Dagbani. Despite a belief within the media sphere that it is practically impossible to broadcast using all official languages, this tendency raises the question of majority and minority rights and could pose a threat to the nascent democracy. Ethnicity plays a prominent role in the political and socio-economic formation of Ghana as it defines or determines political, socio-cultural and economic entitlements (see Akpojivi and Fosu 2016).

Furthermore, outside broadcasting in some of the local languages—predominantly Ewe and Akan—other ethnic and local dialects are ignored and this was not envisaged in the media reform processes. According to a senior media practitioner 'we have over 50 dialects in the country, but most media broadcast in the dominant dialects, do we assume that everybody speaks or understands these dominant dialects? Some group of people have definitely been left out, and they continue to be left out until something is done' (Interview 2010). Akpojivi and Fosu (2016) allege that the status quo is still the same as the media have continued to broadcast in the dominant languages. The scenario is further compounded by the fact that there is no indigenous vernacular newspaper as all the dailies are still published in English.

Lastly, the major challenge to the attainment of universal access to the media is lack of infrastructure. Media reforms embarked upon opened the space for active participation and proliferation of the media organizations to the extent that the NCA no longer considers applications for new broadcasting licenses due to the lack of space (see NCA Report 2017). Except for GBC which broadcasts to all ten regions (GBC News 2010), all the other media organizations (radio and television) are concentrated in urban areas such as Kumasi, Accra and Tema (See Hasty 2005). This is because of the huge cost of building and establishing the required infrastructure and the need to have quick returns on investment. According to Afari-Yeboah of the Ghana Media Standards Improvement Project, 'because of the economic nature of the country, everybody is looking towards Accra or Kumasi which are more economically viable, so if you want the media to operate from the rural areas, how will the publishers and owners make their money back?' (Interview 2010). The same is applicable to the newspapers as Ghana does not have full nationwide coverage. This makes universal access a mirage for Ghana because of 'limited economic resources, the long distance between towns and villages, difficult terrain, and the scarcity of primary power or unreliable power generation' (Akwule 1992: 15). This difficulty in achieving universal access can be attributed to the failure of the various policies to recognize these inherent cultural factors and address them. For instance, the policies call for a massive investment in infrastructure without laying out a framework and setting out a mechanism on how this massive infrastructure can be achieved without 'liberalization' which usually is centred around the interests of economic profit.

Nevertheless, the emergence of new media technologies made accessibility easier, as more people can participate in media and societal debates

(Fosu and Akpojivi 2015), and this results in improvements in democratic cultures, such as accountability (Henckes 2016; Stringer 2014). However, these technologies are limited to the elites who can afford the devices and have the required skills and knowledge to operate the devices.

Media Accountability

In the discourse on media freedom the idea of media accountability is often ignored or sidelined. The idea of media accountability is interconnected to the other themes of media freedom, public trust and universal access already discussed, as there is the need to balance freedom with responsibility, and hold the media accountable for their actions in relation to the attainment of public trust and ease with which people can access and participate in media and societal discourse (Kadhi 1999 cited in Nyamnjoh 2005). There is no universally acceptable definition of 'media accountability' due to the contestation and perspective with which people view it. Nevertheless, I approached media accountability from the perspective of the relationship between the media and other stakeholders in the media sphere (Andrea and Shaw 2009) and the need for the media to be answerable to these stakeholders and society for their actions (directly or indirectly) (McQuail 2005).

Following the reform processes of 1992, there have been numerous complaints and outcries against the media for acting irresponsibly. These include accusations such as sensationalism, false reportage and bias (Hasty 2005), and this has led to a high number of libel cases against the media. This problem necessitated the GJA to tag the 2010 annual GJA awards 'Unethical journalism and corruption in the media' in order to help create awareness and tackle this problem. The above situation raises the fundamental question of who watches the watchdog to ensure that it does not abuse its powers or underperform. This is to avoid Kasoma's assertion that the media is becoming the accuser, the jury and the judge (cited in Nyamnjoh 2005: 83).

The provision contained in Chapter 12 of the constitution can be inferred to be the cause of the high number of irresponsible incidents by media practitioners because of their interpretation of absolute freedom, and if this trend is not controlled it could lead to governments wanting to regulate the media, as witnessed in South Africa where the ruling party, the African National Congress (ANC), has considered establishing the Media Appeal Tribunal (MAT), and the Secrecy Bill (see Daniels 2012).

Consequently, the NMC and GJA are straddled with the responsibility of managing this menace. The NMC, which is charged with the responsibility of ensuring and promoting accountability, designed and implemented several guidelines for political reporting, for the print media and for broadcasting. These guidelines provide the framework in which the media are held answerable according to the beliefs of the public. Karikari (1994) noted that because the mass media are public institutions they should be held accountable as this will help address the issue of media freedom balance that has always confronted societies.

Both the NMC and GJA have approached media accountability from the perspective of self-regulation due to the constitutional provision and contestation surrounding the issue of regulation (see Duncan 2014). To this effect, all media practitioners are expected to adhere to the GJA code of ethics which stipulates the do's and don'ts for every practicing media practitioner. The GJA code of ethics was adopted on July 27, 1994. Article 1 of the code requires all journalists to give truthful reports that are unbiased, accurate and balanced. Hence journalists are required to cross-check their facts before publication and carry out their watchdog role with a high sense of responsibility devoid of inducement (GJA Code of Ethics 1994). This code has been criticized for two reasons. Firstly, all practicing media practitioners are expected to abide by the code. However, the code does not address the issue of non-compliance and the consequences of breaching it. Secondly, the code is accused of not reflecting Ghana's realities but Western ideologies and realities (Nyamnjoh 2005). According to the executive secretary of the GJA, Bright Blewu, the Anglo-Saxon nature of the code is as a result of the support (training and funding) received from Western agencies such as the Friedrich-Ebert-Stiftung (FES), Danish International Development Agency (DANIDA) and the United States Agency for International Development (USAID) by the association and regulator (NMC) (Interview 2010).

These two issues have further necessitated the question of how accountability can be achieved when the realities reflected in the policy document differ from the reality in Ghana. This will pose serious challenges to the media reform process. These two challenges will be the focus of this discussion. Firstly, as earlier mentioned, the framing of the GJA code of ethics along Western ideas ignores the interplay of cultural and socio-economic value impact on media accountability. The prevalent practice and culture of bribe taking among media practitioners, popularly known as 'soli' (for solidarity), ridicules the aims and objectives of the GJA code of ethics. Some media practitioners see 'soli' as a normal and ethical practice and others view it as unethical. For example, Aflred Ogbamey, the managing editor of *Concord* newspaper, believes that soli is ethical depending on one's understanding of ethics, and the act of 'soli' does not impact on media activities as understood by the GJA code of ethics (Interview 2010). On the other hand, Edward Nyarko, editor at GBC, believes that 'soli' is unacceptable and unethical because it influences and lowers journalistic practices and standards (Interview 2010).

The above contestation not only questions the effectiveness of the NMC self-regulation principle as a tool to enforce accountability due to differences in ethical standards but believes that the ineffectiveness of the GJA code of ethics is a result of the incorporation of Western beliefs. Nyamnjoh (2005: 87) argues that the universal ideologies of ethical practices contained in most African countries' codes of ethics will be impossible to implement due to corruption and the circumstances in which the media operate in Africa, which is significantly different from the West. Ghana's media environment is not economically viable like in most Western societies, thus enabling 'soli' to flourish. According to Ajoa Yeboah Afari, coordinator of the Ghana Media Standards Improvement Project, 'most media owners do not have the resources to sustain their operations, because after hurriedly establishing their various media organisations due to the liberalization that occured in 1992, most of them ran out of resources. Consequently, journalists are poorly paid with monthly earnings of $25–$50, and some go without pay for several months' (Interview 2010). This is a typical climate in most media houses in Africa (see Nyamnjoh 2005), and in such situations media practitioners are accustomed to 'soli' to meet their everyday needs and challenges. Therefore, to enact a code of ethics that requires media practitioners to avoid corruption and be objective without recognizing these specific realities and challenges in the media environment is a mockery of the process.

Secondly, the interpretation of Article 167 of the constitution poses serious challenges to enforcing media accountability. This provision allows for independence and freedom of the media devoid of interference. This most often is interpreted to mean the NMC has no powers to check the activities of the media. According to the chairman of the NMC, Kabrah Blay-Amihere, 'the framers of the 1992 constitution had no intention to hinder free speech as the parameters of freedom enshrined in the 1992 constitution allows for freedom and rejects attempts to criminalize free speech' (Interview 2010). Such perception or interpretation reduces the NMC to a mere registrar of newspapers and monitor of electronic and print media content without any enforcement powers to sanction erring media which do not keep to professional standards, in the form of withdrawal of their license or any other means which might act as an impediment to their operations as stated in Article 173. Therefore, the NMC uses moral and ethical appeals as an accountability mechanism for media practitioners.

This approach has been widely criticized as it is perceived to have contributed to the continued irresponsibility of the media as they believe that they cannot be sanctioned by the NMC due to the complexities in the interpretation of constitutional provisions. To Karikari 'there are many problems in the Ghanaian media when it comes to the issue of professionalism and accountability because people don't see the commission as having powers to enforce high journalism standards because of their principle of moral suasion, i.e. having teeth that cannot bite' (Interview 2010). This is problematic for the media environment as Ben Ephsen, editor of the *Daily Dispatch*, sums it up by stating 'if I am invited by the National Media Commission over an act of irresponsibility or unethical conduct, I can decide not to go because the commission has no powers to sanction and effect their judgement, this trend continues' (Interview 2010). Similarly, a senior media practitioner asked: 'what good is it to have a regulatory body (NMC) without an enforcing power, a body depending solely on self-regulation? All journalists have their bias, and self-regulation is not the key to addressing this bias as what is objective to me may not be to another' (Interview 2010). The above assertion indicates that despite media practitioners always wanting to advocate for Western principles and ideas in the industry, they are, however, unwilling to adhere to the ethics of the profession and subject themselves to external bodies for accountability, as required by the media policies in Ghana, especially the GJA code.

Lastly, the major policy contestation that hinders media accountability is the conflict of functions between the NMC and the NCA. It is unclear who is charged with the responsibility of regulating the media since the NCA issues licenses and the NMC monitors the media as stipulated in the constitution. Media monitoring is one of the fundamental functions of the NMC, but the process of content regulation has been made complex and difficult because the institutional structure assigns a different body (NCA) which is not charged with monitoring media content but with the responsibility of allocating frequencies (Buckley et al. 2005: 28). This is problematic because it is difficult to separate content from frequency. George Sarpong adds that the 'NMC is the institution established by the constitution to deal with media regulatory matters and the NCA handles communication spectrum. The conceptual problem with this is that it is difficult to separate frequency control from content regulation, and that in a sense poses a problem' (Interview 2010).

This is in line with Buckley et al.'s (2005: 30) idea that frequency is part of content as frequency provides the platform on which content is broadcast, and the fear of licenses being revoked encourage broadcasters to act ethically (see Akpojivi 2012). Consequently, this has made it difficult for the NMC to regulate the media and promote accountability, hence the idea that there is a vacuum in media regulation. This vacuum was created by the failure of policymakers to recognize the realities in Ghana with regard to policy formulation to address the complexities associated with regulation. This vacuum can be addressed if the NCA's functions are merged with those of the NMC as this will lead to an increase in accountability and the NMC will be able to effectively regulate and monitor content. However, this will require Article 167 of the constitution to be reviewed to accommodate the current complexities.

Bibliography

Adebayo, O. (2001). *West Africa's Political Economy in the Next Millennium: Retrospect and Prospect, CODESRIA Monograph Series*. Dakar: CODESRIA.

African Charter on Human and Peoples' Rights. (1986). Online: http://www.umn.edu/humanart. Accessed 15 Jan 2009.

Aidan W. (2010, August 21). *Speech Delivered at the 15th GJA Awards*.

Ake, C. (2000). *The Feasibility of Democracy in Africa*. Dakar: CODESRIA.

Akpojivi, U. (2012). Community Radio Regulation and Its Challenges in Ghana. *Journal of African Media Studies, 4*(2), 193–207.

Akpojivi, U. (2014). Democratizing the Media in the New Democracies of Ghana and Nigeria: Challenges and Prospects. *Ecquid Novi: African Journalism Studies, 35*(3), 87–105.

Akpojivi, U., & Fosu, M. (2016). Indigenous Language Broadcasting in Ghana: Retrospect and Prospect. In A. Salawu & M. Chibita (Eds.), *Indigenous Language Media, Language Politics and Democracy in Africa*. New York: Palgrave Macmillan.

Akwule, R. (1992). *Global Telecommunications the Technology, Administration and Policies*. London: Focal Press.

Alhassan, A. (2005). Market Valorisation in Broadcasting Policy in Ghana: Abandoning the Quest for Media Democratization. *Media Culture and Society, 27*(2), 211–228.

Andrea, M., & Shaw, C. (2009). *Accountability and the Public Interest in Broadcasting*. London: Palgrave Macmillan.
Arthur, A. (1997, September 8–10). *Media Ownership and Control in Ghana: Past, Present and Future Perspective*. Paper Presented at the Regional Workshop on Media Ownership and Control in West and Central Africa, Yaounde.
Bacchi, C. L. (1999). *Women Policy and Politics, the Construction of Policy Problems*. London: Sage Publications.
Barnett, C. (1999). The Limits of Media Democratization in South Africa: Politics, Privatization and Regulation. *Media Culture & Society, 21*, 649–671.
Boadi, G. (2009). Another Step Forward for Ghana. *Journal of Democracy, 20*(2), 138–152.
Boafo, K. (1987). Democratizing Media Systems in African Societies: The Case of Ghana. *Africa Media Review, 2*(1), 24–37.
Boafo-Arthur, K. (1998). The International Community and Ghana's Transition to Democracy. In K. Ninsin (Ed.), *Ghana: Transition to Democracy*. Dakar: CODESRIA.
Bourgault, L. (1995). *Mass Media in Sub-Saharan Africa*. Bloomington: Indiana University Press.
Buckley, S., Apenteng, B., Bathily, A., & Mtimde, L. (2005). *Ghana Broadcasting Study: A Report for the Government of Ghana and the World Bank*. Online: siteresources.worldbank.org. Accessed 1 Feb 2006.
Chari, T. (2016). *Press-Citizen Interface in a Fragile Society: Mapping Press and Citizens Discourse on Election Violence* (Ph.D Thesis). University of Witwatersrand.
Chomsky, N., & Herman, E. (2002). *Manufacturing Consent: The Political Economy of the Mass Media*. New York: Pantheon Books.
Coleman, S., & Ross, K. (2010). *The Media and the Public "Them and "Us" in Media Discourse"*. West Sussex: Wiley-Blackwell.
Coleman, S., Blumler, J., Dutton, W., Shipley, A., Steibel, F., & Thelwall, M. (2011). *Leaders in the Living Room The Prime Ministerial Debate of 2010: Evidence, Evaluation and Some Recommendations*. Oxford: Reuters Institute for the Study of Journalism, University of Oxford.
Daily Guide. (2016). *NPP Blows Gov't Cover Over GHC449m Scandal*. Online: http://dailyguideafrica.com/npp-blows-govt-cover-gh%C2%A2449m-scandal/. Accessed 21 Sep 2017.
Daniels, G. (2012). *Fighting for Democracy: The ANC and the Media in South Africa*. Johannesburg: Wits University Press.
Daniels, G. (2014). How Far does Twitter Deepen Democracy through Public Engagement? An Analysis of Journalists' Use of Twitter in Johannesburg Newsroom. *Journal of African Media Studies, 6*(3), 299–311.
Diamond, L. (2008a). Consolidating Democracy. In L. LeDUC, R. Niemi, & P. Norris (Eds.), *Comparing Democracies 2 New Challenges in the Study of Elections and Voting*. London: Sage Publications.

Diamond, L. (2008b). Progress and Retreat in Africa the Rule of Law Verse the Big Man. *Journal of Democracy, 19*, 138–149.

Duncan, J. (2014). A Political Economy of the Press Self-Regulation: The Case of South Africa. *Media, Culture and Society, 36*(2), 167–182.

Ekpu, R. (1990). Nigeria's Embattled Fourth Estate. *Journal of Democracy, 1*(2), 106–116.

Eribo, F., & Jong-Ebot, W. (1997). *Press Freedom and Communication in Africa*. Trenton: Africa World Press Inc.

Feintuck, M. (1999). *Media Regulation, Public Interest and the Law*. Edinburgh: Edinburgh University Press.

Fosu, M., & Akpojivi, U. (2015). Media Convergence Practices and Production in Ghana and Nigeria: Implications for Democracy and Research in Africa. *Journal of Applied Journalism and Media Studies, 4*(2), 277–292.

GBC News. (2010). *GBC Celebrates 75th Anniversary*. Accra: GBC.

Ghana Journalists Association. (1994). *GJA Code of Ethics*. Accra: GJA.

Golding, P., & Murdock, G. (1986). The New Communications Revolution. In J. Curran, J. Ecclestone, G. Oakley, & A. Richardson (Eds.), *Bending Reality the State of the Media*. London: Pluto Press.

Government of Ghana. (1993). *National Media Commission Act 1993*. Accra: Government Printers.

Hasty, J. (2005). *The Press and Political Culture in Ghana*. Indiana: Indiana University Press.

Heath, C. (1999). Negotiating Broadcasting Policy Civil Society and Civil Discourse in Ghana. *International Communication Gazette, 61*(6), 511–521.

Henckes, R. (2016). *#Accountability? The Changing Dynamics of Political Accountability Through Social Media in Nigeria* (Bachelor Thesis). Leiden University.

Higgins, M. (2008). *Media and Their Public*. Berkshire: Open University Press.

Jacobson, T. (2004). Participatory Communication for Development and the African Philosophy Debate. In C. Okigbo & F. Eribo (Eds.), *Development and Communication in Africa*. Boulevard: Rowman & Littlefield Publishers, Inc.

Jebuni, C., & Oduro, A. (1998). Structural Adjustment Programme and the Transition to Democracy. In K. Ninsin (Ed.), *Ghana: Transition to Democracy*. Dakar: CODESRIA.

Joy FM. (2017). Broadcasting Law Will Strengthen NMC-Oppong Nkrumah. Online. https://www.myjoyonline.com/politics/2017/april-7th/broadcasting-law-will-strengthen-nmc-oppong-nkrumah.php. Accessed 12 May 2017.

Kafewo, S. (2006). *Ghana Research Findings and Conclusions in African Media Development Initiative*. London: BBC World Service Trust.

Karikari, K. (1994). *Independent Broadcasting in Ghana: Implications and Challenges: Proceedings of the National Conference on the Promotion and Privatization of Radio and Television Broadcasting in Ghana*. Accra: Ghana University Press.

Karikari, K. (1998). The Press and the Transition to Multi-Party Democracy in Ghana. In K. Ninsin (Ed.), *Ghana: Transition to Democracy*. Dakar: CODESRIA.
LaMay, C. (2007). *Exporting Press Freedom Economic and Editorial Dilemmas in International Media Assistance*. London: Transaction Publishers.
Lewis, P. (2006). Community Media: Giving a Voice to the Voiceless. In P. Lewis & S. Jones (Eds.), *From the Margins to the Cutting Edge Community Media and Empowerment*. New Jersey: Hampton Press Inc.
McQuail, D. (2005). *McQuail's Mass Communication Theory* (5th ed.). London: Sage Publications.
Milton, A. (2000). *The Rational Politician Exploiting the Media in New Democracies*. Aldershot: Ashgate.
Ministry of Communication Ghana. (2005). *National Telecommunication Policy*. Accra: Government Printers.
Mosaka, N., & Kamaimba, E. (1998). Botswana. In A. Opoku-Mensah et al. (Eds.), *Up in the Air? The State of Broadcasting in Southern Africa analysis & Trend in Six Countries*. Harare: PANOS.
National Media Commission. (2000). *Ghana National Media Policy*. Accra: NMC.
National Media Commission. (2006). *Ghana Media Review: Media Monitoring Report*. Accra: National Media Commission.
NCA. (2017). New Licenses No Longer Available. Online. https://www.nca.org.gh/newsrelease. Accessed 12 Sep 2017.
Nyamnjoh, F. (2005). *Africa's Media Democracy and the Politics of Belonging*. London: Zed Books.
Nyarko, J., & Akpojivi, U. (2017). Intimidation, Assault, and Violence Against Media Practioners in Ghana: Considering Provocation. *Sage Open 7*(1), 1–12.
Obadare, E. (2006). Playing Politics with the Mobile Phone in Nigeria: Civil Society, Big Business and the State. *Review of African Political Economy, 33*(107), 93–111.
Packenham, R. (1973). *Liberal America and the Third World: Political Development Ideas in Foreign Aid and Social Science*. New Jersey: Princeton University Press.
Radsch, C. (2013). *The Revolutions Will Be Blogged: Cyberactivism and the 4th Estate in Egypt*. Doctoral Dissertation, American University.
Republic of Ghana. (2003). *The Ghana ICT for Accelerated Development {ICT4AD} Policy*. Accra: Government Printers.
RSF. (2016). Who Owns the Media? Online. https://rsf.org/en/news/who-owns-media-ghana. Accessed 5 Oct.
Sarpong, G. (2010). A New Way of Measuring Media Performance. In *Monitoring for Broadcasting*.
Stringer, R. (2014). *The Power of Talk Media Accountability in Three African Countries*. London: BBC.
Teeter, D., & Loving, B. (2004). *Law of Mass Communications Freedom and Control of Print and Broadcast Media* (11th ed.). New York: Foundation Press.

Thapisa, A., & Birabwa, E. (1998). Mapping Africa's Initiative at Building an Information and Communications Infrastructure. *Internet Research, 8*(1), 49–58.

Tomaselli, K., & Tomaselli, R. (1989). Between Policy and Practice in the SABC 1970–1981. In R. Tomaselli, K. Tomaselli, & J. Muller (Eds.), *Studies on the South African Media Broadcasting in South Africa*. London: James Currey Ltd.

Ugboajah, F. (1985). *Mass Communication, Culture, and Society in West Africa*. Munich: Hans Zell.

Ugboajah, F. (1986). Communication as Technology in Africa Rural Development. *Africa Media Review, 1*(1), 1–19.

Umeh, C. (1989). The Advent and Growth of Television Broadcasting in Nigeria: Its Political and Education Overtones. *Africa Media Review, 3*(2), 54–66.

UNDP. (2015). *Ghana Millennium Development Goals 2015 Report*. Accra: UNDP.

Universal Declaration of Human Rights (1948). Online: http://www.un.org/en/documents/udhr. Accessed 12 Oct 2009.

Voltmer, K. (2006). The Mass Media and the Dynamics of Political Communication in Processes of Democratization: An Introduction. In K. Voltmer (Ed.), *Mass Media and Political Communication in New Democracies*. London: Routledge.

William, R. (1979). Institutions of the Technology. In A. Mattelart & S. Siegelaub (Eds.), *Communication and Class Struggle: Capitalism, Imperialism*. New York: International General.

Zongo, G. (2001). *ICTs For Development in Africa*. Online: www.unssc.org/web1/programmes/glnp. Accessed 12 Oct 2006.

CHAPTER 4

Media Reforms, Democratization in Nigeria: From Policy Ambition to Implementation

Like the previous chapter, this chapter is an examination of the media reform processes but in Nigeria. This examination is salient as there are numerous contestations surrounding the reform process and its impact on the democratization processes. Campbell (2011) in his book, *Nigeria Dancing on the Brink* alleged that Nigeria was not sincere about the reform process and this, according to him, is positioning Nigeria towards dancing on the brink of becoming a 'failed state'. Other scholars such as Wale Adebanwi and Ebenezer Obadare (2013) have examined the democratic processes and challenges to the democratization process. The major challenge has been that political actors are unwilling to implement initiatives that will allow full reform. Hence Ake posited that the reform processes mean 'little more than an opening for elites who were previously excluded from power to compete' for power (2000: 73), and initiate measures that will make them hold onto this power.

Therefore, this chapter will examine the media reforms that were embarked upon following the re-democratization processes. It will begin by analyzing the role of foreign actors and influence in the media reform process. This will be followed by a discussion of the rationale behind the media policies that followed the reform process, and an evaluation of the impact of these policies on the media environment and the challenges confronting policy implementation.

U. Akpojivi, *Media Reforms and Democratization in Emerging Democracies of Sub-Saharan Africa*,
https://doi.org/10.1007/978-3-319-75301-0_4

Foreign Influence on Nigeria's Media Reform

As earlier discussed, the Universal Declaration of Human Rights of 1948 and the African Charter on Human and Peoples' Rights 1986 have influenced the conceptualization of media freedom and policy formulation in Africa. As Ekpu (1990: 113) argues, freedom or media freedom is regarded as 'one of the greatest pillars of civilisation', and withholding this freedom from individuals is to challenge the 'very essence' of humanity (Mandela 1990: 32–33). Although this freedom speaks directly to individual freedom of expression and not media, it is germane to note that the media derive their freedom from the individual's freedom provision since the ability of an individual to receive and affect information can only be obtained with the aid of the media.

Nevertheless, to address this problem of media rights being inadequately covered at the supranational policy level, the United Nations Educational Scientific and Cultural Organization's (UNESCO) conference in Windhoek in 2001 led to the formulation of the African Charter on Broadcasting. The purpose of this charter is to address the inadequacies of previous supranational policies such as the African Charter on Human and Peoples' Rights, and provide for the protection of media freedom. For the first time in the history of the continent the mass media were accorded rights and protected from economic and political pressures. The general principles of the charter state that the media should be protected from all forms of interference (economic or political) and regulatory authorities were charged with the task of securing the independence of the media. In addition, the charter provides for a fair and transparent licensing process that should be carried out in line with the public interest (African Charter on Broadcasting 2001).

Outside these supranational policies, the Nigerian media environment can be regarded as lacking an adequate policy framework for guiding the media spheres. Apart from the National Broadcasting Code (2006), other policy document such as the National Mass Communication Policy of 1987 was formulated by the military regime of President General Babangida and does not reflect current democratic trends. Likewise, the National Telecommunication Policy (2000) focused on the development of telecommunication infrastructure for mobile and fixed landline services and discussed little or nothing about broadcasting. Nevertheless, despite the lack of a comprehensive policy framework, the push for re-democratization might have influenced the formulation of policies that will open up the media sphere and democratic space. This, according to Diamond et al. (1997: 1), is because Nigeria's drive to democracy can only be assessed based on the implementation of liberal policies that open up the media sphere (see Ake 1979, 2000).

Consequently, Ake (2000) argues that the Nigerian government have been unwilling to implement reforms due to their desire to hold unto old authoritarian enclaves. Thus, their rhetorical approach to reform and democracy (see Milton 2000). However, this position has been dismissed by government officials who believe that the lack of comprehensive media policies is due to the desire of the state to study these ideas from Western governments or organizations before incorporating them into policies that will guide the media environment. According to a senior media officer in the presidency, the 'government is studying these reforms and how they work in these countries before accepting to put them into practice as the quick acceptance and implementation of every ideology handed down to us by these powerful countries and organisations, presents the likelihood of running into problems with implementation' (Interview, 2010). This idea was equally shared by a senior policymaker at the Ministry of Information who posited that the government has the desire to formulate and implement full media reforms, but is studying the environment to ascertain the necessary measures to take in order to determine the right measures (Obi Adindu, Interview, 2010).

A look at the media landscape shows that not much has changed in the 18 years since the re-democratization process began, as the media environment is still faced with an inadequate framework. This could be attributed to the power struggle between political actors and other stakeholders (media, civil societies, etc.) and this struggle to push ideology in the reform process is what slows the process down because of the state's desire to protect its 'authoritarian enclaves' in the face of other stakeholders wanting open liberal reforms (Haggard and Kanfman 1997: 267). However, it should be noted that despite the power struggle between the different stakeholders, the long period of military regime has contributed to the on-going policy contestation process in Nigeria. Therefore, it can be posited that the media reform process is controlled and contested due to struggles by the different actors to control the process and promote their ideas. This can be seen in the media policies and laws governing the media environment and their rationale, as the goals of most media policies in Nigeria tend to promote 'deeply held authoritarian beliefs and culture'. This shows that the media reform process is highly contested, and this contestation is centered on ideologies; in other words, to what extent should liberal policies be formulated and implemented as part of the reform process and to what degree should authoritarian ideas and control of the media be allowed? The following sections on policy rationale and impact of policies on the media environment will provide further details.

Media Reforms and Policy Framework

Following the re-democratization that started in 1999, the government formulated and implemented the 1999 constitution and the National Telecommunication Policy 2000. In addition to these two documents, there are other fundamental documents such as the Official Secrets Act of 1990, the National Broadcasting Commission Decree of 1991 and the National Mass Communication Policy of 1987 that influence the activities of the mass media daily. Therefore, we need to examine the ideas within these documents and evaluate how they impact on the media environment.

Below is a brief discussion of the different policy documents in Nigeria.

The 1999 Constitution of the Federal Republic of Nigeria The 1999 constitution ushered Nigeria into the democratic era after 29 years of military rule. Like the constitution of most democratic countries, it states the do's and don'ts that govern the country. The constitution has been subjected to numerous contestations that have resulted in three sets of amendments in 2010, 2011 and in 2015, with about 71 changes in the 2015 amendment. Despite these amendments, the constitution has been disputed and it is believed by many that it does not reflect the interests of the people as it was formulated by the military regime of General Abdulsalaam Abubakar without public consultation (Aguda 2007). The constitution starts with 'we the people of the Federal Republic of Nigeria….provide for a constitution for the purpose of promoting the good government and welfare of all persons in our country, on the principles of freedom, equality and justice, and for the purpose of consolidating the unity of our people'. This has been contested as the public was not consulted during the formulation process undertaken by the military in May 1999 and it could be argued that this has contributed to the problematic nature of the constitution that has influenced the constant amendment and lopsided nature of its framework (Donald Duke 2017).

The constitution, to a large extent, is built on ideas from the 1960 and 1979 constitutions that were influenced by the provisions of the Universal Declaration of Human Rights and the African Charter on Human and Peoples' Rights. The explicit provision of the bill of rights in Section 39,

Subsections 1 and 2 of the constitution provides for this. According to the Bill of Rights, 'every person shall be entitled to freedom of expression, including freedom to hold opinion and to receive and impact ideas and information without interference. Without prejudice to the generality of subsection (1) of this section, every person shall be entitled to own, establish and operate any medium for the dissemination of information, ideas and opinions…'. This provision can be regarded as the standard normative human rights bestowed upon citizens. It is on this provision that the mass media in Nigeria derive their freedom and independence as there is no explicit provision for media freedom or independence. Nevertheless, Section 22 charged the media with the task of being a watchdog as, according to the section, 'the press, radio, television, and other agencies of the mass media shall at all times be free to uphold the fundamental objectives contained in this chapter and uphold the responsibility and accountability of the government to the people' (1999 Constitution).

This provision shows the inadequacies of the constitution as the mass media in Nigeria are charged with performing watchdog functions without a provision to protect their rights to exercise these functions. Baker (2007) posits that these watchdog functions are essential in a democratic country, as constituted authorities should be held responsible and accountable for their actions. However, the ability of the media to hold these authorities responsible and accountable for their actions is dependent on the freedom and independence of the media from political and economic influence (Humphreys 1996). And, as this is not provided for within the framework of the constitution, the question of how the media can carry out these functions arises. In addition, a major criticism of the constitution is what Tom (2004) called its 'give and take nature'. Section 39, Subsection 3 of the constitution states that:

> Nothing in this section shall invalidate any law that is reasonably justified in a democratic society. (a) for the purpose of preventing the disclosure of information received in confidence, maintaining the authority and independence of courts or regulating telephony, wireless broadcasting, television or the exhibition of cinematography films, or (b) imposing restrictions upon persons holding office under the government of the federation or of a state, members of the armed forces of the federation or members of the Nigerian police force or other government security services or agencies established by law.

The above provision restricts freedom of expression granted in Section 39, Subsections 1 and 2 under the guise of protecting national interest and privacy of the public, which is a controversial issue as most often national interest or public interest entails government interest. And this is more evident based on the fact that the constitution was formulated without public consultation. Consequently, the belief that government has not been sincere about the reform process as the necessary liberal provisions to facilitate media freedom and independence needed for the media to carry out their watchdog functions is lacking due to the 'give and take nature' of the constitution (Tom 2004).

The National Telecommunication Policy 2000 The National Telecommunication Policy 2000 is an amended version of the 1998 policy formulated by the Ministry of Communication. The reason for the amendment was to address the inadequacies of the 1998 version which were not in line with current democratic realities (National Telecommunication Policy 2000). This policy document is alleged to have been drafted based on relevant stakeholders' engagement, unlike the 1998 policy which was implemented without public engagement. Those involved in drafting the amended National Telecommunication Policy 2000 were the former vice president of Nigeria, Alhaji Atiku Abubakar, 22 members from the Telecommunications Sector Reform Implementation Committee (TSRIC) and stakeholders from media owners, civil societies, media practitioners and regulators.

The focus of the policy was on the development of the telecommunications infrastructure. According to the policy document, its objective is to 'achieve the modernisation and rapid expansion of the telecommunications network and services, and this will enhance national economic and social development, and integrate Nigeria internally, as well as, into the global telecommunications environment' (National Telecommunication Policy 2000). The basis for a modern infrastructure was rooted in the previous antecedence and realities of poor infrastructure as, like most African countries, Nigeria suffered from an underdeveloped infrastructure due to a long period of military regimes. Such authoritarian regimes imposed economic sanctions and monopolizations (see Okigbo and Eribo 2004). Consequently, the policy stated that 'Nigeria needs a more proactive policy that recognises international best standards…a policy that will help establish an open, transparent, future-oriented and proactive regulatory framework' as a means to facilitate an efficient, reliable and universal service to the public (National Telecommunication Policy 2000).

One way of achieving this is through the liberalization of the sector which can be attained by embracing liberal democracy. Hence, Ake (2000) argues that liberal democracy is now synonymous with market openness and development. This is a dominant assertion pushed across countries by organizations such as the Bretton Wood Institute and the World Bank and is highlighted in international telecommunication summits such as the World Summit on the Information Society (WSIS 2003, 2005). To Zongo (2001: 4) a good and reliable telecommunication infrastructure 'is a formidable tool to better address the various developmental issues in a rapid and cost effective manner'. Despite the focus of the policy on telecommunication infrastructural development, one could argue that in this era of convergence an issue of universality can be linked to broadcasting. The African Charter on Broadcasting, while elucidating this idea of convergence, stated that 'the right to communicate includes access to telephone, email, internet and other telecommunication systems', and convergence will enhance the speedy flow of information within societies and meet the information needs of society (African Charter on Broadcasting 2001; Bourgault 1995). To this effect, the policy calls for the creation of a universal service fund that will help to finance infrastructural development.

Therefore, it can be argued that the National Telecommunication Policy 2000 was largely influenced by the ideas of liberalization that were pushed forward during the democratization process and this was rooted in the historic background of the country (i.e. poor infrastructural development). Okonjo-Iweala (2012) supported this argument by stating that the need to overturn these problems and to correct the West's impression of Nigeria and its reform processes led to an active liberalization agenda by the government. Hence, Chakravartty and Sarikakis (2006) argue that developing countries see embracing this idea of liberalization as a means to development, or what Ake reasoned to be perceived as developed (1979, 2000).

The Official Secrets Act of 1990 This act, also known as the Official Secrets Act of 1990 Cap. 335, was originally enacted in 1962. The preamble of the act states that it is an 'act to make further provisions for securing public safety and for the purposes connected therein'. From the above provision it can be argued that the Official Secrets Act concerns itself with the protection of state information, and a mechanism to be followed in the disclosure of state information. Therefore, the act became a viable tool in interpreting and enforcing Section 39, Subsection 3 of the 1999 constitution that restricts the Bill of Rights on receiving and impacting on information. According to Section 1 of the act 'subject to subsection (3) of this section a person who (a) transmits any classified matter to a person to whom he is not authorised on behalf of government to transmit or (b) who obtains, reproduces or retains, as the case may be shall be guilty of an offence' (Official Secrets Act 1990).

Consequently, any media practitioner in possession of government information which is classified, or likewise any person who discloses such information, is subject to 14 years of imprisonment if convicted, as contained in Section 2(b) of the Official Secrets Act 1990. Tom (2004) and Ekpu (1990) argue that due to the complexity in conceptualizing public and national interest, the Official Secrets Act becomes a tool for the government to withhold certain information from the public. Ojo further argued that the act is a deliberate action of the government to censor certain information under the guise of protecting national security, and this is evident in the unwillingness of government officials to disclose vital information to the state, hence consolidating a culture of secrecy. Nevertheless, it was believed that the enactment of the Freedom of Information Act (FOI) (2011) will help change this culture of secrecy as a result of the Official Secrets Act. Akpojivi (2011) argued that despite the enactment of the FOI Act, the media environment will still be restricted due to the numerous restrictive clauses contained in this act. Therefore, the act is restricted to disclosure of mere administrative information and not necessarily information that will assist in holding government accountable (Akpojivi 2011). This idea will be discussed further in subsequent sections in the examination of media freedom and independence.

Therefore, it can be argued that the Official Secrets Act is just an instrument used by government to control the flow of information and the ability of the media to exercise their duties. Therefore, the opportunity to address these lapses using the FOI was rejected, and by promulgating numerous restrictive clauses, the government has continued to hold on to its enclave as these clauses will enable it to treat information needed for democratic advancement as classified. This justifies Ake's (2000) position that the Nigerian government has always desired to hold on to its authoritarian enclave despite its desire for Western progress and development.

National Broadcasting Commission Decree of 1991 This decree led to the establishment of the National Broadcasting Commission (NBC) which is charged with the responsibility of regulating the broadcasting industry and formulating policies that will govern the media industry. In 1999, this decree was amended to recognize the democratic reality, so is now known as the National Broadcasting Commission Act No. 55 of 1999 (see Jibo and Okoosi 2003). In line with its responsibilities, NBC formulated the National Broadcasting Code which stipulates the framework guiding the activities of the broadcasting media. This code, according to the chief public affairs officer, Jimada Maimuna is reviewed every two years in line with current trends (Interview, 2010). Despite, this biennial review, the central objective or principle of the code is to promote broadcast that is in accordance with the national interest. This notion of national interest is a very common theme across the various policies governing the media environment and has generated much debate.

As earlier stated, this idea of national interest could easily be abused and the policy document did not state what constitutes national interest and the criteria that will be followed to determine what is of national interest and the extent to which public interest supersedes national interest. Although the volatile nature of the Nigerian state could have influenced the idea of broadcasting to reflect national interest, as Nigeria is often subject to political, ethnic and religious contestations which are rooted in the foundational ideas informing the composition of the Nigeria state (see Osaghae 1998). Ake (2000) argues that Nigeria is a project which has yet to become a reality due to the numerous ethnic, cultural and political contestations that have made Nigerians very divisible. Hence, this may explain the National Broadcasting Commission Act calling for broadcasting to serve as nation building, and the regulator (NBC) is to ensure that broadcast media organizations adhere to this guideline. However, the regulator (NBC) lacks autonomy as it is under the Ministry of Information, and the president of the Republic appoints board members; so, this idea of national interest in broadcasting could be perceived as a tool of the state in controlling broadcasting due to broadcasting's powerful influence. This will be explored further in detail under the section on media regulation.

National Mass Communication Policy of 1987 Despite the date of this policy document, it can be regarded as the only policy document in Nigeria that clearly states the political and cultural role of the media in the development of the Nigerian state. The policy document was formulated under pressure from the International Monetary Fund (IMF) and the World

Bank on General Babangida to reform and liberalize due to the political and economic crisis confronting the country (see Anyanwu 1992). Hence, Ake (2000) argues that the military regime of General Babangida embraced these reforms due to pressure so as to be seen as democratic with the intention of accessing financial assistance. This is evident in the policy formulation process as it was derived from a two-week seminar organized by the Federal Ministry of Information and Culture in partnership with media professionals and academics in 1987. The findings and recommendations from the seminar coupled with deliberations from the National Council on Information and Culture and ideas from other stakeholders influenced the content of the policy document (National Mass Communication Policy 1987). This was to create the idea of embracing democratic principles on the one hand but holding onto stiff principles that would allow the protection of the government's authoritarian enclave on the other hand (see Ake 2000).

This is evident in the policy provision, as the policy document calls for the usage of mass media for national development and nation building. The policy objectives state that the mass media are central to the socio-economic, political and cultural developments of the country; consequently, the mass media should facilitate this development process (National Mass Communication Policy 1987). To this end, the policy identified three dominant media institutions—print media, electronic media and communication technology—and the roles they are expected to play. The policy classified the print media as the oldest means of communication and states that the print media can be used 'to mobilise and rally the population for development purposes…and are known to have contributed meaningfully to the educational process in some countries' (National Mass Communication Policy 1987). Therefore, government should encourage active participation of the public in the print industry by enacting legislation that will liberalized the industry, and granting subsidies to facilitate the development of the sector (National Mass Communication Policy 1987).

For broadcasting, the policy regards this sector as very sensitive due to its limitless potential and the significant role broadcasting plays in the lives of its citizens. Therefore, the policy calls for all broadcasting organizations to embrace 'national motivation, mobilisation and the attainment of the nation's most cherished national objectives within the context of national communications as their primary task' (National Mass Communication Policy 1987). Due to this sensitivity, the policy calls for strict control of the broadcast media; it should be monopolized by the state and the content should mainly promote national development. This provision of monopolizing of the broadcast sector has been overtaken in time, following the liberalization and privatization of the broadcasting industry in 1992, through the Nigeria Privatisation Decree of 1992. It can be argued that the policy goal of broadcasting protecting national interests is still dominant and geared towards addressing the socio-cultural and political tensions that often characterized the Nigerian state. Lastly, the policy considers communication technology as a pivotal tool in addressing the digital divide that exists between the rural and urban areas due to the infrastructural gap. Hence the policy calls for the integration of traditional forms of communication with modern forms. To this end, the policy requires both the federal and the state governments to establish and focus on community radio and a community viewing center to reach out to rural people excluded from the communication and development process. This is in line with Ugboajah's (1985) idea of 'oramedia' where modern means of communication are integrated with traditional means, such as town criers, to help bridge the information gap between the information haves and have nots.

From the above, it can be argued that this policy document reflects the contestation of the Nigerian state towards reform. This is seen in the struggle to allow full reform on the one hand but, on the other hand, hold on to authoritarian legacies as the government has a strong desire to control media content via the notion of national interest and development. According to Ronning and Kupe (2000: 138), the media in Africa tend to display contradictions as media policies that were implemented during the reform process were a 'reflection of this discrepancy between a democratic and an authoritarian impetus'.

A Discussion: From Policy Ambition(s) to Implementation

From the above discussion on the rationale behind the media policies in Nigeria, there are common themes that cut across the different media policies that have been reviewed. These themes include freedom and independence, universal access, media accountability and media as a public trust, and these will form the basis of the discussion. This is because these themes shape the context and structure of the media policies already discussed.

Independence and Freedom of the Media

There is one dominant theme that cuts across all the policy documents in Nigeria: the need for the state to control the media (i.e. what is said and how it is said) or its unwillingness to allow full reforms due to what Ronning and Kupe termed 'contradictions' in the reform process. Media freedom and independence is understood from Section 22 of the 1999 constitution which charged the media and practitioners with the responsibility of holding the state accountable and responsible for its actions. This freedom according to Olagunju et al. (1993) is salient in an emerging democracy such as Nigeria that is confronted with corruption and abuse of power that had been the basis for truncating previous democratic regimes. Therefore, this freedom entrusted the idea of social responsibility to the media, in other words the responsibility for ensuring that democratic principles are sustained by acting as the active fourth estate of the realm. This is considered a fundamental role of the media as, according to a senior media officer within the presidency, 'what better freedom can the media in Nigeria require other than to have the responsibility of promoting transparency, responsibility and accountability in government which is a major problem in Nigeria' (Interview, 2010).

While the above attest to the media playing a significant role in building and sustaining Nigeria's democracy, there have been questions of how the media can achieve this when they have no constitutional rights to promote accountability and responsibility. Tom (2004) argues that the mass media are not guaranteed constitutional rights to exercise their functions of holding governments accountable. As the media derive their rights from Section 39 of the constitution that pertains to the human rights of freedom of expression and opinion (Okwori and Adeyanju 2006), this can be problematic seeing that media rights are intricately different from each other, although they are similar in terms of conceptualization (see Barendt and Hitchens 2000). The failure of the policymakers and the state to allow for full reform by providing for media freedom can be attributed to the government's desire to hold onto power due to the notion of national interest as a result of the complexity of the Nigerian state owing to political, ethnic and religious tensions. Nyamnjoh (2005) posited that these issues have always presented huge challenges to emerging democracies in consolidating democracy, hence the conceptualization and formulation of policies along the social responsibility perspective to protect and promote national development and unity.

This concept has been dismissed by media practitioners who believe that it's main aim is to censor the media. To most media practitioners the lack of such freedom has influenced their understanding of media freedom in line with the absolute rights perspective. According to Abdullahi Tasiu, a BBC Correspondent in Nigeria, the conceptualization of media freedom should revolve around the ability of the media to carry out their constituted functions. However, the 1999 constitution does not provide for this, leading to the question of how there can be responsibility without rights (Interview, 2010). It can be argued that the media practitioners' understanding of media freedom is rooted in Western ideas of freedom, based on what they perceived to be obtainable in Western countries (Eribo and Jong-Ebot 1997: xi). And once this is not obtainable, there is dispute between the state and media practitioners. This dispute is due to the long struggle between the media and the state for media rights to be accommodated in the constitutional provision and this right has been constantly ignored from the first republic to date. Therefore, to provide a nuanced discussion of the media freedom and independence debate, this discussion will look at the government-media relationship and the media ownership structure.

Government-Media Relationship

As mentioned earlier, the environment in which the mass media operates determines its effectiveness in living up to its responsibility of holding governments accountable and responsible as enshrined in the constitution. Right from independence the relationship between the media and the state has not been easy but rather dominated by tensions over interest. Paterson (2011) argues that this is a common problem in emerging democracies due to previous antecedence as prior relationships were hostile because of the authoritarian nature of the state, and this culture might influence the process of re-democratization. The embrace of democracy in 1999 resulted in a dynamic shift of principles and governance style and in the government's relationship with the media. The starting point of this shift was the institutionalization of a constitution that established a framework for the kind of relationship that should exist between the media and the government. As the chairman of the *Guardian* newspaper described: 'the embrace of democracy in 1999 changed the pattern of interaction between the government and the media, as prior to 1999 the military ruled Nigeria with decrees and laws while the constitution was suspended. However, with the restoration of the constitution in 1999, arbitrary abuse of power has become unfashionable as it is now against state policy' (Interview, 2010).

The fundamental factor underpinning this change in relationship between the media and the government are Sections 39 and 22 of the constitution that allow for freedom of expression and holding government accountable for their actions. These provisions make the media an actor in building and sustaining Nigeria's democracy. As Baker (2007) argues, the watchdog role assigned to the media via the constitution will aid the democratization process as the mass media could play a key role in holding government accountable and responsible for its actions, hence reinforcing democratic culture and principles. This idea infers that there has been a shift in the relationship between the government and the media, from outright oppression and censorship to freedom to engage with the state (see Akpojivi 2014). However, this idea is worrisome as this freedom was granted based on the reform process, but on a practical level there is little or no freedom granted. The media environment is still characterized by policies that restrict media activities or governments (especially that of President Buhari) have openly expressed the idea of regulating the media and new media.

Despite 18 years into the re-democratic culture, the mass media and practitioners enjoy 'qualified freedom' (Ojo 2003). According to Ojo, the media in Nigeria enjoy 'qualified freedom' because the machinery needed for them to carry out their constitutional responsibilities is not available. The machinery that Ojo is referring to is the framework; the available framework provides uncertainty due to the complex provisions within it. The deputy news editor of *Vanguard* newspaper, Obateru Taye, states that 'the basic infrastructures needed to facilitate the media environment and media freedom, i.e. laws and framework to establish the media environment, are either lacking or inadequate as there are no changes with regard to policy' (Interview, 2010). A lucid review of the framework shows that technically the media has no rights to carry out its constituted functions as stipulated in Section 22. Although, some scholars might argue that Section 39, which speaks of human rights, could be used by the mass media, this right was withdrawn in Section 39, Subsection 3(A and B) on the basis of national interest. Hence Tom (2004) classified the environment as 'give and take'. This clause regarding national interest, according to scholars such as Humphreys (1996) and Andsager et al. (2004), is a very common phenomenon in every democratic country as there cannot be absolute freedom. However, the problem is that within the Nigerian context this concept of national interest is not well defined.

The constitution or any other policy document did not explicitly state what constitutes national security or interest and who determines it. This ambiguity has contributed to the difficulty of the mass media and how media practitioners relate with government. The Media Rights Agenda (2002a) states that the media are faced with the challenge of living up to their constitutional role because their access to information is restricted by the available laws and policies that restrict media freedom and promote national interests and building. Under this condition, the mass media cannot function or achieve the constitutional function of holding government accountable and responsible for its actions due to lack of information. For example, in 2017 President Buhari sought medical treatment in the United Kingdom for over 100 days, and the mass media were pressuring the state to disclose his medical condition and the cost of his treatment to the state. Similar incidents happened to late President Yar' Adua in 2010 as he was pressed to disclose the nature of his illness and the cost to the national treasury. In both circumstances, the state cited national interest as the basis for not disclosing the nature of the illness and the cost of treatments to the state. This is further compounded by the Official Secret Act 1990 which poses a threat to the free flow of information by defining some sets of information as 'classified'.

This classified information might be of interest to the public and may contribute to the promotion of accountability by exposing the ills within government establishments. Under the provisions of the act, anybody that discloses classified information is liable to 14 years' imprisonment for both the discloser and recipient of such information. Therefore, Tom (2004) argues that under such conditions, the mass media are rendered ineffective as they need information to carry out their function. The Freedom of Information Act (FOI) 2011 passed by President Goodluck Johnathan was celebrated due to the expectation that this Act would bring about a shift from the culture of secrecy to one of openness, and enhance the operations of the mass media. According to *NEXT* newspaper in its editorial following the passing of the FOI Bill into law, the paper held that FOI Act is crucial to democratic sustenance and will change the pattern of government-media relationships as government and public records, and other information, will be freely available for public consumption and this will fundamentally change the way things have previously been done in Nigeria.

Such an editorial reflects the mood of the media industry and Nigerians who have waited anxiously for the passing of the bill for 12 years as it is believed that the FOI Act will change the dynamics of the relationship between the media and government as the media could access more documents and information and hold government accountable. While it is true that the emergence of the FOI Act will lead to a change in relationship, this single document alone cannot change the culture of secrecy that has been embedded in the Nigerian state for over 50 years (Akpojivi 2011). Also, the act will not be effective as there are still many restrictive clauses within it which means we are back to the status quo. For instance, Sections 12, 13, 15, 16, 17, 18 and 20 of the FOI Act prevent the disclosure of personal information, financial, commercial, technical and scientific information, third-party information, trade secrets, law enforcement investigation, and conduct of international affairs. These restrictions could have an impact on media practices but this has not generated debate within the Nigerian polity due to the fact that other Western countries have an FOI Act which is restrictive. According to the assistant editor of *Source* magazine, Igho Akeregha, the available provisions within the FOI will be sufficient for the practice of journalism in Nigeria as there is no FOI Act in the world that guarantees absolute freedom of information (Interview, 2010).

While he is right that there is no country in the world that has absolute freedom of information, each country differs and policies are tailored to address a country's unique needs. And due to the history of Nigeria having been built around secrecy and military regimes, policies should be formulated to address these. For example, in Ghana the FOI Bill has not been passed into law due to numerous contestations that have not addressed the needs and aspirations of Ghanaian society. Consequently, going by the current FOI Act, it can be posited that the act will not significantly affect media activities as issues that affect democracy and transparency of government fall under the restrictive clauses. Therefore, Akpojivi (2011) sees the act as a tool for disclosing administrative information and not necessarily information that will advance the democratic project by enabling the media to live up to thier constituted function.

This position has been shared by critical policymakers and media analysts. For instance, a senior officer within the Ministry of Information, Francis Agbo, stated that 'the FOI Act is populist nonsense, as the present state of the act will not impact on the media environment; there are no implementation or enforcement regimes and it is just a law to please a segment of the society without any detailed reform' (Interview, 2010). The act does not categorically state its implementation strategy, and it vaguely requires the court in Nigeria to rule over failure of public institutions to disclose information and the Attorney General of the Federation (AGF) is to be in charge of the act's administrative process. This is problematic because the Nigerian judiciary is characterized by lingering litigations that take years to resolve and the AGF is a government official instead of an independent administrative body that could be perceived to be free from interference. Therefore, the whole essence of the act is defeated as it is limited regarding the release of vital government information, or encouraging transparency and accountability.

With the emergence of new media, the dynamics of the media environment have changed. Citizens are now empowered to hold governments accountable directly without the backing of the mainstream media. Browne (2015) argues that people feel more empowered to engage with the media and government on salient issues, as they are free to question and criticize government actions and politics without the need for an intermediary. The new media technology is believed to have caused a paradigm shift by enhancing freedom as people are free to discuss issues that affect them (Anonymous, Interview, 2017). This perceived freedom, devoid of censorship from mainstream media or the government, has led to a more active citizen focused journalism. For instance, the emergence of Sahara Reporters, a citizen journalism news organization, has to a large extent re-defined journalism practices in Nigeria. It is always the first to break news of corruption, misgovernance and social ills in society before the mainstream media. For example, the two major corruption stories of 2017—the discovery of $43 million abandoned in an apartment in Lagos and the certificate scandal of Senator Dino Melaye—were first reported on by Sahara Reporters before the mainstream media. In addition, on certain occasions, the mainstream media depended and relied on Sahara Reporters for controversial news stories. Fosu and Akpojivi (2015), in their study of media practices in Ghana and Nigeria, argue that the mainstream media are also tapping into the potential of these technologies by integrating new media technologies into their journalism practices. The convergence of these technologies has allowed the mainstream media the opportunity to engage with their audience via calls, texts, WhatsApp and tweets. This strengthens the democratic process due to active citizen's participation but complicates the relationship between the media and government. For instance, more media houses, both print and broadcast, are integrating new media technologies into their practices. According to an anonymous source, 'the Punch, Vanguard, African Independent Television, This Day and the like have all managed to garner lots of followers and readers due to the adaptation of social media platforms by these organisations' (Interview, 2017). This move has been considered a threat by the government, consequently it has started monitoring and regulating new media usage. According to the director of defense information, Major General John Enenche, the Nigeria military now monitors new media usage in Nigeria as this is in response to the need to control information that is circulated and viewed as threatening the unity of the country by causing trouble (Channels Television 2017). There is no doubt that the government finds these new technologies threating due to its inability to control what is disseminated and at what time. This was one of the reasons given by the state for the need to monitor new media technology usage in Nigeria as the state believes that national interest or unity of the country will be at risk if ideas are allowed to flow freely through these technologies without government control. This reveals the complexities of the government-media relationship in Nigeria, as the government continues to display a double standard regarding media reforms. It allows the media to operate within old repressive laws. New laws are also formulated but these maintain the status quo or old ideology of protecting national interest while giving the impression of liberalizing the media environment.

Media Ownership Structure

As mentioned previously, media ownership is a very important debate in the discourse on media freedom as the ability of the mass media to fulfill its constitutional responsibilities is tied to its ownership structure. According to Baker (2007), media ownership is significant in any democratic society because it affects the diversity of media content, and the ability to attain a marketplace of ideas. Most of the policy documents in Nigeria discussed earlier did not explicitly address ownership structure or the need to protect the media from the vested political and economic interests. However, the ideas of liberalizing the telecommunication industry as stated in the National Telecommunication Policy 2000 and the ideas of free speech contained in Section 39 of the 1999 constitution cannot be ignored.

Most studies, including Jibo and Okoosi (2003) and Ojo (2003) among others, have looked at media ownership structure since the re-democratization era that started in 1999. However, these studies have failed to look at how the change in the ownership structure following the implementation of liberalization has affected the operations of media practitioners and media content, which will be the focus of this discussion. The ownership of the media prior to independence has continued to shape the structure of media ownership. According to Nyamnjoh (2005), the structure of press ownership during nationalism was private as the different nationalist leaders established their individual media to agitate for independence and protect the interests of their different regions during negotiations.

This structure has continued in Nigeria where the vast majority of newspaper organizations are privately owned. This is also in accordance with Section 3.4(2) of the National Mass Communication Policy 1987, which discourages the state from owning newspapers and having a monopoly of the print industry. According to Ruben Abati, chairman of the *Guardian* newspaper 'the historic past of private ownership of the early press by nationalists has continued to influence the current ownership pattern of the press' (Interview, 2010). Consequently, there are few government-owned newspapers due to the government's unsuccessful attempts at publishing as government newspapers are largely considered as propaganda instruments. However, the case is different for broadcasting which has a history of state ownership. The history of broadcasting in Nigeria shows that broadcasting was established by the different regions starting off with the Western region, moving then to the Eastern and Northern regions, to project the different regions' ideas during the struggle for independence (Bourgault 1995). The liberalization of the broadcasting sector by General Ibrahim Babangida, in 1992, witnessed the active participation of the private sector; therefore making the broadcasting sector both state and privately owned (Akpojivi 2014). This was further facilitated by Section 39(2) of the constitution that states 'without prejudice to the generality of subsection (1), every person shall be entitled to own, establish and operate any medium for the dissemination of information, ideas and opinion…' (1999 constitution).

Scholars such as Ekpu (1990), Ojo (2003) and Okwori and Adeyanju (2006) argue that this provision facilitated massive investment in the media industry as a result of the constitutional framework. Despite this reform, the media environment has not changed significantly as the government still controls the broadcasting sector regarding ownership and regulatory mechanisms. For instance, there are more federal and state-owned broadcasting stations than privately owned broadcasting stations. One fundamental reason behind this is that despite the constitutional provisions of Section 39(2), the section further stated that '… no person other than the president of the federation or of a state or any other person or body authorised by the president on the fulfilment of conditions laid down by an Act of the National Assembly shall own, establish or operate a television or wireless broadcasting station for any purpose whatsoever' (Section 39(2) 1999 constitution). According to the NBC, every application comes to it, after which it makes recommendations to the minister of information and communication, who then forwards such recommendations to the president for either approval or refusal (Jimada Maimuna, Interview, 2010).

While this might be considered a normal process, the process itself is problematic. NBC as a regulator is not an independent body but under the direct control of the minister of communication. Within Nigeria, where there is politic of patronage, there exists what Bayart (2010) termed 'the politics of the belly' where political office holders have to please their masters in order to keep their jobs. In addition, Tom (2004: 95) argues that the president may use his discretionary powers to either approve or reject an application. Based on the fact that Nigerian leaders could abuse their powers, the president could decline an application which he views to be unsupportive of his ideologies. This may influence the ownership structure of the media significantly and how those with licenses operate, as Emerson (1982) and Ziegler and Asante (1992) argue that economic and political forces could influence the activities of the media in a democratic state.

For an emerging democracy such as Nigeria, the fundamental question is how the media can move beyond these vested interests and fulfill their responsibilities. According to a senior media correspondent at the state house, it will be practically impossible for the mass media in Nigeria to move beyond these vested interests as he asked 'Who owns these media that are operational in Nigeria? Have the mass media been able to rise above the primordial levels of ownership interests? (Simeon Alozieuwa, Interview, 2010). The above questions from Simeon highlight how difficult it is to separate media ideology from media owners' beliefs. This is worrisome because none of the policy documents explicitly provide a framework that protects the media from the media owners' vested interests. Section 9(5) of the NBC Decree No. 5 of 1999 only criminalizes cross-media ownership and prevents media concentration but does not address owners' interference. Following the wake of liberalization and democratization in 1999, most of these media owners are politicians or people who have friends in government and business circles to promote their interests. Because of the close ties between the media owners and political and economic actors, the operations of the media are significantly affected. According to the co-founder of *Newswatch* magazine, Dan Agbese, 'the owners of these private media are Nigerians who have political and economic interests, they have friends in government and in the business world, so the media know how far they can go in holding government accountable to the people. If they go too far the political and business interests of their owners could be affected' (Interview, 2010).

Such statements clearly indicate the interplay between media ownership and the daily operations of the media as they cannot 'bite the finger that feeds them'. For instance, there have been numerous instances where media owners have directly interfered with the operations of their organizations. For example, Steve Ayorinde, the editor of *Punch* newspaper once alleged that the managing director Azubuike Ishiekwene had been refusing to publish stories which he thought were unsuitable for the political and economic interests of the newspaper (Olumhense 2010). Similarly, Ekpu (1990) alleged that the owner of *Concord* newspaper, late Chief MKO Abiola, asked his editor to apologize to the president over a news report which Abiola considered not to be in his business and political interests. The above situation does not exclude the government-owned media. According to a senior media officer within the presidency, those who work for government-owned organizations such as the Nigeria Television Authority (NTA) and the Federal Radio Corporation of Nigeria (FRCN) are obliged to protect government interests. He said, 'a question always asked in mass media studies is how one can effectively watch, monitor and reprimand the government when he or she is being paid by the same government' (Mitaire Ikpen, Interview, 2010). The above reveals the complexities associated with media ownership and the ability of the media to be free to exercise its functions.

This raises the question of how the media can be regulated to protect and guarantee its freedom devoid of these political and economic interests and contestations. Chakravartty and Sariakis (2006) argue that regulation is needed especially in a liberalized era in order to achieve a balance. Regulation is carried out by two organizations, the Nigeria Press Council (NPC), which regulates the press and NBC which regulates the electronic media. However, the decree establishing the NPC and the functions ascribed to the NPC—acting as ombudsman to oversee the activities of the press—has been challenges by media practitioners such as Ray Ekpu (co-founder *Newswatch* magazine), Nduka Obaigbena (owner of *This Day* newspaper) and the Newspaper Proprietors Association of Nigeria (NPAN) as they considered the framework of the NPC to be in a breach of Sections 22 and 39 of the 1999 constitution. The court said:

> The clear wording and spirit of the Nigerian Press Council law set out not only to professionalise the journalism practice, but also to establish a regime on how the press in Nigeria is to conduct itself in the manner of performing its operations… and the law has the potential to restrict the expression of opinion of individual members of the press and stall the development of ideas that have universally characterised the development of ideas. (*Vanguard Newspaper* 2010; *see also* Iriekpen 2010)

The ruling is significant as the judge emphasized freedom of speech as more important than the need to build high professional standards within the journalism profession. However, based on collective bargaining and consensus between the Nigeria Union of Journalists (NUJ) and the NPAN, NPC's status has been amended and revised into the Nigerian Press Council Act No. 85 (www.presscouncil.gov.ng). This new act allows the NPC to monitor the activities of the press and address complaints against the press.

The case is, however, different from electronic media as the NBC regulates the electronic media in line with the National Broadcasting Code that focus on national unity. The primary objective of the code is to ensure that all broadcasting is to be in the national interest, equitable and fair. These concepts have generated huge controversy as they were not properly defined. What constitutes an equitable and fair broadcast or a broadcast of national interest? Equitable or fairness means different things to different people, especially in a post-colonial state such as Nigeria, and the NBC determines the yardstick or criterion in determining what is fair, equitable and of national interest based on context. Nevertheless, the NBC held that 'there is only one meaning of fairness and equity, as what is fair is fair, and equity is as clear as it is; the idea is to try as much as possible to make all sides of the story as clear as possible and this is how we determine fair and equitable coverage' (Jimada Maimuna, Interview, 2010).

Practically, this is not as simple as it has been portrayed. Broadcast houses have been sanctioned by the NBC for being unfair and inequitable in their coverage despite the contrary claims from these broadcast houses that they presented balanced, fair and equitable coverage. There have been many instances where media houses have questioned the NBC over its sanctions. This is principally due to lack of transparency surrounding the process and the influence of the government over the activities of NBC, being that it is under the direct control of the minister and the presidency. The president appoints the NBC board members and the NBC office is located within the state house, 'Aso Rock Ville'. This reflects the complexities associated with the media reform processes in Nigeria as the state wants to maintain its enclave of control.

Media as a Public Trust

The idea of the media acting as a public trust is highly contested in a democratic society. This is because there are different roles the media could play as a public trust in protecting the interests of the citizens over the state. While scholars like Davies and Shields (1999) and Ross (1998), among others, suggest that government should manage the media as a way of protecting the public trust on behalf of the citizens, others believe that because of the centrality of the media to societal discourse, it should be protected from both state and private interests. McQuail (1992) argues that the ability of the media to win the public's trust is dependent on them satisfying the needs and interest of the public. Therefore, Entman (1989: 17) argues that the ability of the mass media to act as a public trust should be judged based on their ability to satisfy and maintain the public interest despite political and economic pressures. In this era of media reforms facilitated with neoliberal policies, the media struggle to maintain the balance between the needs of citizens, government and private actors despite a democratic society demanding a well-informed citizenry.

Following the reform processes, there are no policy documents that explicitly require the media to act or serve the public trust. However, Section 22 of the 1999 constitution requires the media to hold government accountable and responsible to the public. Therefore, it can be inferred that this provision recognizes that the media have a role of public trust by ensuring accountability and transparency in society, and by so doing, maintaining professional and ethical standards as contained in the preamble of the Nigerian Journalists Code of Ethics of 1998. Ojo (2003) and Musa and Mohammed (2004) argue that, following the reform processes during democratization, the various interests of the different actors are more visible, and the lack of a detailed policy to address public trust explains the complexities associated with the concept of public trust and the ability of the media to achieve the public's trust.

One fundamental issue with the concept of the media acting as a public trust is which public trust should the media achieve? Is the public homogeneous with all having similar interests or tastes? These questions are relevant in Nigeria, a heterogeneous country, where there are more than 250 ethnic groups and languages, and ethnicity plays a large role in the political and economic fabric of the country (see Achebe 1984, 2012; Osaghae 1998). Osaghae (1998), while expounding on the complexities of the heterogeneous nature of the Nigerian state and the birth of suspicion, argues that right from the first republic there have been ethnic tensions and rivalry among the different ethnic groups as each ethnic group and political parties seeks to protect a specific interest and not a collective interest. And this suspicion and rivalry has made it practically impossible for the media to meet the diverse interests of the different ethnic groups as the media instead now act as a propaganda tool for the different ideologies of the ethnic groups. For instance, the *New Age* newspaper is known to be associated with the Hausa people, the *Nigerian Tribune* for the Yoruba ethnic group and the *Vanguard* for the Itsikiri ethnic group. Due to the fragmentation of the public, it is therefore unclear which public trust the media should seek to protect and serve. According to Coleman and Ross (2010), the diverse nature of society has placed the mass media in a state of dilemma over which public to serve and democracy has made it compulsory for the media to serve the needs of all publics as a social actor.

Consequently, the concept of public trust within the Nigerian media environment is a mirage. As a senior officer within the Ministry of Information and Communication puts it 'when you say public trust, where is the public? Which public? There is a narrow public and broader public. Politically, we have the majority public, i.e. Hausa, Yoruba, and Igbo public, and the minority public, i.e. South-South and Middle-Belt public. We even have a diverse religious public, so which public should the media identify with? Because each of these publics have their own interest they seek to promote' (Obi Adindu, Interview, 2010). This is not a new phenomenon that started in 1999 following the re-democratization process but has been a deep-rooted issue right from pre-independence and is evident in the composition of the Nigerian state and has continued to manifest itself in different forms in this reform and re-democratized era. Eribo (1997) argues that the division of the public along ethnic and religious lines right from pre-independence, when different regions and nationalists established media to promote their different ideologies, has hindered the media from acting as a public trust. This is further compounded by the fact that outside private ownership of the media serving a specific narrow interest, the government-owned media (i.e. national broadcasters NTA and FRCN) serve the interests of the ruling government first before the public despite the mandate of national interest as stipulated in Decree No. 24 of 1977 which established them. For example, every government whether military or civilian has used the NTA and the FRCN as a propaganda tool to project or promote its selfish ideology. During the era of General Abacha, the NTA boldly presented him as the only candidate that could bring about development during the transition period by using the slogan 'who the cap fits'.

Although the decree establishing NTA and FRCN has been repealed following the 1979 constitution, Umeh (1989) argues that the state-owned media organization should go beyond serving the needs of the government or acting as a propaganda tool but help integrate the various ethnic groups as by so doing it can win the public's trust. This is in line with McQuail's (2005) argument that the media are an institution whose sustenance is dependent on their reputation before the public. And the reputation of any media organization is dependent on how the public perceive such an organization as acting in their interests, by providing credible information and programming and fulfilling its functions in relation to democracy. Thus, Higgins (2008) posited that the public distrust for any media will lead to a gradual loss of public trust. Two ways in which this could be averted is by the media providing the public with what they want and by stating the relationship between media owners and media. A cursory examination of all policy documents in Nigeria indicate that these have not been effectively considered. The NBC has a mandate to carry out research activities to develop the broadcasting industry (NBC 2010), but there is no evidence that it is doing so. Detailed examination of its operations show there are no reports outside the broadcasting code. In addition, the media houses have not embarked on research to ascertain the needs of the public and how these needs could be met. The need for audience research in a heterogeneous society such as Nigeria cannot be emphasized enough as Andrew and Shaw (2009) argue that research on media activities and public needs will afford the regulator and media organizations the opportunity to formulate policies that will be beneficial to the wider needs of society.

Furthermore, no policy document provides a framework for establishing the kind of relationship that should exist between the media and their owners, and Okwori and Adeyanju (2006) argue that this has contributed to poor programming and the inability of the media to meet the needs of the public due to their owners' interference. And this is a common phenomenon in Nigeria, as indicated by the earlier examples provided in the media ownership section. Consequently, the assistant editor of *Source* magazine, Igho Akeregha, said that 'the greatest factor affecting the practice of the mass media in terms of public trust is ownership, whether government or private, because the interests of media owners are often considered by the respective media organisations, and this determines the kind of information they bring to the public space (sic)' (Interview, 2010). Thus, there is the need for a detailed broadcasting policy in Nigeria that will help establish the working relationship between the media and their owners, and outline how the media can achieve the public's trust in a fragmented state such as Nigeria.

Universal Access to the Media

In the discourse of media freedom, universal access to the media is a vital component of the ideas pertaining to media freedom. Every media reform process seeks to address accessibility of the media by the public, in other words the public being able to access media content and participate. The concept of universal access is both an economic and infrastructural issue and is salient in Nigeria, following the long period of infrastructural deficit due to an era of military regime (see National Telecommunication Policy 2000). Golding and Murdock (1986: 185) while emphasizing the need for universal access to the media argue that 'no one should be barred from communicating publicly or from acquiring communication because of characteristics which they are powerless to control', as access is considered a fundamental human right.

The concept of universal access is another mirage or 'white elephant project' in Nigeria because it is unattainable due to Nigeria's lack of infrastructure, policy framework and the resources to facilitate this universal access. This is evident in the consistent failure of the Nigerian state to achieve its own deadlines of digital migration that were set for 2012, 2015 and 2017 (Adepetun 2017). This will be discussed in detailed later in this section. Nigeria has an estimated population of more than 182 million (National Population Commission 2017) and, according to the World Bank, 51% of this population resides in rural areas with limited amenities (https://data.worldbank.org/indicator/SP.RUR.TOTL.ZZS). In addition, according to the National Bureau of Statistics' Nigeria Report of 2017, 81.15 million Nigerians are unemployed and actively looking for jobs. Furthermore, the minister of education, Alhaji Adamu Adamu, stated that between 65 and 75 million Nigerians are illiterate as at 2017 (Vanguard Newspaper 2017). The above statistics reveal the enormous challenges confronting the Nigerian state in relation to the attainment of universal access of the media irrespective of geographical location.

Consequently, media practitioner Simeon Alozieuwa asserts that the project of universal access to the media is a long one that will take time to achieve, as until the relevant policy framework has been put in place the idea of universal access will remain largely theoretical. Policywise, the National Telecommunication Policy 2000 identified that the era of monopolization hindered infrastructural development, hence the need to embrace total liberalization. Nigeria liberalized the broadcasting sector in 1992, and President Obasanjo during his tenure (1999–2007) allowed for total liberalization (privatization, commercialization and liberalization) as this was seen as an interventionist strategy to open the sector up to massive infrastructural development (Okonjo-Iweala 2012). The National Council on Privatisation and the Bureau of Public Enterprises were established as policy making and implementation agencies to drive and enforce this goal. This is in line with the National Telecommunication Policy 2000 goal that massive investment in telecommunication infrastructure via liberalization and privatization will promote socio-economic and political development that will put Nigeria in the global market where information is readily available (see National Telecommunication Policy 2000).

This has recorded some success as there was an increase in communication infrastructural development (Ojo 2004) due to both government and private sector participation (Ekpu 1990). For instance, there has been a significant increase in private radio and television stations in Nigeria coupled with print media. Such massive investment has resulted in the Media Foundation for West Africa (2008) recognizing that Nigeria has the most heterogeneous and developed media landscape in Africa. However, a lucid review indicates that these media organizations are centered in urban and commercial cities. For example, the print media are predominately concentrated around Lagos, while broadcast media are situated in economically viable urban areas dictated by a quick return on investment (Bourgault 1995; Nyamnjoh 2005). All the major newspapers in Nigeria such as the *Guardian*, *Vanguard*, *Punch*, *Next* and the *Nation* are located in Lagos while *This Day* and *Leadership* are located in Abuja. Similarly, most state-owned newspapers such as the *Pointer* and *Cross River Watch* are located in the capital cities of these states. To Akwule (1992) the common reasons behind the concentration of the media around urban areas are limited resources (technical or manpower), a reliable power supply and the need for a quick return on investment, which is not feasible in rural areas. According to NBC, the license fees for broadcasting in a 'Category A location in the federal capital territory (Abuja), Lagos and Port Harcourt are N20 million for radio, N15 million for television and N10 for million cable. For Category B (i.e. any location in other states) it is N15 million for radio, N11.25 million for television and N7.5 million for cable. Direct to Home (multichannel) is N25 million'. These fees are renewable every five years (http://www.nbc.gov.ng/pages/license-fees-schedule-and-renewal). In addition, these media organizations are required to promote Nigerian local content. For instance, requirements are 80% local content for radio and 60% local content for television in line with the NBC broadcasting code. These require substantial capital which is not readily available after paying the huge license fees.

The fee structure is beyond the reach of most business people who might be interested in establishing media organizations following the liberalization of the airwaves. Consequently, they resort to banks to seek loans to finance media ownership and this could explain the low penetration rate of the media in Nigeria and the need to be centered in urban areas.

The print industry is not excluded from these high charges as the industry was once subjected to value added tax (VAT) on import dues on materials needed for the print industry. Nigeria is import oriented so the materials needed for newspaper production are largely imported. According to the chairman of the *Guardian* newspaper, Ruben Abati, VAT on imported printing materials was only stopped in 2008 after a long period of lobbying by media owners (Interview, 2010). Despite this respite, the cost of importing these print products into the country is very high following the economic crisis and there are other hidden factors such as custom fees (Okonjo-Iweala 2012). Okwori and Adeyanju (2006) argue that this huge cost in production is transferred to readers, which has invariably resulted in a low readership affecting the sustainability of these print titles. For example, the average newspaper costs between N200 to N250, and magazines between N250 and N300, which is above the reach of the ordinary citizen (Media Foundation of West Africa 2008). And this is affecting the circulation of newspapers in Nigeria as no newspaper in Nigeria has a circulation figure above 200,000. *Punch* and *Vanguard* have the highest circulation figures at 80,000 and 130,000 respectively.

The total circulation figure compared to the total population shows that there is a huge gap in terms of accessibility and reach. According to

Ruben Abati, there are towns in Nigeria where people cannot access a daily newspaper. They receive it two days after publication, and this is unhealthy for the sustenance of democracy (Interview, 2010). The co-founder of *Newswatch* magazine, Dan Agbese, while elaborating on the above idea, stated that 'the right of rural dwellers to access the media is a major failure of the media in Nigeria since we are concentrated in urban areas to the detriment of the rural areas because of infrastructural issues. Nobody gets to know what is happening in the rural areas and rural dwellers do not get to know what is happening outside their borders either, they have been totally ignored' (Interview, 2010). Despite these challenges to universal access to the media, there is a common phenomenon whereby people with access to the media (i.e. newspapers or transistor radios) share with others who cannot afford them. This is known as 'free readers associations'—an association made up of people who cannot afford to buy newspapers resorting to standing at the vendors' tables, reading or glancing at the headlines of all newspaper titles, or borrowing them from colleagues or friends to read (Media Foundation for West Africa 2008).

Likewise, sharing is common in rural areas where not everyone can afford a radio as the average cost of a good radio is between \$70 and \$100 (Bourgault 1995). The person with a cheap transistor radio that does not require electricity places the radio in a strategic position for all to listen to in order to keep up to date with what is happening in society. Hasty (2005), in her study, alleged that this is a very common practice in developing emerging democracies. This fosters a sense of community as Ake (1993) stated that most rural people believe in community (i.e. 'an interconnected whole') and not individualization, as this influences or shapes their sense of participation in democratic processes. This will be elaborated upon in the concluding chapter. From the above, it can be argued that despite the challenges and difficulties in achieving universal access, ordinary citizens are thinking of innovative ways to satisfy their information needs.

However, the emergence of new media and information communication technology (ICT) has increased accessibility as liberalization has led to the growth and expansion of the ICT sector in Nigeria (see Dunn 2011). Statistics show that Nigeria's telecommunication industry is regarded as the fastest growing on the African continent (Akpore 2007) as anyone with new media devices can now access and participate in media discourse. This has led to what scholars call 'citizen journalism' and

Paterson (2013) argues that these devices and technologies have a grave impact on journalism practices and significantly affect both media and societal discourses. Media organizations such as Channels Television, African Independent Television (AIT), WAZOBIA FM and EKO FM have integrated the use of these technologies in their programming and activities, so reaching out to a wider audience and giving room to people to freely participate (Fosu and Akpojivi 2015). This enhances transparency and accountability and changes the dynamics of the relationship between state and citizens due to interactivity. Norris and Odugbemi (2010) argue that these technologies will help empower citizens and address the numerous challenges associated with democratic governance as such technologies would readily expose wrong doing and ills in society without the pressure from economic and political actors associated with the mainstream media. Okonjo-Iweala (2012), while citing the impact of these technologies on ordinary citizens in relation to universal access, stated that those in rural areas that were once neglected can, with the aid of mobile devices (phones), access information that would aid their activities and enable connections with other communities.

Although some progress has been recorded with universal access, this progress has been slow. One reason for this is the lack of a coherent policy framework to drive the process. According to Okonjo-Iweala (2012), the reforms embarked upon during the re-democratization process have not yielded the necessary goals due to opposition to the reforms. Although policies have been implemented to gear the process, these are inadequate and have not outlined mechanisms or structures which should be followed to achieve policy goals. A good example of this is the inability of the Nigerian state to pursue and achieve digital migration by 2015 in accordance with the International Telecommunication Union (ITU) objective. Despite three deadlines of 2012, 2015 and 2017 Nigeria is yet to achieve this goal owing to the lack of a detailed policy framework that recognizes the full implication of such migration on the audience and their access to the media (Adepetun 2017).

Most policies and discussions are just centered around infrastructure for the media organization forgetting that the technological, content development and financing aspects should also be considered so that no citizen is hindered or denied the full digital experience of migration (Adepetun 2017). And this is a very common problem in Nigeria as policies do not recognize the political, economic and cultural challenges that might impact on policy goals and objectives as the policymaking process is usually done in a haphazard way in order to be perceived as being democratic (see Osaghae 1998). Okonjo-Iweala (2012) alleges that this is a common problem with policy or reform processes in Nigeria as there is always an 'unfinished agenda'. This can be seen in the liberalization and privatization policy during President Obasanjo's era as the process witnessed controversy and criticism, such as the NITEL and Transcorp deals, which to date still bring into question the reform and policy framework process.

Media Accountability

Following the re-democratization era, one fundamental issue in the media reform process is the ability to balance the freedom of the mass media and promote accountability within the media sphere. Questions often asked are: who watches the watchdog? And who are the mass media accountable to? These questions, although simple, reflect the complex working relationship that exists between the media, media owners, regulators and the general public (see Andrea and Shaw 2009). McQuail (2003: 74) states that the issue of media accountability 'arises when a publication is charged with offences that go beyond what the freedom of the press allows or what society can tolerate'. This puts the public at the heart of media accountability as the media are dependent on the public for their survival.

Due to the nature of the Nigerian state and media ownership structure, which often encourages media content to be sensationalized and biased, media accountability is very important (Musa and Mohammed 2004; Ekpu 1990). Therefore, Ette (2000) argues that without effective media accountability the democratic process of Nigeria could be endangered. A cursory look at the various policy documents earlier examined indicates that media accountability was not addressed. However, the NUJ Code of Ethics ratified in 1998 at Ilorin is the only policy framework for media accountability in Nigeria. Although the NBC broadcasting code provides the general framework for broadcasting content, it is more related to media regulation than enforcing accountability.

According to the NUJ code of ethics preamble, 'journalism entails a high degree of public trust, and to earn and maintain this trust, it is morally imperative for every journalist and every news medium to observe the highest professional and ethical standards in the exercise of their duties' (NUJ Code of Ethics 1998). The above means that accountability can be achieve via the promotion of high professionalism and journalistic standards. Consequently, journalists are required to give a balanced, detailed and accurate reportage, shun corrupt practices, cross-check facts and carry out their watchdog functions with a high sense of responsibility. Accountability is believed to be achieved or facilitated when every journalist adheres to these guidelines (Owens-Ibie 1994).

It is worth stating that the content of the NUJ code of ethics is framed according to Western ideologies of ethics governing journalists in Western societies. Nyamnjoh (2005) argues that this is a common phenomenon for emerging or transitioning democracies because it is believed that such replication will help advance media practices and democratic processes. The Western ideologies are perceived to be the standard to which every journalist must adhere. A senior BBC correspondent in Nigeria held that every journalist aspires to operate within the ideas of the West because these ideas are viewed as perfection and will help advance journalistic practices (Interview, 2010). But Nyamnjoh (2005) argues that the framing of a media code of ethics in African countries along Western beliefs and principles is problematic with regard to implementation. According to him, the objectives of promoting accountability will seldom be achieved because of the interplay of cultural practices such as corruption. This idea was equally supported by the deputy news editor of *Vanguard* newspaper, Taye Obateru, who states that 'accountability can be hardly achieved because the ideas in the NUJ Code of Ethics are different from the realities in the media environment' (Interview, 2010).

This idea that the realities encapsulated in the policy document are different from the realities of the media environment is further established by the strategies of the code of ethics in promoting accountability. According to the code of ethics, self-regulation and certification of journalists will help to attain accountability. Self-regulation is believed to be the best mode of protecting the freedom of media practitioners from interference (Duncan 2014). Attempts to regulate the media by the state through a media tribunal or government regulatory agencies are often criticized and viewed as attempts by the state to interfere in the media's activities (see Daniels 2012). The NUJ code of ethics calls for self-regulation where every practicing journalist adheres to the code of ethics and complaints against the conduct of any journalist will be investigated by the Nigerian Press Council which is charged with the responsibility of monitoring press activities and investigating complaints against the press (Nigeria Press Council Act 1992).

While the call for self-regulation is understandable because it is seen as freedom from political and economic pressures (Wasserman and de Beer 2006), it is only registered journalists who are required to adhere to the principles of the code of ethics. This is very problematic since not all practicing journalists are members of the NUJ. In addition, the total number of practicing journalists in Nigeria is unknown as there is no reliable record or statistics to that effect (Okwori and Adeyanju 2006). Based on this, it will be extremely difficult to enforce accountability when members or non-members breach the code of ethics. As the chairman of *Guardian* newspaper Ruben Abati puts it, 'the problem with enforcing accountability in Nigeria is that we have so many journalists that are not part of NUJ, and the majority of these journalists are not aware of the code of ethics' (Interview, 2010). The inability to determine the number of practicing journalists makes the issue of self-regulation problematic as it raises questions as to how the NPC or the NUJ would be able to monitor what is happening in the media sphere (i.e. who is saying what and under which platform?). Andrea and Shaw (2009) argue that for self-regulation to be effective all practicing journalists must abide by a code of conduct or ethics, as erring media practitioners could be sanctioned.

According to Section 17 of the Nigerian Press Council Act, erring media practitioners could be asked to tender an apology/correction or be fined N2000 and media house N30,000. However, the act made no provision for non-compliance as these directives or sanctions from the council could be dismissed as not all media practitioners are registered with the NUJ. This is a major loophole in media accountability as it gives the impression that the press is above the law or societal structures, hence not accountable to anybody. The situation is slightly different with broadcasting as the NBC has used the content regulation approach to enforce accountability as this could be seen as the rationale behind the revocation of broadcasting licenses (see Media Rights Agenda and Article 19 Reports).

Apart from self-regulation, the Nigerian Press Council Act requires the certification of journalists. That is, the act requires that before someone becomes a journalist he/she must be registered with the NUJ and must have received formal training in an NUJ approved institution (Section 19, Nigerian Press Council Act). This certification will enable the council and the NUJ to effectively monitor who is publishing what content. While this is a veritable means of trying to enforce and promote media accountability, it goes against Section 39 of the Nigerian 1999 constitution that allows everyone freedom of speech without interference and this idea of certification could be seen as interference. Although, many media practitioners see this certification as a way of improving the image of the profession, in Nigeria it is seen as an all-comers job. According to a senior media correspondent at the state house, Simeon Alozieuwa, 'almost everyone is now a media practitioner due to the uncontrolled entry into the profession which has given room to irresponsible journalism and led to the difficulty in enforcing accountability' (Interview, 2010). This means that there are many journalists who are yet to be certified and who may not be operating according to a code of ethics.

Outside the idea of this certification seen as licensing, the inability of the NUJ to fight for a better wage for its members, as is done in other countries, has contributed to the challenge of certifying journalists and an unethical practice which is akin to taking a bribe. The taking of bribes, also known as 'brown envelope' or 'transport', is a very common practice within the Nigerian media environment due to poor working conditions. According to Okwori and Adeyanju (2006: 10), journalists are paid between N25,000 and N30,000 ($160–$200) per month and some go without pay for months. The NUJ code of ethics, like any other code, admonishes journalists not to collect bribes as this impacts on their work; and media freedom is engendered in the 'conditions of corruption, poverty and fear' (International Federation of Journalists). But because the media environment is largely underfunded due to the expensive nature of media, media practitioners have no choice but to continue being 'brown envelope' journalists. As the assistant editor of *Source* magazine puts it: 'the NUJ code forbids journalists from taking bribes, but in a situation where workers in over 60% of the media houses in Nigeria have not been paid for months, the necessary motivation to work is lost, so what do we expect from these journalists?' (Igho Akeregha, Interview, 2010). The situation is even more dire following the poor economic conditions that have led to recession and employers (state or private) are unable to pay their workers for months. Some workers are owed between nine and 18 months' salary (Sahara Reporters 2017). Therefore, Olorunyomi Dapo, the chief executive officer of Premium Times Media likened Nigerian media practitioners to the Nigerian police force, which is currently regarded as the worst in Africa due to their highly corrupt activities (Sahara Reporters 2017).

This therefore establishes Nyamnjoh's (2005) argument that it is practically impossible to implement Western ideologies encapsulated in policy documents that do not recognize the unique features inherent in postcolonial states.

Bibliography

Achebe, C. (1984). *The Trouble with Nigeria.* Oxford: Heinemann Publishers.

Achebe, C. (2012). *There Was a Country: A Personal History of Biafra.* London: Penguin Books.

Adebanwi, W., & Obadare, E. (2013). *Democracy and Prebendalism in Nigeria: Critical Interpretations.* New York: Palgrave Macmillan.

Adepetun, A. (2017, June 9). Nigeria: The Nation Misses Yet Another Digital Migration Deadline. *The Guardian Newspaper.*

African Charter on Broadcasting. (2001). Online: http://portal.unesco.org/ci/en. Accessed 12 Jan 2010.

African Charter on Human and Peoples' Rights. (1986). Online: http://www.umn.edu/humanart. Accessed 15 Jan 2009.

Aguda, O. (2007). The Need for a National Conference. Online: www.hg.org. Accessed 8 Dec 2007.

Ake, C. (1979). *Social Science as Imperialism: The Theory of Political Development.* Ibadan: Ibadan University Press.

Ake, C. (1993). The Unique Case of African Democracy. *International Affairs, 69*(2), 239–244.

Ake, C. (2000). *The Feasibility of Democracy in Africa.* Dakar: CODESRIA.

Akpojivi. U. (2011, June 27). The FOI Act: Beyond the Euphoria. *Guardian Newspaper.*

Akpojivi, U. (2014). Rethinking Media Pluralism: An Examination of the Nigerian Media Ecology. *Journal of Global Communication, 7*(1), 29–37.

Akpore, S. (2007, April 14). Nigeria May Rule Africa's Mobile Telephone Market. *Guardian Newspaper.*

Akwule, R. (1992). *Global Telecommunications the Technology, Administration and Policies.* London: Focal Press.

Alozieuwa, S. (2010, August 19). *Media, Ownership influence and Crisis/Conflict Situation in a Multi-Ethnic Society: Toward a Framework for Democratic Consolidation in Nigeria.* Paper Presented at Africa Media and Democracy Conference titled: *Mediating Democracy in Africa.*

Andrea, M., & Shaw, C. (2009). *Accountability and the Public Interest in Broadcasting.* London: Palgrave Macmillan.

Andsager, J., Wyatt, R., & Martin, E. (2004). *Free Expression and Five Democratic Publics Support for Individual and Media Rights.* New Jersey: Hampton Press Inc.

Baker, E. (2007). *Media Concentration and Democracy Why Ownership Matters.* Cambridge: Cambridge University Press.

Barendt, E., & Hitchens, L. (2000). *Media Law Cases and Materials.* Harlow: Pearson Longman.

Bayart. (2010). The State in Africa: The Politics of the Belly (2nd ed). Cambridge: Polity Press.

Bourgault, L. (1995). *Mass Media in Sub-Saharan Africa*. Bloomington: Indiana University Press.

Browne, E. (2015). Social Media and Governance. GSDRC Helpdesk Research Report. Online. http://www.gsdrc.org. Accessed 15 Sep 2017.

Campbell, J. (2011). *Nigeria Dancing on the Brink*. New York: Rowman & Littlefield Publishers Inc.

Chakravartty, P., & Sarikakis, K. (2006). *Media Policy and Globalization*. Edinburgh: Edinburgh University Press.

Channels Television. (2017, August 23). *We now Monitor Social Media for Anti-Government and Anti-Military Information*. Online: https://www.channelstv.com/2017/08/23/now-monitor-social-media-anti-government-anti-military-information-military/

Coleman, S., & Ross, K. (2010). *The Media and the Public "Them and "Us" in Media Discourse"*. West Sussex: Wiley-Blackwell.

Daniels, G. (2012). *Fighting for Democracy: The ANC and the Media in South Africa*. Johannesburg: Wits University Press.

Davies, H., & Shields, V. (1999). Public Trust and Accountability for Clinical Performance: Lessons from the National Press Reportage of the Bristol Hearing. *Journal of Evaluation in Clinical Practice, 5*(3), 335–342.

Diamond, L., Greene, A., & Oyediran, O. (1997). The Politics of Transition Without End. In L. Diamond, A. Greene, & O. Oyediran (Eds.), *Transition Without End: Nigerian Politics and Civil Society Under Babangida*. London: Lynne Rienner Publisher.

Duke, D. (2017, September 30). *Hard Copy*. Channels TV.

Duncan, J. (2014). A Political Economy of the Press Self-Regulation: The Case of South Africa. *Media, Culture and Society, 36*(2), 167–182.

Dunn, H. (2011). ICT Policy-making and International Trade Agreements in the Caribbean. In R. Mansell & M. Raboy (Eds.), *The Handbook of Global Media and Communication Policy*. West Sussex: Wiley-Blackwell.

Ekpu, R. (1990). Nigeria's Embattled Fourth Estate. *Journal of Democracy, 1*(2), 106–116.

Emerson, T. (1982). The First Amendment in the Year 2000. In S. Halpern (Ed.), *The Future of Our Liberties: Perspectives on the Bill of Rights*. Westport CT: Greenwood.

Entman, R. (1989). *Democracy Without Citizens Media and the Decay of American Politics*. Oxford: Oxford University Press.

Eribo, F. (1997). Internal and External Factors Affecting Press Freedom in Nigeria. In F. Eribo & W. Jong-Ebot (Eds.), *Press Freedom and Communication in Africa*. Trenton: Africa World Press Inc.

Eribo, F., & Jong-Ebot, W. (1997). *Press Freedom and Communication in Africa*. Trenton: Africa World Press Inc.

Ette, M. (2000). Agent of Change or Stability? The Nigerian Press Undermines Democracy. *The Harvard International Journal of Press/Politics, 5*(3), 67–86.

Federal Government of Nigeria. (1987). *Nigeria Mass Communication Policy.* Lagos: Federal Government Press.

Federal Government of Nigeria. (1990). *Official Secret Act.* Lagos: Federal Government Press.

Federal Government of Nigeria. (1992). *Nigerian Press Council Act No. 85 of 1992.* Lagos: Federal Government Press.

Federal Government of Nigeria. (2011). *Freedom of Information Act.* Lagos: Federal Government Press.

Fosu, M., & Akpojivi, U. (2015). Media Convergence Practices and Production in Ghana and Nigeria: Implications for Democracy and Research in Africa. *Journal of Applied Journalism and Media Studies, 4*(2), 277–292.

Golding, P., & Murdock, G. (1986). The New Communications Revolution. In J. Curran, J. Ecclestone, G. Oakley, & A. Richardson (Eds.), *Bending Reality the State of the Media.* London: Pluto Press.

Haggard, S., & Kaufman, R. (1997). The Political Economy of Democratic Transitions. *Comparative Politics, 29*(3), 263–283.

Hasty, J. (2005). *The Press and Political Culture in Ghana.* Indiana: Indiana University Press.

Higgins, M. (2008). *Media and Their Public.* Berkshire: Open University Press.

Humphreys, P. (1996). *Mass Media and Media Policy in Western Europe.* Manchester: Manchester University Press.

Iriekpen, D. (2010, July 27). Court Declares Press Council Law Oppressive. *This Day Newspaper.*

Jibo, M., & Okoosi, A. (2003). The Nigerian Media: An Assessment of Its Role in Achieving Transparent and Accountable Government in the Fourth Republic. *Nordic Journal of African Studies, 12*(2), 180–195.

Mandela, N. (1990). African National Congress. *Journal of Democracy, 1*(4), 32–35.

McQuail, D. (1992). *Media Performance Mass Communication and the Public Interest.* London: Sage Publication.

McQuail, D. (2003). *Media Accountability and Freedom of Publication.* Oxford: Oxford University Press.

McQuail, D. (2005). *McQuail's Mass Communication Theory* (5th ed.). London: Sage Publications.

Media Foundation for West Africa. (2008). *Media Alert West Africa 2008: Annual State of the Media Report.* Accra: Media Foundation for West Africa.

Media Rights Agenda. (2002a). *Print Monitor Report 2002.* Lagos: Media Rights Agenda.

Ministry of Communication Federal Republic of Nigeria. (2000). *National Policy on Telecommunication.* Abuja: Federal Government Press.

Ministry of Communication Nigeria. (2000). *National Telecommunication Policy.* Abuja: Federal Government Press.

Musa, M., & Mohammed, J. (2004). The Political Economy of Media Ownership in Nigeria. In T. Pradip & Z. Nain (Eds.), *Who Owns the Media Global Trends and Local Resistances*. London: Zed Books.
National Broadcasting Commission. (2006). *Nigeria Broadcasting Code*. Abuja: Regent.
National Population Commission. (2017). Online. http://population.gov.ng/. Accessed 1 Nov 2017.
NBC. (2010). *NBC Vs AIT: Restraining Order Lapses*. Online: www.nbc.gov.ng. Accessed 10 Feb 2010.
Nigeria Union of Journalists. (1998). *Code of Ethics for Nigerian Journalists*. Asokoro: Nigeria Press Council.
Norris, P., & Odugbemi, S. (2010). Evaluating Media Performance. In P. Norris (Ed.), *Public Sentinel: News Media and Goveranance Reform*. Washington, DC: The World Bank.
Nyamnjoh, F. (2005). *Africa's Media Democracy and the Politics of Belonging*. London: Zed Books.
Ojo, E. (2003). The Mass Media and the Challenges of Sustainable Democratic Values in Nigeria: Possibilities and Limitations. *Media Culture & Society, 25*(6), 821–840.
Ojo, T. (2004). Old Paradigm and Information & Communication Technologies for Development Agenda in Africa: Modernization as Context. *Journal of Information Technology Impact, 4*(3).
Okigbo, C., & Eribo, F. (2004). *Development and Communication in Africa*. Oxford: Rowman & Littlefield.
Okonjo-Iweala, N. (2012). *Reforming the Unreformable: Lessons from Nigeria*. Cambridge: MIT Press.
Okwori, Z., & Adeyanju, A. (2006). *African Media Development Initiative Nigeria Research Findings and Conclusions*. London: BBC World Service Trust.
Olagunju, T., Jinadu, A., & Oyovbaire, S. (1993). *Transition to Democracy in Nigeria (1985–1993)*. Ibadan: Safari Books Limited.
Olumhense, S. (2010). *The Nigeria Mass Media on Trail*. Online: www.saharareporter.com/column. Accessed 21 Mar 2010.
Ororunyomi, D. (2017, November 9). The Level of Bribery in Journalism Today Is Worse Than the Police. *Sahara Reporters*.
Osaghae, E. (1998). *Nigeria Since Independence: Crippled Giant*. Bloomington: Indiana University Press.
Owens-Ibie, N. (1994). Press Responsibility and Public Opinion in Political Transition. *Africa Media Review, 8*(1), 69–80.
Paterson, C. (2011). *Press Carnage and US Responsibility*. Paper Presented at the ICA Conference Boston.
Paterson, C. (2013). Journalism and Social Media in the African Context. *Ecquid Novi African Journalism Studies, 34*(1), 1–6.

Ronning, H., & Kupe, T. (2000). The Dual Legacy of Democracy and Authoritarianism: The Media and the State in Zimbabwe. In J. Curran & M. Jin-Park (Eds.), *De-Westernising Media Studies*. London: Routledge.

Ross, C. (1998). Joseph Sax and the Idea of the Public Trust. *Ecology Law Quarterly, 25*(351), 351–362.

Tom, D. (2004). The Watchdog Inside a Cage: The Nigerian Press and Censorship Laws. *Ethiope Research Abraka Journal of the Arts, Law and Social Sciences, 1*(2), 91–118.

Ugboajah, F. (1985). *Mass Communication, Culture, and Society in West Africa*. Munich: Hans Zell.

Umeh, C. (1989). The Advent and Growth of Television Broadcasting in Nigeria: Its Political and Education Overtones. *Africa Media Review, 3*(2), 54–66.

Vanguard Newspaper. (2010, August 6). Nigerian Press Council Act Violates rights of Free Speech.

Vanguard newspaper. (2017). Illiteracy Rate in Nigeria Alarming-FG. Online. http://www.vanguardngr.com/2017/09/illiteracy-rate-nigeria-alarming-fg/. Accessed 2 Oct 2017.

Wasserman, H., & de Beer, A. (2006). Conflicts of Interest? Debating the Media's Role in Post Apartheid South Africa. In K. Voltmer (Ed.), *Mass Media and Political Communication in New Democracies*. London: Routledge.

World Summit on the Information Society "Geneva Report 2003". Online: http://www.itu.int/wsis/documents/index.html. Accessed 12 Oct 2007.

World Summit on the Information Society "Tunis Report 2005". Online, http://www.itu.int/wsis/documents/index.html. Accessed 12 Oct 2007.

Ziegler, D., & Asante, M. (1992). *Thunder and Silence the Mass Media in Africa*. Trenton: Africa World Press Inc.

Zongo, G. (2001). *ICTs For Development in Africa*. Online: www.unssc.org/web1/programmes/glnp. Accessed 12 Oct 2006.

CHAPTER 5

Comparative Analysis: Common Patterns or Disparity?

From the discussions in Chaps. 3 and 4 about the reform processes (i.e. policy formulation to implementation), we need to examine the media reform processes in Ghana and Nigeria to establish whether there are common patterns or disparities between them. This is to ascertain how both countries have approached media reforms and democratization processes, and determine the extent to which previous antecedence (i.e. political, economic and cultural) have influenced the processes. This knowledge is fundamental as according to Price (2010) it will help explain why there is a disconnect between theory and practice, especially in Africa where scholars such as Ake (1979) and Nyamnjoh (2005) have argued that the realities in Africa differ from normative conceptions of the West.

There is no doubt that the ideas of democracy and media freedom are interconnected and are considered germane to the development of Ghana and Nigeria. According to Johannsen (1994), while establishing this interconnectedness, stated that democracy thrives on freedom of speech and media as this will enable citizens to make informed decisions that will advance the democratic project (cited in Daniels 2012: 22). This has informed the democratization project or the push for re-democratization which Huntington (1991) termed the 'third wave of democracy', which is now part of the foreign policy/project of Western nations such as the United States and Britain (Packenham 1973). Because of the importance of media freedom

U. Akpojivi, *Media Reforms and Democratization in Emerging Democracies of Sub-Saharan Africa*,
https://doi.org/10.1007/978-3-319-75301-0_5

to the democratization processes, media reforms are highly contested by the various national and international actors. To Nordenstreng (2011: 84) this contestation is a result of the struggle for or against the hegemonic ideology, in other words a 'tactical argument in [the] socio-economic and ideological struggle' that reflects the foundational principles of freedom in the United States which is being pushed onto the global scene. Ake (2000) adds that even in democratic African states, African leaders are in a struggle based on their desire to reform in order to promote development and likewise the desire to reject these reforms because of the belief that they promote Western principles and ideas. The implementation of such reforms means a loss of autonomy and further dependency on the West for a policy framework, which is problematic.

From both case studies previously discussed, it can be argued that the media reform process and the call for re-democratization for both countries were largely influenced by Western ideologies and organizations. Ninsin (1998) argues that Ghana's move to democracy and the implementation of media reforms was Western oriented as the country was made to embrace these reforms and democracy as a condition for continuous support. Kafewo (2006: 3) adds that because Ghana is a poor country that depends on Western technical assistance and financial assistance (i.e. loans), the country had no choice but to quickly embrace these ideas. This is evident in the liberal and neo-liberal policies that were formulated such as the Constitution, National Media Policy, National Telecommunication Policy and the Ghana Journalists Association (GJA) Code of Ethics.

The implementation of these policies has significantly impacted on the media sphere and democratic culture as people are more vocal and readily available to participate in both media and national discourse that affect them (see Fosu and Akpojivi 2015; Akpojivi and Fosu 2016) due to openness. In addition, the history of the country having endured long military regimes that promoted suppression and economic crisis further contributed to the warm embrace of liberal and neo-liberal policies. However, this was not carefully planned as other socio-economic, political and cultural factors are hindering the realization of the full potential of these policies, as evident in the recent attempts by the government to control the activities of the media (see Nyarko and Akpojivi 2017). For instance, consider the debate surrounding the interpretation of Article 162(3) of the constitution as to whether the press but not other forms of mass media are exempted from licensing. This debate is also centered on the complexity between the regulatory bodies, the National Media Commission (NMC) and the National

Communication Authority (NCA), over their functions and which has the powers to monitor media content. Furthermore, the recent attempt by the state, as argued by Nyarko and Akpojivi (2017), to intimidate and restrict the activities of media practitioners indicate that government is attempting to re-define the relationship between the media and government and this is not in agreement with neo-liberal policy goals and agenda.

Therefore, it can be argued that policymakers in Ghana adopted a policy framework without the active participation and engagement of the public to identify the compatibility of these policy goals with the socio-economic, political and cultural realities. The realities in Ghana are different from the Western realities encapsulated in the policy documents. Consequently, the government and private owners still interfere with media operations and corruption has become the norm with journalists collecting 'soli', and this is against the policy goals.

On the other hand, Nigeria's drive to media reform and re-democratization can be regarded as complex due to pressure from both internal and external actors. The internal actors range from civil societies to the mass media, and sanctions during the military regimes facilitated the reform process (Diamond et al. 1997). This was as a result of political turmoil and economic depression caused by trade restrictions enforced by Western countries. Although the Nigerian government allowed for reform, this process has not been sincere as the government, despite the reforms, still seeks to promote its authoritarian enclave using instruments of national interest and security. Therefore, Tom (2004) argues that the media reform process in Nigeria is not comprehensive due to its nature of 'give and take' and this is evident in all the policy documents (e.g. the Constitution, the Official Secret Act, the National Mass Communication Policy and the NBC Broadcasting Code). Ake (1996: 9), while elaborating on the above, states that the Nigerian government right from independence has never been sincere when it comes to the development of the country as 'their minds were absorbed in the struggle for power and survival'.

This struggle for power and survival has influenced media reform processes as despite 18 years into re-democratization, the policies in Nigeria do not promote viable media growth and development as the government is still unwilling to allow full reform. Mgbejume (1991) argues that the unwillingness of government to embrace full reform has necessitated the desire to formulate policies that protect national interests or give the government power to maintain the status quo. This unwillingness is tied to the historical antecedence of the Nigerian state and the role of the mass media. Nyamnjoh (2005) states that the history of the role of the press during the independence struggle, where the press were active instruments for nationalists in the fight for independence, has contributed to the government's desire to control the media. Likewise, Uko (2004) posited that the Nigerian press has always 'romanced' the different governments i.e. military or civilian, and such romance has made the press less critical of governments action and policy, consequently, enabling the government to continue formulating policies that are not holistic but haphazard.

In both countries (Ghana and Nigeria), the ideas of media freedom, public trust, universal access to the media and media accountability were recurring themes within the formulated policy documents which have been addressed in the preceding two chapters. Mansell and Raboy (2011) posit that these themes originate from Western frameworks that are pushed or transplanted into global media and communication policies. Despite the globalized nature of these themes, their applicability in both countries was affected by the interplay of socio-economic, political and cultural factors.

Following the reform and democratization process, media freedom and independence became a topical debate as the opening up of the media sphere was considered a pivotal tool in the democratic process and development of the media (Ojo 2003; Karikari 1998). All of Ghana's media policies promoted this idea of media freedom and independence. This led to a significant improvement in the form of proliferation of media houses and the participatory nature of journalism and programming, as citizens were actively encouraged to contribute to both media and national discourses (Fosu and Akpojivi 2015; Hasty 2005). The independent regulatory agency, the NMC, was established to insulate the media from interference, therefore advancing the frontiers of freedom in Ghana. However, it was established that due to the inherent culture of secrecy from previous political antecedence of censorship, media practitioners are still careful and sensitive about what they say and how they say it, especially those from state owned organizations. And there have been contestations to policy interpretation in relation to regulation of the media. Who has the power to interdict the board members of state-owned media organizations, and who can regulate media content? are some of the salient questions currently confronting the media sphere. Also, lately, there has been an increase in intimidation and harassment of media practitioners in Ghana and this is rooted in the antecedence of political control right from independence (see Ake 1996).

In Nigeria, the era of democratization and media reform opened the media sphere to investment as there has been a proliferation of media houses. Despite this proliferation, media freedom and independence is limited as policy frameworks are restrictive and do not guarantee freedom and independence. Sections 39 and 22 of the constitution allow for individual freedom of expression and media responsibility to act as a watchdog. However, the media cannot fulfill its constitutional responsibility due to the 'give and take' nature of the policy framework (Tom 2004). In addition, the government's desire to control media activities is seen in the various policies as limiting freedom in the guise of national interest, coupled with the government appointing members to the regulatory body, the National Broadcasting Commission (NBC). Due to political patronage (Tomaselli and Tomaselli 1989) and 'politics of the belly' (Bayart 2010) these appointees have the responsibility to promote the government's interest over public interest. According to a senior media officer within the Presidency, 'whoever is appointed naturally owes the government the obligation of protecting their interest even when it ought not to be' (Mitaire Ikpen, Interview, 2010). This has become a common practice in Nigeria as these political appointees defy the public interest and promote and defend the government's interest, thus attesting to Bayart's (2010) idea of the 'politics of the belly'.

On media acting as public trust, this concept is difficult to achieve in both countries as political and economic interests affect the ability of the media to act as public trust. In Ghana, despite the policy provisions attesting to the issue of public trust, these policies have not adequately addressed how government and private interests could be effectively managed. Karikari (1998) argues that the state-owned media houses are less critical of the government as they seek to please it. Likewise, privately owned media are subject to owners' interests and biases as the ideological interests (political and economic) of these owners influence media activities. In addition, the public's trust in the media is difficult to achieve due to the proliferation of media that followed the media reforms. This has facilitated active competition, and the various policy documents did not provide a mechanism or state the extent to which owners can interfere in the operation of the media.

In Nigeria, there are no detailed policy provisions in relation to the realization of public trust. The Nigerian Press Council Act stipulates that media practitioners should act in an ethical way to win the public's trust. However, this relates more to media accountability than public trust. Likewise, Section 22 of the constitution could be interpreted as promoting public trust. Nevertheless, the heterogeneous nature of the Nigerian state, with over 250 ethnic groups and 400 languages, has posed the question: which sector of the public trust should the media win? In addition, the proliferation of media houses coupled with a vast majority of these media houses being owned by politicians has made it impossible for the media to win public trust (see Okwori and Adeyanju 2006). The vested economic and political interests of media owners are played out in mass media activities hence making the concept of public trust a theoretical concept that is unachievable.

Lastly, both countries' regulators, the NMC and the NBC, have not carried out audience research to determine what the public wants. Meeting the needs of the public is fundamental to the attainment of public trust, but there is no evidence or statistic which shows that the NMC, the NBC or the media organizations are engaged in audience research to understand the needs of the public. Fosu and Akpojivi (2015) argue that the inability of both the regulators and media organizations to embark on audience research has led media organizations to assume that they know what the public wants; hence the over politicization of programming.

Universal access to the media was one key argument contained in the policy documents of both countries. Policies were formulated to open up the media industry and encourage massive investment. As stated earlier, although these policies have facilitated the proliferation of the media houses in both countries, these media houses are concentrated in urban areas, thus making it difficult for rural communities, which accommodate the vast majority of the populace, to access and participate in media activities. In Nigeria, the high cost of licensing and establishing media organizations has hindered growth and development of the media as the majority of the media organizations are owned by the government, while the few privately owned media are centered in urban areas for a quick return on investment. In Ghana, the use of the mother tongue (i.e. the indigenous language) was identified as a way of achieving universal access to the media as this would help address the high illiteracy rate that has posed a challenge to accessibility and participation in media discourse (Kafewo 2006). But this has consequently led to the dominance of Akan and Ewe in broadcasting, neglecting the other dialects.

The emergence of new media technologies such as mobile phones and social media has, to a large extent, increased accessibility in both countries; ordinary people once excluded have been given a voice. The emergence and convergence of these technologies has increased media penetration, as people can now listen to the radio and watch television on their mobile devices. Print media organizations, for example, now have online news versions; likewise electronic media now broadcast live streams. Aker and Mbiti (2010: 208) argue that mobile phones and new media technologies are 'evolving from [a] simple communication tool into service delivery platforms', and this is evident in how the public now engage the government and enforce accountability and democratic principles. Fosu and Akpojivi (2015) highlight this impact by stating that almost every media organization has integrated these technologies into their platforms, thus changing the dynamic of the relationship between governments, the media and the public (see Browne 2015). This has resulted in both countries attempting to regulate new media technologies. The attempt to regulate is centered on the idea that the new media pose a threat to government actions due to the ease with which the public can get information and critique government actions by enforcing accountability.

Media accountability has been a great challenge to both countries due to the interplay of cultural and economic factors. Both countries formulated a code of ethics which was framed along Western ideas without recognizing the inherent cultural factors. Both the Ghana Journalists Association (GJA) and the Nigeria Union of Journalists (NUJ) believe in self-regulation and this is to avoid government interference. However, this has led to irresponsibility of some media practitioners in both countries who collect bribes known as 'soli' and 'brown envelopes' respectively, which has impacted on the media profession. News stories that are false and biased are published. The idea of certification of journalists by the NUJ as a way of promoting accountability has questioned the legality of Section 39 of the Nigerian constitution. Likewise, the inability to ascertain the total number of media practitioners has made it difficult for the NUJ and the Nigerian Press Council to monitor the activities of media practitioners in accordance with the Nigeria Press Council Act. Similarly, in Ghana, the failure of the National Media Commission's ombudsman to enforce decisions made it difficult for media practitioners to adhere to the commission's guidelines and judgements. The NMC now depends on moral suasion to appeal to media practitioners to act responsibly, and this is considered as ineffective.

The above has shown that there is disparity in both countries in terms of their approach to media reform and democratization. While Ghana was open minded by embracing liberal and neo-liberal ideas in their policies, Nigeria, on the other hand, approached the reform process cautiously as policies were incomprehensive and not holistic. Despite both countries' approach to media reform, the inherent socio-economic, political and cultural factors have determined and influenced the success of reform processes. The impact of these socio-economic, political and cultural factors on the realization of the different policy documents in both countries shows the similarity. These factors shape policy formulation and policy content in both countries, as most of the policies formulated were designed to address problems confronting the society.

Bibliography

Ake, C. (1979). *Social Science as Imperialism: The Theory of Political Development*. Ibadan: Ibadan University Press.

Ake, C. (1996). *Democracy and Development in Africa*. Washington DC: The Brookings Institution.

Ake, C. (2000). *The Feasibility of Democracy in Africa*. Dakar: CODESRIA.

Aker, J., & Mbiti, I. (2010). Mobile Phones and Economic Development in Africa. *Journal of Economic Prospect, 24*(3), 207–232.

Akpojivi, U., & Fosu, M. (2016). Indigenous Language Broadcasting in Ghana: Retrospect and Prospect. In A. Salawu & M. Chibita (Eds.), *Indigenous Language Media, Language Politics and Democracy in Africa*. New York: Palgrave Macmillan.

Bayart, J. (2010). *The State in Africa: The Politics of the Belly* (2nd ed.). Cambridge: Polity Press.

Browne, E. (2015). Social Media and Governance. GSDRC Helpdesk Research Report. Online. http://www.gsdrc.org. Accessed 12 May 2015.

Daniels, G. (2012). *Fighting for Democracy: The ANC and the Media in South Africa*. Johannesburg: Wits University Press.

Diamond, L., Greene, A., & Oyediran, O. (1997). The Politics of Transition Without End. In L. Diamond, A. Greene, & O. Oyediran (Eds.), *Transition Without End: Nigerian Politics and Civil Society Under Babangida*. London: Lynne Rienner Publisher.

Fosu, M., & Akpojivi, U. (2015). Media Convergence Practices and Production in Ghana and Nigeria: Implications for Democracy and Research in Africa. *Journal of Applied Journalism and Media Studies, 4*(2), 277–292.

Hasty, J. (2005). *The Press and Political Culture in Ghana*. Indiana: Indiana University Press.

Huntington, S. (1991). *The Third Wave: Democratization in the Late Twentieth Century*. Norman: University of Oklahoma Press.

Kafewo, S. (2006). *Ghana Research Findings and Conclusions in African Media Development Initiative*. London: BBC World Service Trust.

Karikari, K. (1998). The Press and the Transition to Multi-Party Democracy in Ghana. In K. Ninsin (Ed.), *Ghana: Transition to Democracy*. Dakar: CODESRIA.

Mansell, R., & Raboy, M. (2011). Introduction: Foundations of the Theory and Practice of Global Media and Communication Policy. In R. Mansell & M. Raboy (Eds.), *The Handbook of Global Media and Communication Policy*. London: Wiley-Blackwell.

Mgbejume, O. (1991). Constraints on Mass Media Policies in Nigeria. *Africa Media Review, 5*(2), 47–57.

Ninsin, K. (1998). Civic Associations and the Transition to Democracy. In K. Ninsin (Ed.), *Ghana: Transition to Democracy*. Dakar: CODESRIA.

Nordenstreng, K. (2011). Free Flow Doctrine in Global Media Policy. In R. Mansell & M. Raboy (Eds.), *The Handbook of Global Media and Communication Policy*. London: Wiley Blackwell.

Nyamnjoh, F. (2005). *Africa's Media Democracy and the Politics of Belonging*. London: Zed Books.

Nyarko, J., & Akpojivi, U. (2017). Intimidation, Assault, and Violence Against Media Practioners in Ghana: Considering Provocation. *Sage Open, 7*(1), 1–12.

Ojo, E. (2003). The Mass Media and the Challenges of Sustainable Democratic Values in Nigeria: Possibilities and Limitations. *Media Culture & Society, 25*(6), 821–840.

Okwori, Z., & Adeyanju, A. (2006). *African Media Development Initiative Nigeria Research Findings and Conclusions*. London: BBC World Service Trust.

Packenham, R. (1973). *Liberal America and the Third World: Political Development Ideas in Foreign Aid and Social Science*. New Jersey: Princeton University Press.

Price, M. (2010, July 4–17). *Lecture on Strategic Communication and Media Freedom*, at the 6th Annenberg/Oxford Summer Institute in Global Media Policy.

Tom, D. (2004). The Watchdog Inside a Cage: The Nigerian Press and Censorship Laws. *Ethiope Research Abraka Journal of the Arts, Law and Social Sciences, 1*(2), 91–118.

Tomaselli, K., & Tomaselli, R. (1989). Between Policy and Practice in the SABC 1970–1981. In R. Tomaselli, K. Tomaselli, & J. Muller (Eds.), *Studies on the South African Media Broadcasting in South Africa*. London: James Currey Ltd.

Uko, N. (2004). *Romancing the Gun: The Press as a Promoter of Military Rule*. Trenton: Africa World Press.

CHAPTER 6

Rethinking Media Reforms in Emerging Democracies: The Unanswered Questions

My argument throughout this book is that media reform in the emerging democracies of Ghana and Nigeria is a complex process that should not just involve the transplanting of Western ideas and frameworks but should involve the active participation of all to formulate policies that will meet the particular needs of these countries. Failure to do this will result in complexity as a result of the interplay between policy ideas and the socio-political, economic and cultural realities of these countries which have been influenced by the history of the political and media spheres. And this could pose a threat to both the reform process and democratization, as these antecedents have continued to play a germane role in the democratic process.

However, the democratic nature of African states will be evaluated by the West and Western organizations based on states' ability to promote freedom of speech and liberalization of the media. This is based on the principles of non-intervention (Nyamnjoh 2005), where emerging democracies have been forced to embrace policies that promote media freedom and independence, as failure to do so results in a severed relationship. The act of embracing these policies without an understanding of the policy processes, the influence of history, and the place of ethnicity, cultural interplay, economic and sectarian agendas, which are the realities in emerging democracies, is simplistic and unrealistic and accounts for complexities in policy and unrealized policy objectives in Ghana and Nigeria.

U. Akpojivi, *Media Reforms and Democratization in Emerging Democracies of Sub-Saharan Africa*,
https://doi.org/10.1007/978-3-319-75301-0_6

Bogues (2012: 30) adds that in conceptualizing freedom nation states, 'grapple with the conundrum that while freedom had been constructed in Western political philosophy and the history of thought primarily as a value and normative ideal…but research is leading to grappling with freedom as practice'. In practice, freedom is difficult to achieve due to its 'abstractification', which is just a concept (see Ake 1979) and could manifest differently in different societies based on context. Therefore, the questions of: what does freedom look like in emerging democracies whose realities are significantly different from the West? Despite the complexities of freedom (i.e. 'abstractification') what constitutes freedom in emerging democracies? What does it mean to reform the media in emerging democracies characterized by economic and political tensions? What approach would aid the reform and democratization project? Do African realities allow for a holistic reform that will facilitate true principles of democracy? If so, how can it be achieved and projected especially in this era of hegemonic ideological control between the West and the South? These questions are salient as there have been uprisings in the Global South over decolonization and transformation issues in which the mass media are considered as tools for promoting Western ideologies and principles (see Ake 1979; Mingjiang 2008). As Chinweizu (1999) argues, the challenge confronting the African continent is to have a media that are realistically African with African ideologies that reflect African realities.

Therefore, making media reforms in emerging democracies an ideological battle. This battle is from two standpoints, ideas and mode. In other words, the media reform process in emerging democracies entails origin and form: whose ideas shape or influence the policy document and how is this policy document arrived at? Is it through active participation of the public or a few elites who gather in the urban (capital) city to depend on the West for a framework or formulate policy based on their limited knowledge of society and the needs of society. The imposition and dependency on the West and foreign organizations for ideas is another form of colonialism or what Noam Chomsky (1979) called neocolonialism. Cusicanqui (2012) argues that attempts by states to embrace reforms (i.e. liberal and modernization) can be seen as re-colonization because of the reproduction of colonial ideas despite independence. This signals the need for decolonization as the elites, who are 'caricatures of the West', are at the forefront of this re-colonization project due to their readiness to easily accept these colonial ideas or push them onto the ordinary citizens during the policy formulation processes.

Kwame Nkrumah (1965) vigorously campaigned against neocolonialism in Africa as he considered it a deadly trap. According to him, post-colonial states are confronted with neocolonialism in the form of economic systems or policies that are driven from the West onto the continent to impoverish the people. This is done to promote Western ideas and values and make them universal, but in so doing ignoring and denying other realties. Ake (1979) in his well-known book, *Social Science as Imperialism* buttressed this further by stating that concepts such as freedom and political theories are ideas from the West to further imperialism, another form of neocolonialism. This is manifested by using aid, technical assistance and financial assistance as bait and an instrument to make emerging democracies accept these ideas. Because these emerging democracies are coming out of political instability and economic restrictions they have no other option but to accept and implement these ideas. This study has shown that such an approach has not been successful in either Ghana or Nigeria as the transplanting of these ideas has not achieved the desired results therefore establishing that these Western ideas are not practicable in other countries (Ake 1979).

Consequently, Cabral (1966) argues for an 'ideological weapon' of struggle against both the external impasse of these ideas and internal factors that necessitate these ideas (political, economic, cultural and social). To Cabral this ideological warfare is part of the way in which 'foreign domination of African homelands' can be eliminated. The domination of Western ideas in policy making processes during media reforms does not mean that there is a lack of ideas that can facilitate or aid policy making and media reform in Africa especially in Ghana and Nigeria, but ideas are based on the ignorance of the elite who do not recognize historical realities (see Cabral 1966). To Wamba-dia-Wamba 'thinking has often been denied to African people. And these people due to deep alienation have often simply adopted models [of] thought elsewhere' (cited in Neocosmos 2016). This is in line with Steve Biko's (1978 [2002]) argument that the mind is the best form of colonialization and re-colonialization (neocolonialism) as the act of thinking, which reflects their realities, will lead to freedom from neocolonialism. Media reform processes in emerging democracies have always been centered on elites (i.e. the 'privileged few') who then decide aspects of reform and the form such reform should follow. This excludes ordinary citizens, who are exposed to the socio-economic, political and economic realities, from active participation in the process. In addition, these elites, due to their inability to think, embrace an established framework that does not recognize the realities of their countries, so promoting dependency and complexities within the reform processes.

One could ask what all these mean for media reform and democratization projects in emerging democracies of Sub-Sahara Africa. It means the need to re-think approaches to media reform and democratization—the need to go beyond the normative approach to understanding reform processes in societies. This does not mean that Marxism is seen as the solution to all the political and media reform issues, as Wamba-dia-Wamba says that 'the Marxist political vision has collapsed, attempts to recalibrate it are in difficulty as they lack historical reference' (cited in Neocosmos 2016). Or as Neocosmos (2016: xiv) puts it 'until the 1980s it had been Marxism that provided a vision of some kind of alternative to the appalling inequalities, exploitation and oppression inherent in capitalism. The decline of Marxist analysis and its replacement in intellectual thinking by what has been called the "language turn" in the social sciences and humanities, has been intimately connected to the worldwide disintegration of Marxism's alternative emancipatory vision'.

In other words, Marxism does not have answers to all the problems and it has failed, so we need to think of an alternative model or approach that will be relevant to the African continent. Therefore, in re-thinking media reforms and democratization in emerging democracies we need to embrace Critical African Thoughts. By this I mean recognizing African realities and experiences and using these experiences to address or solve their problems. Anyanwu termed this 'African Philosophy' which is a critical thinking process in which Africans make sense of their world, and shape and reconstruct it (cited in Peters 1959). Therefore, Critical African Thought is centered around the notion of thinking about critical African values, in other words not easily accepting any ideas, and reflecting on how these values could be utilized to address problems confronting individual states. This departs significantly from former South African president Thabo Mbeki's idea of 'African solutions for African problems'.

Adopting Critical African Thought in media reforms and democratization in emerging democracies involves the need to question and critique the policy decision making process. Who are those involved in the process and why them? What ideas are being considered or pushed through? And how would these ideas improve the democratic culture? What are the other alternatives available? Scholars such as Ngugi wa Thiong'o, Frantz Fanon, Wole Soyinka, and nationalists Kwame Nkrumah and Julius Nyerere recognize Critical African Thought as a silent tool to facilitate the development of African states as it allows for the flow of different alternative ideas. These alternative ideas are only possible via thinking and active engagement with the public, both urban and rural dwellers. According to Ake (1993), participation for Africans is 'communality'. He adds that participation within an African community promotes community, the interconnected whole which suppresses individualism and self-interest. Consequently, recreating a democratic structure that is in line with African realities would help address the needs of society and promote development. As Ake (1993: 244) puts it, for this communal nature of participation 'democracy has to be recreated in the context of the given realities and in political arrangements which fit the cultural context, but without sacrificing its values and inherent principles'. Hence in re-thinking media reforms in Ghana and Nigeria the process has to be recreated in line with the realities of both countries to advance the democratic project.

Bibliography

Ake, C. (1979). *Social Science as Imperialism: The Theory of Political Development.* Ibadan: Ibadan University Press.

Ake, C. (1993). The Unique Case of African Democracy. *International Affairs, 69*(2), 239–244.

Biko, S. (1978). *I Write What I Like.* London: Bowerdean Press.

Bogues, A. (2012). And What About the Human? Freedom, Human Emancipation and the Radical Imagination. *Boundary, 2, 39*(3), 29–46.

Cabral, A. (1966, January). *The Weapon of Theory.* Addressed to the First Tricontinental Conference of the peoples of Asia, Africa, and Latin America held in Havana.

Chinweizu. (1999). Towards the African Renaissance Media. In M. W. Makgoba (Ed.), *African Renaissance.* Cape Town: Tafelberg Publishers Limited.

Chomsky, N. (1979). *The Washington Connection and Third World Fascism.* New York: South End Press.

Cusicanqui, S. R. (2012). Ch'ixinakax utxiwa: A Reflection on the Practices and Discourse of Decolonization. *South Atlantic Quarterly., 111*(1), 95–109.

Mingjiang, L. (2008). China Debates Soft Power. *The Chinese Journal of International Politics, 2*(2), 287–308.

Neocosmos, M. (2016). *Thinking Freedom in Africa: Toward a Theory of Emancipatory Politics.* Johannesburg: Wits University Press.

Nkrumah, K. (1965). *Neo-Colonialism, the Last Stage of Imperialism.* London: Thomas Nelson & Sons, Ltd.

Nyamnjoh, F. (2005). *Africa's Media Democracy and the Politics of Belonging.* London: Zed Books.

Peters, R. S. (1959). *Authority, Responsibility and Education.* London: G Allen and Unwin.

Bibliography

Abdulraheem, A. (2006, December 28). Case for Freedom of Information Law in Nigeria. *Punch Newspaper*.

Achebe, C. (1984). *The Trouble with Nigeria*. Oxford: Heinemann Publishers.

Achebe, C. (2012). *There Was a Country: A Personal History of Biafra*. London: Penguin Books.

Adebanwi, W., & Obadare, E. (2013). *Democracy and Prebendalism in Nigeria: Critical Interpretations*. New York: Palgrave Macmillan.

Adebayo, O. (2001). *West Africa's Political Economy in the Next Millennium: Retrospect and Prospect, CODESRIA Monograph Series*. Dakar: CODESRIA.

African Charter on Broadcasting. (2001). Online: http://portal.unesco.org/ci/en. Accessed 12 Jan 2010.

African Charter on Human and Peoples' Rights. (1986). Online: http://www.umn.edu/humanart. Accessed 15 Jan 2009.

Aginan, M. (2005). Media in Globalizing Africa: What Prospect for Democratic Communication? In R. Hackett & Y. Zhao (Eds.), *Democratizing Global Media One World Many Struggles*. Oxford: Rowman & Littlefield Publishers Inc.

Aguda, O. (2007). The Need for a National Conference. Online: www.hg.org. Accessed 8 Dec 2007.

Ahmed, A. (2006). Freedom of the Press and Its Constraints: A Study of Press Regulations in Bangladesh. *Canadian Journal of Media Studies, 1*(1), 1–36.

Aidan W. (2010, August 21). *Speech Delivered at the 15th GJA Awards*.

Ainslie, R. (1966). *The Press in Africa: Communications Past and Present*. London: Gollancz.

U. Akpojivi, *Media Reforms and Democratization in Emerging Democracies of Sub-Saharan Africa*,
https://doi.org/10.1007/978-3-319-75301-0

Ake, C. (1979). *Social Science as Imperialism: The Theory of Political Development.* Ibadan: Ibadan University Press.

Ake, C. (1982). *A Political Economy of Africa.* London: Longman.

Ake, C. (1991). Rethinking African Democracy. *Journal of Democracy, 2*(1), 32–44.

Ake, C. (1993). The Unique Case of African Democracy. *International Affairs, 69*(2), 239–244.

Ake, C. (1996). *Democracy and Development in Africa.* Washington DC: The Brookings Institution.

Ake, C. (2000). *The Feasibility of Democracy in Africa.* Dakar: CODESRIA.

Aker, J., & Mbiti, I. (2010). Mobile Phones and Economic Development in Africa. *Journal of Economic Prospect, 24*(3), 207–232.

Akpojivi. U. (2011, June 27). The FOI Act: Beyond the Euphoria. *Guardian Newspaper.*

Akpojivi, U. (2012). Community Radio Regulation and Its Challenges in Ghana. *Journal of African Media Studies, 4*(2), 193–207.

Akpojivi, U. (2014). Democratizing the Media in the New Democracies of Ghana and Nigeria: Challenges and Prospects. *Ecquid Novi: African Journalism Studies, 35*(3), 87–105.

Akpojivi, U., & Fosu, M. (2016). Indigenous Language Broadcasting in Ghana: Retrospect and Prospect. In A. Salawu & M. Chibita (Eds.), *Indigenous Language Media, Language Politics and Democracy in Africa.* New York: Palgrave Macmillan.

Akpore, S. (2007, April 14). Nigeria May Rule Africa's Mobile Telephone Market. *Guardian Newspaper.*

Akwule, R. (1992). *Global Telecommunications the Technology, Administration and Policies.* London: Focal Press.

Alhassan, A. (2005). Market Valorisation in Broadcasting Policy in Ghana: Abandoning the Quest for Media Democratization. *Media Culture and Society, 27*(2), 211–228.

Alhassan, A. (2006). *Broadcasting Regulation in Nigeria and the Prohibition of Live Rebroadcast of Foreign News by Local Stations.* Paper Presented at Communication Law and Policy Section of the 56th Annual Conference of the International Communication Association, Germany.

Alozieuwa, S. (2010, August 19). *Media, Ownership influence and Crisis/Conflict Situation in a Multi-Ethnic Society: Toward a Framework for Democratic Consolidation in Nigeria.* Paper Presented at Africa Media and Democracy Conference titled: *Mediating Democracy in Africa.*

Ambrose, B. (1995). *Democratization and the Protection of Human Rights in Africa: Problems and Prospects.* London: Praeger.

Amupala, J. (1989). *Development Radio in Namibia and Tanzania: A Comparative Study.* Tampere: University of Tampere Press.

Andrea, M., & Shaw, C. (2009). *Accountability and the Public Interest in Broadcasting*. London: Palgrave Macmillan.

Andsager, J., Wyatt, R., & Martin, E. (2004). *Free Expression and Five Democratic Publics Support for Individual and Media Rights*. New Jersey: Hampton Press Inc.

Anokwa, K. (1997). Press Performance Under Civilian and Military Regimes in Ghana: A Reassessment of Past and Present Knowledge. In F. Eribo & W. Jong-Ebot (Eds.), *Press Freedom and Communication in Africa*. Trenton: Africa World Press, Inc.

Ansu-Kyeremeh, K., & Karikari, K. (1998). *Media Ghana: Ghanaian Media Overview, Practitioners and Institutions*. Accra: University of Ghana Printing Press.

Anyanwu, J. (1992). President Babangida's Structural Adjustment Programme and Inflation in Nigeria. *Journal of Social Development in Africa, 7*(1), 5–24.

Arat, Z. (1988). Democracy and Economic Development: Modernization Theory Revisited. *Comparative Politics, 21*(1), 21–36.

Arthur, A. (1997, September 8–10). *Media Ownership and Control in Ghana: Past, Present and Future Perspective*. Paper Presented at the Regional Workshop on Media Ownership and Control in West and Central Africa, Yaounde.

Bacchi, C. L. (1999). *Women Policy and Politics, the Construction of Policy Problems*. London: Sage Publications.

Baker, B. (2001). Democratization in Sub-Saharan Africa. In J. Haynes (Ed.), *Towards Sustainable Democracy in the Third World*. London: Palgrave Publishers.

Baker, E. (2007). *Media Concentration and Democracy Why Ownership Matters*. Cambridge: Cambridge University Press.

Banda, F. (2010). Media Reforms in Africa – A Theoretical Commentary. In D. Moyo & W. Chuma (Eds.), *Media Policy in a Changing Southern Africa Critical Reflections on Media Reforms in the Global Age*. Pretoria: University of South Africa Press.

Bardoel, J., & d'Haenens, L. (2008). Reinventing Public Service Broadcasting in Europe: Prospects, Promises and Problems. *Media Culture and Society, 30*(3), 337–355.

Barendt, E. (1985). *Freedom of Speech*. Oxford: Clarendon Press.

Barendt, E., & Hitchens, L. (2000). *Media Law Cases and Materials*. Harlow: Pearson Longman.

Barnett, C. (1999). The Limits of Media Democratization in South Africa: Politics, Privatization and Regulation. *Media Culture & Society, 21*, 649–671.

Bayart, J. (2009). *The State in Africa: The Politics of the Belly* (2nd ed.). Cambridge: Polity Press.

Beadle, G. (1963). *Television: A Critical Review*. London: Geoge Allen & Unwin.

Benn, S., & Peters, R. (1966). The Philosophic Problem of Liberty. In P. Radcliff (Ed.), *Limits of Liberty: Studies of Mill's On Liberty*. California: Wadsworth Publishing Company Inc.

Bennett, W., & Serrin, W. (2007). The Watchdog Role of the Press. In D. A. Graber (Ed.), *Media Power in Politics*. Washington DC: CQ Press.

Berger, A. (2000). *Media and Communication Research Methods an Introduction to Qualitative and Quantitative Approaches*. London: Sage Publications.

Berger, G. (2002). Theorizing the Media-Democracy Relationship in Southern Africa. *Gazette The International Journal for Communication Studies, 64*(1), 21–45.

Berlin, I. (1966). The Notion of Negative Freedom. In P. Radcliff (Ed.), *Limits of Liberty: Studies of Mill's On Liberty*. California: Wadsworth Publishing Company Inc.

Bicket, D., & Wall, M. (2009). BBC News in the United States: A Super-alternative News Medium Emerges. *Media Culture and Society, 31*(3), 365–384.

Black, D. (1976). *The Behaviour of Law*. Bingley: Emerald Group Publishing Limited.

Blake, C. (1997). Democratization: The Dominant Imperative for National Communication Policies in Africa in the 21st Century. *Gazette, 59*(4/5), 253–269.

Blankson, I. (2007). Media Independence and Pluralism in Africa Opportunities and Challenges of Democratization and Liberalization. In I. Blankson & P. Murphy (Eds.), *Negotiating Democracy Media Transformations in Emerging Democracies*. Albany: State University of New York.

Blumler, J. (1992a). Introduction: Current Confrontations in West European Television. In J. Blumler (Ed.), *Television and the Public Interest Vulnerable Values in West European Broadcasting*. London: Sage Publications.

Blumler, J. (1992b). Public Service Broadcasting Before the Commercial Deluge. In J. Blumler (Ed.), *Television and the Public Interest Vulnerable Values in West European Broadcasting*. London: Sage Publications.

Blumler, J. (1992c). Vulnerable Values at Stake. In J. Blumler (Ed.), *Television and the Public Interest Vulnerable Values in West European Broadcasting*. London: Sage Publications.

Blumler, J., & Rien, H. (1992). Toward Renewed Public Accountability in Broadcasting. In J. Blumler (Ed.), *Television and the Public Interest Vulnerable Values in West European Broadcasting*. London: Sage Publications.

Boadi, G. (2004a). Africa: The Quality of Political Reform. In G. Boadi (Ed.), *Democratic Reform in Africa the Quality of Progress*. Colorado: Lynne Rienner Publishers Inc.

Boadi, G. (2004b). Introduction. In G. Boadi (Ed.), *Democratic Reform in Africa the Quality of Progress*. Colorado: Lynne Rienner Publishers Inc.

Boadi, G. (2009). Another Step Forward for Ghana. *Journal of Democracy, 20*(2), 138–152.

Boafo, K. (1987). Democratizing Media Systems in African Societies: The Case of Ghana. *Africa Media Review, 2*(1), 24–37.

Boafo, K. (1991). Communication Technology and Dependent Development in Sub-Saharan Africa. In G. Sussman & J. Lent (Eds.), *Transnational Communications: Wiring the Third World*. Newbury Park: Sage.

Boafo-Arthur, K. (1998). The International Community and Ghana's Transition to Democracy. In K. Ninsin (Ed.), *Ghana: Transition to Democracy*. Dakar: CODESRIA.

Bogues, A. (2012). And What About the Human? Freedom, Human Emancipation and the Radical Imagination. *Boundary, 2, 39*(3), 29–46.

Bollinger, L. (1986). *The Tolerant Society: Freedom of Speech and Extremist Speech in America*. New York: Oxford University Press.

Bourgault, L. (1993). Press Freedom in Africa: A Cultural Analysis. *Journal of Communication Inquiry, 17*(2), 69–92.

Bourgault, L. (1995). *Mass Media in Sub-Saharan Africa*. Bloomington: Indiana University Press.

Braman, S. (2006). *Change of State Information, Policy, and Power*. London: The MIT Press.

Brewer, G., & deLeon, P. (1983). *The Foundations of Policy Analysis*. Illinois: Dorsey Press.

Buckley, S., Apenteng, B., Bathily, A., & Mtimde, L. (2005). *Ghana Broadcasting Study: A Report for the Government of Ghana and the World Bank*. Online: siteresources.worldbank.org. Accessed 1 Feb 2006.

Bureau of Public Enterprises. (2010). Commercialization and Privatization Rationale. Online: www.bpeng.org/privatization. Accessed 15 Jan 2010.

Buse, K. (2008). Addressing the Theoretical, Practical and Ethical Challenges Inherent in Prospective Health Policy Analysis. *Health Policy and Planning, 23*, 351–360.

Cabral, A. (1966, January). *The Weapon of Theory*. Addressed to the First Tricontinental Conference of the peoples of Asia, Africa, and Latin America held in Havana.

Callamard, A. (2010). Accountability, Transparency, and Freedom of Expression in Africa. *Social Research, 77*(4), 1211.

Cammack, P. (1994). Political Development Theory and the Dissemination of Democracy. *Democratization, 1*(3), 353–374.

Cammaerts, B. (2011). Power Dynamics in Multi-stakeholder Policy Processes and Intra-civil Society Networking. In R. Mansell & M. Raboy (Eds.), *The Handbook of Global Media and Communication Policy*. London: Wiley-Blackwell.

Campbell, J. (2011). *Nigeria Dancing on the Brink*. New York: Rowman & Littlefield Publishers Inc.

Center for Democracy and Governance. (1998). *Democracy Dialogue*. Washington, DC: U.S. Agency for International Development.

Chakravartty, P., & Sarikakis, K. (2006). *Media Policy and Globalization*. Edinburgh: Edinburgh University Press.

Channels Television. (2017, August 23). *We now Monitor Social Media for Anti-Government and Anti-Military Information*. Online: https://www.channelstv.com/2017/08/23/now-monitor-social-media-anti-government-anti-military-information-military/

Chari, T. (2016). *Press-Citizen Interface in a Fragile Society: Mapping Press and Citizens Discourse on Election Violence* (Ph.D Thesis). University of Wit watersrand.

Chinweizu. (1999). Towards the African Renaissance Media. In M. W. Makgoba (Ed.), *African Renaissance*. Cape Town: Tafelberg Publishers Limited.

Chomsky, N. (1993). *Necessary Illusions Thought Control in Democratic Societies*. London: Pluto Press.

Chomsky, N., & Herman, E. (2002). *Manufacturing Consent: The Political Economy of the Mass Media*. New York: Pantheon Books.

Chuma, W., & Moyo, D. (2010). Policying the Media in Southern Africa in the Global Era: An Introduction. In D. Moyo & W. Chuma (Eds.), *Media Policy in a Changing Southern Africa Critical Reflections on Media Reforms in the Global Age*. Pretoria: University of South Africa Press.

Clapham, C. (1993). Democratization in Africa: Obstacles and Prospects. *Third World Quarterly, 14*(3), 423–438.

Clark, C. (2005). The Press the Founders Knew. In T. Cook (Ed.), *Freeing the Presses the First Amendment in Action*. Louisiana: Louisiana State University Press.

Coker, I. (1960). "The Nigerian Press: 1929–1959", in Committee on Inter-African Relations "Report on the Press in West Africa", prepared for the International Seminar on Press and Progress in West Africa. University of Dakar.

Coleman, S., & Ross, K. (2010). *The Media and the Public "Them and "Us" in Media Discourse"*. West Sussex: Wiley-Blackwell.

Coleman, S., Blumler, J., Dutton, W., Shipley, A., Steibel, F., & Thelwall, M. (2011). *Leaders in the Living Room The Prime Ministerial Debate of 2010: Evidence, Evaluation and Some Recommendations*. Oxford: Reuters Institute for the Study of Journalism, University of Oxford.

Committee on Inter-African Relations. (1960, May 31–June 4). Report on the Press in West Africa. Prepared for the International Seminar on Press and Progress in West Africa. University of Dakar.

Committee to Protect Journalists Reports. Online: www.cpj.org/reports/. Accessed 13 Jan 2010.

Curran, J. (1979). Press Freedom as a Property Right: The Crisis of Press Legitimacy. *Media Culture & Society, 1*, 59–82.

Cusicanqui, S. R. (2012). Ch'ixinakax utxiwa: A Reflection on the Practices and Discourse of Decolonization. *South Atlantic Quarterly., 111*(1), 95–109.

Dahl, R. (1956). *A Preface to Democratic Theory*. London: The University of Chicago Press.

Dahl, R. (1971). *Polyarchy Participation and Opposition*. London: Yale University Press.

Daily Guide. (2016). *NPP Blows Gov't Cover Over GHC449m Scandal*. Online: http://dailyguideafrica.com/npp-blows-govt-cover-gh%C2%A2449m-scandal/. Accessed 21 Sep 2017.

Daniels, G. (2012). *Fighting for Democracy: The ANC and the Media in South Africa*. Johannesburg: Wits University Press.

Davies, H., & Shields, V. (1999). Public Trust and Accountability for Clinical Performance: Lessons from the National Press Reportage of the Bristol Hearing. *Journal of Evaluation in Clinical Practice, 5*(3), 335–342.

De Gale, C. (1999). *Ghana Media Report*. Available online at: http://journ.ru.ac.ac/amd/Ghana.htm. Accessed 20 Feb 2007.

De Sola Pool, I. (1963). Mass Media and Politics in the Modernization Process. In L. Pye (Ed.), *Communications and Political Development*. Princeton: Princeton University Press.

Diamond, L. (1993). Introduction: Political Culture and Democracy. In L. Diamond (Ed.), *Political Culture and Democracy in Developing Countries*. London: Lynne Rienner Publishers.

Diamond, L. (2008a). Consolidating Democracy. In L. LeDUC, R. Niemi, & P. Norris (Eds.), *Comparing Democracies 2 New Challenges in the Study of Elections and Voting*. London: Sage Publications.

Diamond, L. (2008b). Progress and Retreat in Africa the Rule of Law Verse the Big Man. *Journal of Democracy, 19*, 138–149.

Diamond, L., Greene, A., & Oyediran, O. (1997). The Politics of Transition Without End. In L. Diamond, A. Greene, & O. Oyediran (Eds.), *Transition Without End: Nigerian Politics and Civil Society Under Babangida*. London: Lynne Rienner Publisher.

Donkor, P. (2007). *Self Censorship in Ghana Broadcasting Corporation (GBC)* (M. A. Dissertation). University of Leeds.

Duke, D. (2017, September 30). *Hard Copy*. Channels TV.

Duncan, J. (2014). A Political Economy of the Press Self-Regulation: The Case of South Africa. *Media, Culture and Society, 36*(2), 167–182.

Dunn, H. (2011). ICT Policy-making and International Trade Agreements in the Caribbean. In R. Mansell & M. Raboy (Eds.), *The Handbook of Global Media and Communication Policy*. West Sussex: Wiley-Blackwell.

Ebo, L. (1994). The Ethical Dilemma of African Journalists: A Nigerian Perspective. *Journal of Mass Media Ethics, 9*(2), 84–93.

Edetaen, O. (2009). Paper Presented at the Awareness Seminar on the Press Ombudsman organized by the Newspaper Proprietors' Association of Nigeria (NPAN), in association with the Nigeria Union of Journalists (NUJ), the Nigerian Guild of Editors (NGE) and other stakeholders.

EFA Global Monitoring Report. (2011). *The Hidden Crisis Armed Conflict and Education*. Paris: UNESCO.

Ekpu, R. (1990). Nigeria's Embattled Fourth Estate. *Journal of Democracy, 1*(2), 106–116.

Emerson, T. (1982). The First Amendment in the Year 2000. In S. Halpern (Ed.), *The Future of Our Liberties: Perspectives on the Bill of Rights.* Westport CT: Greenwood.

Entman, R. (1989). *Democracy Without Citizens Media and the Decay of American Politics.* Oxford: Oxford University Press.

Eribo, F. (1997). Internal and External Factors Affecting Press Freedom in Nigeria. In F. Eribo & W. Jong-Ebot (Eds.), *Press Freedom and Communication in Africa.* Trenton: Africa World Press Inc.

Eribo, F., & Jong-Ebot, W. (1997). *Press Freedom and Communication in Africa.* Trenton: Africa World Press Inc.

Ette, M. (2000). Agent of Change or Stability? The Nigerian Press Undermines Democracy. *The Harvard International Journal of Press/Politics, 5*(3), 67–86.

Federal Government of Nigeria. (1987). *Nigeria Mass Communication Policy.* Lagos: Federal Government Press.

Federal Government of Nigeria. (1990). *Official Secret Act.* Lagos: Federal Government Press.

Federal Government of Nigeria. (1999a). *1999 Constitution of the Federal Republic of Nigeria.* Lagos: Federal Government Press.

Federal Government of Nigeria. (1999b). *Nigeria Criminal Code.* Lagos: Federal Government Press.

Federal Government of Nigeria. (1999c). *National Broadcasting Commission Act No. 55.* Lagos: Federal Government Press.

Federal Government of Nigeria. (2011). *Freedom of Information Act.* Lagos: Federal Government Press.

Federal Republic of Nigeria. (1999). *The Nigeria Press Council Act.* Lagos: Federal Government Press.

Feintuck, M. (1999). *Media Regulation, Public Interest and the Law.* Edinburgh: Edinburgh University Press.

Findahl, O. (1999). Public Service Broadcasting – A Fragile, Yet Durable Construction. *Nordicom Review, 20*(1), 13–19.

Fiss, O. (1990). Why the State. In J. Lichtenberg (Ed.), *Democracy and the Mass Media.* Cambridge: Cambridge University Press.

Fosu, M., & Akpojivi, U. (2015). Media Convergence Practices and Production in Ghana and Nigeria: Implications for Democracy and Research in Africa. *Journal of Applied Journalism and Media Studies, 4*(2), 277–292.

Freedman, D. (2008). *The Politics of Media Policy.* Cambridge: Polity Press.

Freedom House, Ghana Report 2007. Online: www.freedomhouse.org. Accessed 12 Mar 2009.

Freedom House, Nigeria Report 2007. Online: www.freedomhouse.org. Accessed 12 Mar 2009.

Freedom House, Nigeria Report 2008. Online: www.freedomhouse.org. Accessed 12 Mar 2009.

Freedom House Report on Ghana 2008. Online: www.freedomhouse.org. Accessed 12 Jan 2009.

GBC News. (2010). *GBC Celebrates 75th Anniversary.* Accra: GBC.

Ghana Journalists Association. (1994). *GJA Code of Ethics.* Accra: GJA.

Ghana Web. (2009). Online: www.ghanaweb.com. Accessed 12 Jan 2009.

Ghana Web. (2010). Online: www.ghanaweb.com. Accessed 20 Jan 2010.

Gilson, L., & Erasmus, E. (2008). How to Start Thinking About Investigating Power in the Organizational Settings of Policy Implementation. *Health Policy and Planning, 23*(5), 361–368.

Gilson, L., & Raphaely, N. (2008). The Terrain of Health Policy Analysis in Low and Middle Income Counties: A Review of Published Literature 1994–2007. *Health Policy and Planning, 23*, 294–307.

Golding, P., & Murdock, G. (1986). The New Communications Revolution. In J. Curran, J. Ecclestone, G. Oakley, & A. Richardson (Eds.), *Bending Reality the State of the Media.* London: Pluto Press.

Government of Ghana. (1993). *National Media Commission Act 1993.* Accra: Government Printers.

Government of Ghana. (1996). *National Communication Authority Act 524.* Accra: Government Printers.

Graber, D. (2002). *Mass Media and American Politics.* Washington DC: CQ Press.

Graber, D., McQuail, D., & Norris, P. (1998). Political Communication in Democracy. In D. Graber, D. McQuail, & P. Norris (Eds.), *The Politics of News, the News of Politics.* Washington DC: CQ Press.

Gunaratne, S. (2002). Freedom of the Press: A World System Perspective. *International Communication Gazette, 64*(4), 343–369.

Hachten, W. (1971). *Muffled Drums: The News Media in Africa.* Ames: Iowa State University Press.

Hachten, W. (1987). *The World News Prism: Changing Media, Clashing Ideologies* (2nd ed.). Ames: Iowa State University Press.

Hachten, W. (1993). *The Growth of Media in the Third World: African Failures, Asian Successes.* Ames: Iowa State University Press.

Haggard, S., & Kaufman, R. (1997). The Political Economy of Democratic Transitions. *Comparative Politics, 29*(3), 263–283.

Hasty, J. (2005). *The Press and Political Culture in Ghana.* Indiana: Indiana University Press.

Hayman, G., & Tomaselli, R. (1989). *Studies on the South African Media Broadcasting in the South Africa.* London: James Currey Ltd.

Haynes, J. (2001a). Sustainable Democracy in the Third World. In J. Haynes (Ed.), *Towards Sustainable Democracy in the Third world.* London: Palgrave Publishers.

Haynes, J. (2001b). Conclusion. In J. Haynes (Ed.), *Towards Sustainable Democracy in the Third World*. London: Palgrave Publishers.
Heath, C. (1999). Negotiating Broadcasting Policy Civil Society and Civil Discourse in Ghana. *International Communication Gazette, 61*(6), 511–521.
Hegel. (1896). *Hegel's Philosophy of Right*. (S. W. Dyde, Trans.). London: George Bell and Sons.
Henckes, R. (2016). *#Accountability? The Changing Dynamics of Political Accountability Through Social Media in Nigeria* (Bachelor Thesis). Leiden University.
Henten, A., Falch, M., & Anyimadu, A. (2004). Telecommunications Development in Africa: Filling the Gap. *Telematics and Informatics, 21*(1), 1–9.
Higgins, M. (2008). *Media and Their Public*. Berkshire: Open University Press.
Hill, M. (2005). *The Public Policy Process* (4th ed.). London: Pearson Longman.
Holmes, S. (1990). Liberal Constraints on Private Power?: Reflections on the Origins and Rationale of Access Regulation. In J. Lichtenberg (Ed.), *Democracy and the Mass Media*. Cambridge: Cambridge University Press.
Holmes, S. (1995). *Passion and Constraint on the Theory of Liberal Democracy*. London: University of Chicago Press Ltd.
Humphreys, P. (1996). *Mass Media and Media Policy in Western Europe*. Manchester: Manchester University Press.
Huntington, S. (1991). *The Third Wave: Democratization in the Late Twentieth Century*. Norman: University of Oklahoma Press.
Hutchison, D. (1999). *Media Policy: An Introduction*. Oxford: Blackwell Publishers.
Hyden, G., & Okigbo, C. (2002). The Media and the Two Waves of Democracy. In G. Hyden, M. Leslie, & F. Ogundimu (Eds.), *Media and Democracy in Africa*. New Brunswick: Transaction Publishers.
IFEX. (2011). *Freedom of Information Law Is a Victory for Democracy*. Online: www.ifex.org. Accessed 2 June 2011.
Ifidon, E. (2002). Transitions from Democracy in Nigeria: Toward a Pre-emptive Analysis. *African Journal of Political Science, 7*(1), 109–128.
Iriekpen, D. (2010, July 27). Court Declares Press Council Law Oppressive. *This Day Newspaper*.
Jacobson, T. (2004). Participatory Communication for Development and the African Philosophy Debate. In C. Okigbo & F. Eribo (Eds.), *Development and Communication in Africa*. Boulevard: Rowman & Littlefield Publishers, Inc.
Jakubowicz, K. (2002). Media in Transition the Case of Poland. In M. Price, B. Rozumilowicz, & S. Verhulst (Eds.), *Media Reform Democratizing the Media, Democratizing the State*. London: Routledge.
Jebuni, C., & Oduro, A. (1998). Structural Adjustment Programme and the Transition to Democracy. In K. Ninsin (Ed.), *Ghana: Transition to Democracy*. Dakar: CODESRIA.
Jeffrey, H. (2000). Understanding Ambiguity During Democratization in Africa. In J. Hollified & C. Jillson (Eds.), *Pathways to Democracy: The Political Economy of Democratic Transition*. London: Routledge.

Jensen, M. (2001). *Afriboxes, Telecenters, Cybercafes: ICT in Africa, No 1.* Online: http://tedd.undp.org/coopsouth/2001_oct/097-109.pdf. Accessed 16 May 2007.

Jibo, M., & Okoosi, A. (2003). The Nigerian Media: An Assessment of Its Role in Achieving Transparent and Accountable Government in the Fourth Republic. *Nordic Journal of African Studies, 12*(2), 180–195.

Jones-Quartey, K. (1960). "The Ghana Press", in Committee on Inter-African Relations "*Report on the Press in West Africa*", Prepared for the International Seminar on Press and Progress in West Africa. University of Dakar.

Kafewo, S. (2006). *Ghana Research Findings and Conclusions in African Media Development Initiative.* London: BBC World Service Trust.

Kant, I. (1934). *Critique of Pure Reason.* London: Orion Publishing Group.

Kareithi, P., & Kariithi, N. (2005). Introduction. In P. Kareithi & N. Kariithi (Eds.), *Untold Stories Economics and Business Journalism in African Media.* Johannesburg: Wits University Press.

Karikari, K. (1994). *Independent Broadcasting in Ghana: Implications and Challenges: Proceedings of the National Conference on the Promotion and Privatization of Radio and Television Broadcasting in Ghana.* Accra: Ghana University Press.

Karikari, K. (1998). The Press and the Transition to Multi-Party Democracy in Ghana. In K. Ninsin (Ed.), *Ghana: Transition to Democracy.* Dakar: CODESRIA.

Keane, J. (1991). *The Media and Democracy.* Cambridge: Polity Press.

Kelley, D., & Donway, R. (1990). Liberalism and Free Speech. In J. Lichtenberg (Ed.), *Democracy and the Mass Media.* Cambridge: Cambridge University Press.

Kendall, W. (1966). The Open Society and Its Fallacies. In P. Radcliff (Ed.), *Limits of Liberty: Studies of Mill's On Liberty.* California: Wadsworth Publishing Company Inc.

Kwame, K. (2004). Press Freedom in Africa Challenges and Opportunities. *New Economy.*

LaMay, C. (2007). *Exporting Press Freedom Economic and Editorial Dilemmas in International Media Assistance.* London: Transaction Publishers.

Lasorsa, D. (1997). Agenda Setting and Press Performance: A Social System Approach for Building Theory. In M. McCombs, D. Shaw, & D. Weaver (Eds.), *Communication and Democracy Exploring the Intellectual Frontiers in Agenda Setting Theory.* London: Lawrence Erlbaum Associates Publishers.

Lasswell, H. (1948). *The Structure and Function of Communication and Society: The Communication of Ideas.* New York: Institute for Religious and Social Studies.

Lasswell, H. (1956). *The Decision Process: Seven Categories of Functional Analysis.* College Park: Bureau of Governmental Research: University of Maryland.

Leftwich, A. (1993). Governance, Democracy and Development in the Third World. *Third World Quarterly, 14*(3), 605–624.

Lerner, D. (1958). *The Passing of Traditional Society*. Glencoe: Free Press.

Levi, A. (1966). The Value of Freedom: Mill's Liberty (1859–1959). In P. Radcliff (Ed.), *Limits of Liberty: Studies of Mill's On Liberty*. Belmont: Wadsworth Publishing Company Inc.

Levine, R. (1971). Dreams and Deeds: Achievement Motivation in Nigeria. In R. Melson & H. Wolpe (Eds.), *Nigeria: Moderization and Politics of Communicalism*. East Lansing: Michigan State University Press.

Levitt, R. (1980). *Implementing Public Policy*. London: Croom Helm Ltd.

Levitsky, S., & Way, L. (2010). Why Democracy Needs a Level Playing Field. *Journal of Democracy, 21*(1), 57–68.

Lewis, T. (2004). Democracy, Free Speech and TV: The Cases of BBC and Profile Alliance. *Web Journal of Current Legal Issues*, 1–21.

Lewis, P. (2006). Community Media: Giving a Voice to the Voiceless. In P. Lewis & S. Jones (Eds.), *From the Margins to the Cutting Edge Community Media and Empowerment*. New Jersey: Hampton Press Inc.

Lichtenberg, J. (1990a). Introduction. In J. Lichtenberg (Ed.), *Democracy and the Mass Media*. Cambridge: Cambridge University Press.

Lichtenberg, J. (1990b). Foundations and Limits of Freedom of the Press. In J. Lichtenberg (Ed.), *Democracy and the Mass Media*. Cambridge: Cambridge University Press.

Linz, J., & Stepan, A. (1996). *Problems of Democratic Transition and Consolidation: Southern Europe, South America, and Post-Communist Europe*. Baltimore: Johns Hopkins University Press.

Mabadeje, I. (2004). *The Nigerian Press Under the Military: A Compendium of Cases of Press Freedom Violations in Nigeria (1966–1999)*. Uyo: Robertminder International Ltd.

Macbridge Report. (1980). Many Voices One World. Online: www.unesco.org. Accessed 12 Oct 2007.

Mackay, I. (1964). *Broadcasting in Nigeria*. Ibadan: Ibadan University Press.

Mahmoud, E. (2008). *Interweavement International Media Ethics and Rational Decision-Making*. New York: Custom Publishing.

Mandela, N. (1990). African National Congress. *Journal of Democracy, 1*(4), 32–35.

Mano, W. (2011). Why Radio Is Africa's Medium of Choice in the Global Age. In L. Gunner, D. Ligaga, & D. Moyo (Eds.), *Radio in Africa: Publics, Cultures, Communities*. Johannesburg: Wits University Press.

Mansell, R., & Raboy, M. (2011). Introduction: Foundations of the Theory and Practice of Global Media and Communication Policy. In R. Mansell & M. Raboy (Eds.), *The Handbook of Global Media and Communication Policy*. London: Wiley-Blackwell.

Manyozo, L. (2011). Rethinking Communication for Development Policy: Some Considerations. In R. Mansell & M. Raboy (Eds.), *The Handbook of Global Media and Communication Policy*. London: Wiley-Blackwell.

Marcuse, H. (1969). Repressive Tolerance. In R. Wolff & H. Marcuse (Eds.), *A Critique of Pure Tolerance*. London: Beacon Press.
Mbembe, A. (2017). *Critique of Black Reasoning*. Johannesburg: Wits University Press.
McChesney, R. (2002). *Our Media Not Theirs: The Democratic Struggle Against Corporate Media*. New York: Seven Stories Press.
McChesney, R. (2008). *The Political Economy of the Media, Enduring Issues, Emerging Dilemmas*. New York: Monthly Review Press.
McLuhan, M. (1964). *McLuhan Understanding Media*. London: Routledge.
McQuail, D. (1992). *Media Performance Mass Communication and the Public Interest*. London: Sage Publication.
McQuail, D. (2003). *Media Accountability and Freedom of Publication*. Oxford: Oxford University Press.
McQuail, D. (2005). *McQuail's Mass Communication Theory* (5th ed.). London: Sage Publications.
MDG's. Online: www.un.org/milleuniumgoals/. Accessed 14 Jan 2011.
Media Foundation for West Africa. (2008). *Media Alert West Africa 2008: Annual State of the Media Report*. Accra: Media Foundation for West Africa.
Media Rights Agenda. (2002a). *Print Monitor Report 2002*. Lagos: Media Rights Agenda.
Media Rights Agenda. (2002b). *Airwaves Monitor Report 2002*. Lagos: Media Rights Agenda.
Media Rights Agenda & Article 19. (2001). Broadcasting in Nigeria: Unlocking The Airwaves Report on the Framework for Broadcasting and Telecommunications in Nigeria. Lagos.
Media Sustainability Index. *Africa 2006–2007 Nigeria*. Lagos: IREX.
Meier, W., & Trappel, J. (2002). Media Concentration and the Public Interest. In D. McQuail & K. Siune (Eds.), *Media Policy Convergence, Concentration and Commerce*. London: Sage Publications.
Meiklejohn, A. (1966). Freedom of Speech. In P. Radcliff (Ed.), *Limits of Liberty: Studies of Mill's On Liberty*. Belmont: Wadsworth Publishing Company.
Meiklejohn, A. (2004). *Free Speech and Its Relation to Self-Government*. New Jersey: The Lawbook Exchange, Ltd.
Melkote, S., & Steeves, L. (2001). *Communication for Development in the Third World Theory and Practice for Empowerment* (2nd ed.). London: Sage Publication.
Melody, W. (2011). Whose Global Village? In R. Mansell & M. Raboy (Eds.), *The Handbook of Global Media and Communication Policy*. London: Wiley-Blackwell.
Mgbejume, O. (1991). Constraints on Mass Media Policies in Nigeria. *Africa Media Review, 5*(2), 47–57.
Mill, S. J. (1869). *On Liberty* (4th ed.). London: Longman.
Mill, S. J. (1974). *On Liberty*. London: Penguin Group.

Milton, A. (2000). *The Rational Politician Exploiting the Media in New Democracies*. Aldershot: Ashgate.
Mingjiang, L. (2008). China Debates Soft Power. *The Chinese Journal of International Politics, 2*(2), 287–308.
Ministry of Communication Federal Republic of Nigeria. (2000). *National Policy on Telecommunication*. Abuja: Federal Government Press.
Ministry of Communication Republic of Ghana. (2004). *National Telecommunication Policy*. Accra: Government Printers.
Mosaka, N., & Kamaimba, E. (1998). Botswana. In A. Opoku-Mensah et al. (Eds.), *Up in the Air? The State of Broadcasting in Southern Africa analysis & Trend in Six Countries*. Harare: PANOS.
Moyer, B. (2008, July 11). Is the Fourth Estate a Fifth Column?: Corporate Media Colludes with Democracy's Demise. *In These Times*.
Musa, M., & Mohammed, J. (2004). The Political Economy of Media Ownership in Nigeria. In T. Pradip & Z. Nain (Eds.), *Who Owns the Media Global Trends and Local Resistances*. London: Zed Books.
National Broadcasting Commission. (2006). *Nigeria Broadcasting Code*. Abuja: Regent.
National Communication Authority. (2007). *Guidelines for Operation of Community Radio Stations in Ghana*. Accra: National Communication Authority.
National Communication Authority. (2008). *Annual Report 2008*. Accra: NCA.
National Media Commission. (2000). *Ghana National Media Policy*. Accra: NMC.
National Media Commission. (2006a). *Ghana Media Review: Media Monitoring Report*. Accra: National Media Commission.
National Media Commission. (2006b). *Media and National Development: Proceedings of a Two Day Conference*. Accra: National Media Commission.
National Media Commission. (2009). *Guidelines for Local Language Broadcasting*. Accra: National Media Commission.
NBC. (2009a). Management Structure of the National Broadcasting Commission. Online: www.nbc.gov.ng. Accessed 28 Nov 2009.
NBC. (2009b). Online: www.nbc.gov.ng. Accessed 23 Dec 2008.
NBC. (2010). *NBC Vs AIT: Restraining Order Lapses*. Online: www.nbc.gov.ng. Accessed 10 Feb 2010.
NCA. (2009). *Organisational Structure of National Communication Authority*. Online: http://www.nca.org.gh. Accessed 28 Nov 2009.
NCC. (2010). Online: www.ncc.gov.ng. Accessed 2 Feb 2010.
NCC. (2011). *Industry Performance 2011*. Online: www.ncc.gov.ng/industry-statistic. Accessed 12 Dec 2011.
Neocosmos, M. (2016). *Thinking Freedom in Africa: Toward a Theory of Emancipatory Politics*. Johannesburg: Wits University Press.
Net2 Group of Companies. Online: www.net2tv.kencity.com.gh. Accessed 28 Jan 2011.

Netshitenzhe, J. (2002). *Should the Media Serve the Public or National Interest?*", presentation to the Goedgedacht Forum for Social Reflection, Cape Town. www.gcis.gov.za.

Next Newspaper. (2011, June 3). *Next Editorial Freedom at Last.*

Ngugi, W. (2017, March 2). *Secure the Base: Decolonising the Mind.* Lecture at the University of the Witwatersrand.

Nigeria Press and Practice of Journalism Council Bill. (2009). Abuja: National Assembly.

Nigeria Union of Journalists. (1998). *Code of Ethics for Nigerian Journalists.* Asokoro: Nigerian Press Council.

Ninsin, K. (1998). Civic Associations and the Transition to Democracy. In K. Ninsin (Ed.), *Ghana: Transition to Democracy.* Dakar: CODESRIA.

Nkrumah, K. (1965). *Neo-Colonialism, the Last Stage of Imperialism.* London: Thomas Nelson & Sons, Ltd.

NMC. (2009). *Management Structure of the National Media Commission.* Online: www.nmcghana.org. Accessed 28 Nov 2009.

Nordenstreng, K. (2011). Free Flow Doctrine in Global Media Policy. In R. Mansell & M. Raboy (Eds.), *The Handbook of Global Media and Communication Policy.* London: Wiley Blackwell.

Nordenstreng, K., & Schiller, H. (1993). *Beyond National Sovereignty: International Communication in the 1990s.* Norwood: Ablex Publishers.

NPC. (1991). *1991 Summary of Census.* Online: www.population.gov.ng. Accessed 21 Nov 2009.

Nyamnjoh, F. (2003). *Media Pluralism and Diversity: A Critical Review of Competing Models.* In Broadcasting Policy and Practice in Africa by Article 19.

Nyamnjoh, F. (2004). Media Ownership and Control in Africa in the Age of Globalization. In T. Pradip & Z. Nain (Eds.), *Who Owns the Media Global Trends and Local Resistances.* London: Zed Books.

Nyamnjoh, F. (2005). *Africa's Media Democracy and the Politics of Belonging.* London: Zed Books.

Nyarko, J., & Akpojivi, U. (2017). Intimidation, Assault, and Violence Against Media Practioners in Ghana: Considering Provocation. *Sage Open, 7*(1), 1–12.

Nyerere, J. (2000). *Africa Today and Tomorrow.* Dar Es Salaam: Mwalimu Nyerere Foundation.

Obadare, E. (2006). Playing Politics with the Mobile Phone in Nigeria: Civil Society, Big Business and the State. *Review of African Political Economy, 33*(107), 93–111.

Ochere-Darko, G. (2010, August 19). *Speech delivered at the Africa Media Democracy Conference Accra.*

Ocitti, J. (1999). *Media and Democracy in Africa Mutual Political Bedfellows or Implacable Arch-Foes.* Cambridge: Weatherhead Center for International Affairs.

Ogbondah, C. (2004). Democratization and the Media in West Africa: An Analysis of Recent Constitutional and Legislative Reforms for Press Freedom in Ghana and Nigeria. *West Africa Review, 6*, 1–36.

Ogbondah, C., & Onyedike, E. (1991). Origins and Interpretation of Nigerian Press Laws. *Africa Media Review, 5*(2), 59–70.

Ojo, E. (2003). The Mass Media and the Challenges of Sustainable Democratic Values in Nigeria: Possibilities and Limitations. *Media Culture & Society, 25*(6), 821–840.

Ojo, T. (2004). Old Paradigm and Information & Communication Technologies for Development Agenda in Africa: Modernization as Context. *Journal of Information Technology Impact, 4*(3), 821–840.

Okigbo, C., & Eribo, F. (2004). *Development and Communication in Africa*. Oxford: Rowman & Littlefield.

Okonjo-Iweala, N. (2012). *Reforming the Unreformable: Lessons from Nigeria*. Cambridge: MIT Press.

Okwori, Z., & Adeyanju, A. (2006). *African Media Development Initiative Nigeria Research Findings and Conclusions*. London: BBC World Service Trust.

Olagunju, T., Jinadu, A., & Oyovbaire, S. (1993). *Transition to Democracy in Nigeria (1985–1993)*. Ibadan: Safari Books Limited.

Olumhense, S. (2010). *The Nigeria Mass Media on Trail*. Online: www.saharare-porter.com/column. Accessed 21 Mar 2010.

Olutokun, A., & Seteolu, D. (2001). The Media and Democratic Rule in Nigeria. *Development Policy Management Network Bulletin, 13*(3), 1–8.

Oluwadare, J. (2007). *Amendment of the Nigerian Constitution*. Online: www.hg.org/article. Accessed 12 Jan 2010.

Onwumechili, C. (2007). Nigeria: Equivocating While Opening the Broadcast Liberalization Gates. In I. Blankson & P. Murphy (Eds.), *Negotiating Democracy Media Transformations in Emerging Democracies*. Albany: State University of New York.

Opoku-Mensah, A. (1998). *Up in the Air? The State of Broadcasting in Southern Africa. Analysis and Trend in Six Countries*. South Africa: PANOS.

Ororunyomi, D. (2017, November 9). The Level of Bribery in Journalism Today Is Worse Than the Police. *Sahara Reporters*.

Osaghae, E. (1998). *Nigeria Since Independence: Crippled Giant*. Bloomington: Indiana University Press.

Owens-Ibie, N. (1994). Press Responsibility and Public Opinion in Political Transition. *Africa Media Review, 8*(1), 69–80.

Packenham, R. (1973). *Liberal America and the Third World: Political Development Ideas in Foreign Aid and Social Science*. New Jersey: Princeton University Press.

Paterson, C. (1994b, August). *Broadcasting for National Development in the New South Africa*. Presented to the International Division of the Association for Education in Journalism and Mass Communication.

Paterson, C. (1998). Reform or Re-Colonisation? The Overhaul of African Television. *Review of African Political Economy, 25*(78), 571–583.

Patterson, T. (2000). The United States: News in a Free Market Society. In R. Gunther & A. Mughan (Eds.), *Democracy and the Media: A Comparative Perspective*. Cambridge: Cambridge University Press.

Peters, R. S. (1959). *Authority, Responsibility and Education*. London: G Allen and Unwin.

Pillai, M. (1999–2000). Freedom of the Press: Is the Western Press Listening to its colleagues in the Third World Countries? *Nieman Report*, 53/54.

Population Service International. (2004). www.psi.org. Accessed 20 Jan 2010.

Press Reference. (2007). *Ghana Press, Media, TV, Radio, Newspapers*. Online: www.pressreference.com/Fa-GU/Ghana.html. Accessed 13 Mar 2009.

Price, M. (1998). Free Media Depends on Laws, Institutions, and Culture. In *Democracy Dialogue*. Pennsylvania: USAID's Centre for Democracy and Governance.

Price, M. (2002a). *Media and Sovereignty the Global Information Revolution and Its Challenge to State Power*. Cambridge: MIT Press.

Price, M. (2002b). Bosnia-Hercegovina and Post-conflict Media Restructuring. In M. Price, B. Rozumilowicz, & S. Verhulst (Eds.), *Media Reform Democratizing the Media, Democratizing the State*. London: Routledge.

Price, M. (2010, July 4–17). *Lecture on Strategic Communication and Media Freedom*, at the 6th Annenberg/Oxford Summer Institute in Global Media Policy.

Price, M., & Verhulst, S. (2000). Introduction. In M. Price & S. Verhulst (Eds.), *Broadcasting Reform in India Media Law from a Global Perspective*. Oxford: Oxford University Press.

Price, M., Rozumilowicz, B., & Verhulst, S. (2002). Introduction. In M. Price, B. Rozumilowicz, & S. Verhulst (Eds.), *Media Reform Democratizing the Media, Democratizing the State*. London: Routledge.

Price, M., Al-Marashi, I., & Stremlau, N. (2010). Media in the Peace-Building Process: Ethiopia and Iraq. In P. Norris (Ed.), *Public Sentinel: News Media and Governance Reform*. Washington DC: World Bank Publications.

Radcliff, P. (1966). Introduction. In P. Radcliff (Ed.), *Limits of Liberty: Studies of Mill's On Liberty*. Belmont: Wadsworth Publishing Company Inc.

Radelet, S. (2010). Success Stories from Emerging Africa. *Journal of Democracy, 21*(4), 87–101.

Randall, V. (1993). The Media and Democratization in the Third World. *Third World Quarterly, 14*(3), 625–646.

Report of the African Regional Conference for WSIS Tunis 2005. Online: http://www.itu.int/wsis/documents/index.html. Accessed 12 Oct 2007.

Republic of Ghana. (1992). *The Constitution of the Republic of Ghana 1992*. Accra: Government Printers.

Republic of Ghana. (1993). *The National Media Commission Act 449*. Accra: Government Printers.

Republic of Ghana. (1996). *National Communication Authority Act 524*. Accra: Government Printers.

Republic of Ghana. (2003). *The Ghana ICT for Accelerated Development {ICT4AD} Policy*. Accra: Government Printers.

Republic of Ghana. (2006). *Whistleblower Act 720*. Accra: Government Printers.

Richards, D. (1999). *Free Speech and the Politics of Identity*. Oxford: Oxford University Press.

Riley, J. (1998). *Routledge Philosophy Guidebook to Mill On Liberty*. London: Routledge.

Rogers, E. (1962). *The Diffusion of Innovations*. New York: Free Press.

Ronning, H., & Kupe, T. (2000). The Dual Legacy of Democracy and Authoritarianism: The Media and the State in Zimbabwe. In J. Curran & M. Jin-Park (Eds.), *De-Westernising Media Studies*. London: Routledge.

Ross, C. (1998). Joseph Sax and the Idea of the Public Trust. *Ecology Law Quarterly, 25*(351), 351–362.

Rozumilowicz, B. (2002). Democratic Change: A Theoretical Perspective. In M. Price, B. Rozumilowicz, & S. Verhulst (Eds.), *Media Reform Democratizing the Media, Democratizing the State*. London: Routledge.

RSF Report. (2011). Online: www.en.rsf.org/ghana. Accessed 6 Aug 2011.

Scanlon, T. (1990). Content Regulation Reconsidered. In J. Lichtenberg (Ed.), *Democracy and the Mass Media*. Cambridge: Cambridge University Press.

Schiller, H. (1976). *Communication and Cultural Domination*. New York: White Plains.

Shugerman, E. (2017, October 12). US Withdraws from UNESCO Over 'Anti-Israel Bias'. *Independent Newspaper*.

Silverstone, R. (1999). *Why Study the Media?* London: Sage Publications.

Stringer, R. (2014). *The Power of Talk Media Accountability in Three African Countries*. London: BBC.

Taylor, P. (1997). *Global Communications, International Affairs and the Media Since 1945*. London: Routledge.

Teeter, D., & Loving, B. (2004). *Law of Mass Communications Freedom and Control of Print and Broadcast Media* (11th ed.). New York: Foundation Press.

Tettey, W. (2001). The Media and Democratization in Africa: Contributions, Constraints and Concerns of the Private Press. *Media Culture & Society, 23*(1), 5–32.

Tettey, W. (2006). The Politics of Media Accountability in Africa: An Examination of Mechanisms and Institutions. *International Communication Gazette, 68*(3), 229–248.

Thapisa, A., & Birabwa, E. (1998). Mapping Africa's Initiative at Building an Information and Communications Infrastructure. *Internet Research, 8*(1), 49–58.

The African Preparatory Conference for the WSIS Tunis 2005. Online: http://www.undp.org. Accessed 23 Jan 2009.

Thussu, D. (2000). *International Communication Continuity and Change*. London: Arnold.

Tom, D. (2004). The Watchdog Inside a Cage: The Nigerian Press and Censorship Laws. *Ethiope Research Abraka Journal of the Arts, Law and Social Sciences, 1*(2), 91–118.

Tomaselli, K. (2009). Repositioning African Media Studies: Thoughts and Provocation. *Journal of African Media Studies, 1*(1), 9–21.

Tomaselli, K., & Tomaselli, R. (1989). Between Policy and Practice in the SABC 1970–1981. In R. Tomaselli, K. Tomaselli, & J. Muller (Eds.), *Studies on the South African Media Broadcasting in South Africa*. London: James Currey Ltd.

Tudesq, A. (1983). *La Radio en Afriqua Noire*. Paris: Editions A. Pedone.

Tudesq, A. (1992). *L'Afrique Noire et ses Television*. Paris: Anthropos.

Tunstall, J. (1977). *The Media Are American*. New York: Columbia University Press.

Ugboajah, F. (1985). *Mass Communication, Culture, and Society in West Africa*. Munich: Hans Zell.

Ugboajah, F. (1986). Communication as Technology in Africa Rural Development. *Africa Media Review, 1*(1), 1–19.

Umeh, C. (1989). The Advent and Growth of Television Broadcasting in Nigeria: Its Political and Education Overtones. *Africa Media Review, 3*(2), 54–66.

UNESCO. (2007a). *UIS Statistics in Brief Ghana*. Online: http://stats.uis.unesco.org. Accessed 1 Aug 2009.

UNESCO. (2007b). *UIS Statistics in Brief Education in Nigeria*. Online: http://stats.uis.unesco.org. Accessed 1 Aug 2009.

Ungar, S. (1990). The Role of a Free Press in Strengthening Democracy. In J. Lichtenberg (Ed.), *Democracy and the Mass Media*. Cambridge: Cambridge University Press.

United Nations Development Programme Report 2004. Online: http://www.undp.org. Accessed 23 Jan 2009.

Universal Declaration of Human Rights (1948). Online: http://www.un.org/en/documents/udhr. Accessed 12 Oct 2009.

Van Belle, D. (2000). *Press Freedom and Global Politics*. WestPoint: C.T. Praeger.

Vanguard Newspaper. (2010, August 6). Nigerian Press Council Act Violates rights of Free Speech.

Voltmer, K. (2006). The Mass Media and the Dynamics of Political Communication in Processes of Democratization: An Introduction. In K. Voltmer (Ed.), *Mass Media and Political Communication in New Democracies*. London: Routledge.

Voltmer, K. (2008). Comparing Media Systems in New Democracies: East Meets South Meets West. *Central European Journal of Communication, 1*, 23–40.

Wahl-Jorgensen, K. (2007). *Journalists and the Public Newsroom Culture, Letters to the Editor and Democracy*. New Jersey: Hampton Press Inc.

Walt, G. (1999). Implementing Health Care Reform: A Framework for Discussion. In R. Saltman, J. Figueras, & C. Sakellarides (Eds.), *Critical Challenges for Health Care Reform in Europe*. Philadelphia: Open University Press.

Walt, G., & Gilson, L. (1994). Reforming the Health Sector in Developing Countries: The Central Role of Policy Analysis. *Health Policy and Planning, 9*(4), 353–370.

Walt, G., Shiffman, J., Schneider, H., Murray, S., Brugha, R., & Gilson, L. (2008). Doing Health Policy Analysis: Methodological and Conceptual Reflections and Challenges. *Health Policy and Planning, 23*, 308–317.

WarD, D. (2003). State Aid or Band Aid? An Evaluation of the European Commission's Approach to Public Service Broadcasting. *Media Culture & Society, 25*(2), 233–250.

Wasserman, H., & Boloka, M. (2004). Privacy, the Press and the Public Interest in Post-Apartheid South Africa. *Parliamentary Affairs, 57*(1), 185–195.

Wasserman, H., & de Beer, A. (2006). Conflicts of Interest? Debating the Media's Role in Post Apartheid South Africa. In K. Voltmer (Ed.), *Mass Media and Political Communication in New Democracies*. London: Routledge.

West, H., & Fair, E. (1993). Development Communication and Popular Resistance in Africa: An Examination of the Struggle Over Tradition and Modernity Through Media. *African Studies Review, 36*(1), 91.

William, R. (1979). Institutions of the Technology. In A. Mattelart & S. Siegelaub (Eds.), *Communication and Class Struggle: Capitalism, Imperialism*. New York: International General.

Windhoek Declaration. (1991). http://www.unesco.org/webworld. Accessed 1 Dec 2009.

Winseck, D. (2002). The WTO, Emerging Policy Regimes and the Political Economy of Transnational Communications. In M. Raboy (Ed.), *Global Media Policy in the New Millennium*. Luton: University of Luton Press.

World Summit on the Information Society "Geneva Report 2003". Online: http://www.itu.int/wsis/documents/index.html. Accessed 12 Oct 2007.

World Summit on the Information Society "Tunis Report 2005". Online, http://www.itu.int/wsis/documents/index.html. Accessed 12 Oct 2007.

www.awcfs.org, Professor Alfred Opubor. Accessed 4 Mar 2010.

www.icann.org/en/, Professor Clement Dzidonu Biography. Accessed 6 May 2011.

www.ifj.org, Accessed 7 July 2010.

www.joynews.com, Accessed 26 Sep 2009.

Ziegler, D., & Asante, M. (1992). *Thunder and Silence the Mass Media in Africa*. Trenton: Africa World Press Inc.

Zongo, G. (2001). *ICTs For Development in Africa*. Online: www.unssc.org/web1/programmes/glnp. Accessed 12 Oct 2006.

Index

U. Akpojivi, *Media Reforms and Democratization in Emerging Democracies of Sub-Saharan Africa*,
https://doi.org/10.1007/978-3-319-75301-0

The manufacturer's authorised representative in the EU is Springer Nature Customer Service Centre GmbH, Europaplatz 3, 69115 Heidelberg, Germany. If you have any concerns regarding our products, please contact ProductSafety@springernature.com

Printed and bound by CPI Group (UK) Ltd, Croydon, CR0 4YY

05/10/2026

02228138-0001